BLOOD ON THE GREEN

Punjab's Tryst with Terror

BLOOD ON THE GREEN

Punjab's Tryst with Terror

[From a reporter's notebook]

PPS Gill

Bookwell
Delhi

Blood On The Green

Punjab's Tryst With Terror

By PPS Gill

Cover Design: A P Singh; {apfoto99@gmail.com}

ISBN: 978-93-86578-00-6

First Published in 2017 by:

Bookwell
3/79, Nirankari Colony,
Delhi 110009, India
Ph: 91-11-27601283, 27604536
E-mail: bkwell@nde.vsnl.net.in
bookwelldelhi@gmail.com
Website: www.bookwellindia.com

The book is dedicated
to
all innocent people who lost
their life to terrorism

Contents

Acknowledgements

My first book *Punjab- a Frozen Tear; hopes and despairs of farmers* gave me the confidence to write another one. The Chandigarh-based Centre for Research in Rural and Industrial Development {CRRID} had published it in September, 2015. Before its launch, my teacher, Professor SS Johl, Chancellor of Central University Punjab, who also wrote the *Prologue* of the first book, told me: "*I want you to write about your experiences as a journalist, particularly of your long stay in Amritsar. That will give me more satisfaction. I believe that anyone who has been lucky to have reached some position in life and society must contribute by leaving behind for posterity his thoughts, memoirs and perspective as to how he viewed the world in which one has worked and received so much in return. I am sure you will not disappoint me.*"

He gave the example of his own widely read and acclaimed autobiography *Ranga di Gagar* {Pitcher of Colours}. The book in hand is a product of his encouragement; enticement, if I may say!

I approached my mother Gurbachan Kaur {affectionately called GK} and explained to her the concept of the book and what I intended to write, assuring her that I would circumvent controversies. She had been skeptical when I had first brought up this subject before I eventually settled to write the other book. She cross-questioned me. She had apprehensions! She gave her blessings. However, she has one grouse: she cannot read what I write, as she does not know English.

I owe a debt of gratitude to my teacher Professor Amarjit Singh Hayer for his valuable suggestions and for vetting the book. I acknowledge the time and attention given by Ramesh Inder Singh Mander, a former Indian Administrative Service officer, who went through the manuscript. I have known him since the time he was Additional Deputy Commissioner, Faridkot. We were together at Amritsar, when he was the Deputy Commissioner; and, when he was the Chief Information Commissioner, I was the State Information Commissioner {2007-2012}, Punjab.

My special thanks to the Editor-in-Chief of *The Tribune*, Mr Harish Khare, who was kind enough to accept my request to write the Foreword. He was Media Adviser to the former Prime Minister Dr Manmohan Singh. I owe a debt of gratitude to *Tribune's* Chief Sub-Editor, Ms Harvinder Khetal for editing the book and meticulously going through the manuscript.

I thank Punjabi writer-cum-poet Gurbhajan Gill for the encouragement to pen my memoirs. He had worked with me when I was Additional Director Communication at PAU: Punjab Agricultural University, Ludhiana {2005-06}; he is a recipient of the Punjab Government's *Punjabi Shiromani Kavi Purskar* {2012}.

I also thank Ms Suman Khosla, Editorial Research and Publication Officer, CRRID, for her help in my project. Last, but not the least, my sincere thanks to publisher Mr. M.S. Khurana for doing wonderful job.

Ours is a joint as well as nuclear family, under one roof. I thank every member: my sons Gagandeep and Gauravjit, my daughters-in-law, Amandeep and Simerjeet, respectively; my grandsons, Har Aziz and Arjan, respectively, for making it easy for me to work, despite the responsibilities and tasks they would occasionally entrust me with. I thank my wife, Amarjit – Dolly – for her contribution in keeping records and preserving very methodologically all my news clippings, spanning close to 30 years when I worked with *The Tribune*. This enabled me to retrieve the same during the course of writing this book.

For background material, I clicked *Google* and looked up *Wikipedia.* I solicit this online free-service facility; inaccuracies, flaws, if any, notwithstanding!

PPS Gill

Foreword

Punjab is an enigma. Its history is fascinatingly convoluted. Its politics is Byzantine-perfect. Its political class is a curious mixture of the good, the bad and the ugly. Its economy is almost insolvency institutionalized. Its society is deeply fractured along familiar lines of caste and religion.

Above all, Punjab is a challenge to any historian.

And, this is a challenge that PPS Gill has accepted with gusto and has come out with his honour and reputation as a first-rate chronicler intact.

There have been very many books about Punjab, especially about the 1984 events. Most of these books were written by the angry or the motivated or both. Gill's account of those dramatic months and years bears the imprimatur of a first-hand witness. As *The Tribune* correspondent based in Amritsar, Gill had a ringside view of the "cunning and conniving politicians and their internecine wars". He gives us a fascinating peep into the unholy manoeuvrings among various holy sants, claiming to speak in the name of the Sikh qoum. With equal candour, he writes of the lawlessness of law agencies, specially the central paramilitary forces such as the CRPF.

And, he reminds the reader how hazardous was the reporter's job, under pressure and threat from both the militants and government agencies. Those years hardened the boys into men and tested their professionalism. Gill had the wits to survive it all and do robust reporting.

Gill is a quintessential, old-fashioned political reporter and has an eye for the telling detail. He writes with considerable verve and style, his anecdotes reveal quite a bit. Gill is unsparing in underlining the Akali leaders' recklessness, which subjected the state of Punjab and its people to untold misery.

Punjab and its recent history drive home the inescapable fact: it is easy to start a fight, using intimidation and violence to achieve political or personal goals, but no one – not even the mighty Indian state – can calibrate and control the consequences of violence.

Chandigarh
January, 2017

Harish Khare
Editor-in-Chief
The Tribune

corporate world news etc. This bouquet has compounded the persistent confusion for such is the packaging and presentation that an unsuspecting reader/viewer/listener tends to believe what is offered in print, on screen, on *Air and on line*! And, as to the accountability of the media, debate is still open!

As to the prime time *live* debates on television, less said the better. What cause or purpose do these debates serve, involving, as these do, die-hard spokespersons of political parties professing myriad ideologies, if any, and idiosyncrasies? Every evening these worthies are seen {seldom heard} gesticulating, fretting, fuming and talking simultaneously; of course, at a tangent from the given issue or subject matter. Add to this evening crowing crowd religious preachers and other categories of opinion-makers in their own right.

These debates are akin to a clutch of birds of different feathers, quarreling, squeaking and snapping at each other while scrambling for space to roost on trees at dusk! The same way, these TV savvy political spokespersons make all the *right noises*, in their own perceptions, leaving viewers flustered! And, on some channels, when there are participants from across the international border, couched in Pakistan TV studios, in some of the discussions or debates, it adds only spice to the programmes; no substance.

Amidst this circus of the absurd, as one frustratingly surfs channels, most display multiple runners speeding across the screen, each beaming a different message, which is difficult to read, while anchors, acting more like charged-up activists, shrill and speak on something else. This kind of mad-house journalism makes viewers' diastole and systole to fluctuate alarmingly, causing ulcerous lacerations in the gastronomy!

Information, technology and communication seem to have come at a heavy price for the viewers! And, with the advent of science, technology, innovations, gadgets and gizmos, if the complexion, context, sub-text and content of journalism have changed, so have changed the basic tenets of journalism. Rather than ensuring that the news is true, correct, accurate and in-depth, the race is to be the first, fast and furious: *breaking news*; lest TRP: television rating point dips; and the channel trips!

In this mad media race and fierce competition, social media has carved its own niche. Blogs, micro-blogs, Twitter, Whats App, Face book, Instagram, YouTube and a host of others have given journalism a new dimension, a new direction, a new edge; and new competitors leaving the user/consumer with multiple choices and persistent confusion; leaving him gasping for breath and waiting for a whiff of authenticity and credibility! Yet, newspapers, television channels, social and digital media/medium have learnt to adjust and coexist.

In this age of changing profile of media, are books a casualty? Are books still relevant? While the print editions of books may have received a setback, e-books (read on Kindle etc., and their online availability, courtesy Flip kart, Amazon.com, LinkedIn et al), have created their own market niche. Libraries are also becoming Wi-Fi with a host of stock going digital.

Worldwide, key old and respected, prestigious and popular publications {newspapers/magazines} have taken to online editions, as well, in a big way. The shrinking print editions show that change to new media is as inevitable as it is imminent. As, one day, *Newsweek* decided to stop its print edition; ending eight decades of paper edition. The last print issue was dated December 31, 2012. *Newsweek's* Editor-in-chief, Tina Brown, wrote a farewell piece informing readers to meet them on their iPads or Kindle or phone in the first week of January, 2013. Yes, this signalled a change: *A new chapter opened,* as Tina had titled her write-up, saying: *sometimes, change isn't just good, it is necessary.* One hopes such new transitions in the offing, globally, are for good; as well as necessary!

*

Even the U K- based *The Independent* became the first national newspaper title to move to a digital-format; available online only. *The Tribune*, in a front-page box item on Sunday, March 27, 2016, *'The Independent'* stop press, carried a picture of the last print edition. The photo-caption read: The final print edition of *The Independent* newspaper went on sale on Saturday, {*March 26, 2016*}, ending its 30-year appearance on British newsstands with an exclusive on an assassination plot against a former Saudi King. A poignant wrap-around front page carried the words 'STOP PRESS' in red lettering on a white background, followed by the words 'Read all about it in this, our final print edition – 1986-2016. The newspaper will be available online only'. A detailed four-column report followed, on page 19, wherein inter alia with its final editorial claiming history would be the judge of its *'bold transition….as an example for other newspapers around the world to follow'*.

Earlier, in February, 2016, Evgeny Lebedev, Russian-born British owner of *The Independent* had said: '*The newspaper industry was changing, and that change was being driven by readers. They're showing us that the future is digital.*'

*

My belief is that print media still holds sway over electronic media and may yet last much longer than most people think it would. Not denying, however, the ground reality that electronic or digital media is the future media and the medium.

Such is the speed, spread and sweep of sources of information and knowledge that at times it is difficult to keep pace with what is happening in the wired, weird world: global village; a virtual *worldwide web*! If in his theory of evolution of life, Charles Darwin talked of *survival of the fittest*; in today's digital world it would be *survival of the tech savvy*, what with government services and private sector facilitations going online and getting linked to Aadhaar Card and Pan Card numbers, rendering large sections of the population computer-illiterate, since everything is now getting web-linked or online! That's the reason for stress on *Digital India*!

On top of it all, parents usually hand their children play stations and smart mobiles with games downloaded, as per the desire and demand of the children. (Are these learning tools?) They do this more out of convenience, rather than conviction. Parents do this since they are either unable to spend or do not spend time (what to say quality time) with their children; after all, it is the age of working couples! Parents forget the adverse impact of such devices on a child's health, psyche and brain cells. They also ignore with impunity research findings of studies and surveys on the ill-effects of rays these devices radiate and emit and harm children.

In fact, even adults are vulnerable to harmful effects, if they overuse mobiles or work long hours on computers. Or hold rays-emitting devices with either games or holding very small print devices too close to their eyes. Or operate these in the darkness of the room, when in bed.

One feels outdated, if not obsolete, as one looks over the shoulder to see how far journalism, media and medium have transformed and traversed, how information, technology and communication have impacted life, how mass communication teaching institutions {shops?} have come up across the decades; and what a variety of subjects and sub-texts have been introduced from making of animation films/documentaries to social media to public relations to media advertising to on-line editing to designing websites to training to be TV anchors or Radio-jockeys etc.

I read the views of veteran journalist P Sainath, Ramon Magsaysay award recipient, on the state of the *Indian Media*, which he said was facing a *credibility deficit* {*The Hindustan Times*, August 12, 2015}. He suggested introduction of journalism at school level to create awareness about media and make media more accountable.

In his address at Kurukshetra University on *Emerging trends in the Indian media*, he was quoted having said that in the absence of awareness about media, people were subjected to *misinformation.* Once younger people developed awareness, they would look at the media *critically by understanding the nature, techniques and impact of the mass media.* Also, one tends to quite agree with Sainath when he says that *paid news, selective blackouts of news events, massive reduction on news gathering from the spot and reporting without analysis were among the key challenges before the Indian media.*

*

It is in this backdrop that I write this book. The style chosen for narrative, in telling all, is in the form of anecdotes, recalling not only important events, how those were covered and also analyzing or deconstructing the story behind the story, relating some of those events to developments in the present times; and recapitulating my perceptions and interpretations of happenings that unfolded at that point of time, and how some of them have cast a shadow over contemporary times.

I have, in a way, attempted to summarize the situation, particularly in Amritsar, so as to give a semblance of what the prevailing atmosphere was like then, before and after 1984; i.e. pre-Bluestar and post-Bluestar.

I wish to share my experiences in the field of journalism, which gave me my daily bread for 29 years {1975-2004} that were spent working with *The Tribune*, a prestigious newspaper of the region, published from Chandigarh. {*As editorial advisor, I have had a brief stint with the Chandigarh-edition of Dainik Bhaskar*}.

While with *The Tribune*, my career spanned from Bathinda to Amritsar to Ambala to Amritsar to Chandigarh with assignments abroad: Pakistan, the UK, the

USA; and private tours of Canada and Europe. Working in *The Tribune* gave me an exposure, an insight, as much into the hopes and despairs of the people, as knowledge about socio-economic, religious, ethnic, caste-class conflicts - their up-down swings; about drug-crazy youth; and distress in agriculture coupled with farmer suicides; about disquiet in village-life; about plight and flight of industry, as also into the affairs of the state: political, administrative, financial, economic, and much more.

*

The period spent reporting from Amritsar and Gurdaspur {1983 -1990} has been very rewarding, educative, exciting and crucial, in so far as field experience is concerned. {I had two working spells in Amritsar: first was a short one in 1977, when the city celebrated its 400th foundation day; second from November 1983 to 1990; besides being occasionally sent on assignments from Chandigarh, later.}

The second spell at Amritsar enabled me to look closely at the human psyche, suffering, fear psychosis and endurance, as also how humans swing between agony and ecstasy; in other words, discovering that there is yet another angle to reporting: human and humane, which is more important than sensational reporting. No wonder, development and positive journalism, thus, became my forte, without, of course, compromising on professional ethics; at times even exercising self-restraint. One may call it *self-censorship*! It has helped, it helps. It has worked, it works.

In my journalistic career, spanning nearly three decades, two lessons that I learned way back in 1980s, are still etched in my mind: r*eport what is in the interest of the people, not what interests the people*. This remark by the UK top cop at a press conference in Amritsar has been helpful on many occasions, especially, when reporting on sensitive and emotive issues, involving the two principal communities, the Sikhs and the Hindus; or on matters of the state. The second lesson was: m*ere muck-raking does not take a reporter far*, as *The Tribune* Editor-in-chief V. N Narayanan, would often say, adding: *journalism is one per cent inspiration, 99 per cent perspiration.*

*

The Tribune, dated December 9, 2015, published an item on page 10: *A gentle, unassuming Editor*. It caught my attention. Narayanan, 75, had passed away on

December 5, 2015, while on a visit to his daughters - Ramya and Vindhya - in Singapore. It was an obituary by my former colleague Roopinder Singh; and there he was: mug shot of a smiling editor, who had taught us all, a lot. I remember the coconut sweet dishes his wife Radhan had offered me and my wife at their house in Chandigarh. Roopinder had paid a wholesome and handsome tribute.

As a reporter-observer, one is expected to record for posterity, as well. My *beat* has, by and large, been Punjab. The advent of militancy, which led to murders, mayhem, political vacuum; trust deficit, poor governance, shuffling of governors, long-spells of the President's Rule; unending 24x7 day and night curfews, a trail of bans and restrictions on daily life; snapping of communication lines and much more, gave me a wide angle view and exposure to the state's tryst with destiny!

One also gained experience, moving on from cute potable Olivetti type writer to computer, from pager to mobile, from Morse-code key to Tele-printer to internet. All these have individually and collectively revolutionized not just the media, the profession but also politics, governance and business scene; in fact, *Aam Aadmi's* life itself!

Having been drawn into the vortex of journalism, it is a humble attempt to share a reporter's notebook, filled with on and off record stories and anecdotes. In that sense, the following pages are part biographic, memoirs, travelogues, reportage, experiences and remembrances of yesteryears, all scribbled on yellowing pages or preserved in clippings, which showcase the vignettes of the period of turmoil and chaos; and of tranquility and normalcy in Punjab! Some writing is interpretative commentary in which comparisons between the past and present have been drawn, given the semblance or sameness of the events then and now. There may be some repetition or over-lapping. Bear with that.

Already, exhaustive and rich literature is available, in print and online, on various facets of Punjab tragedy: events, happenings, eye-witness accounts, first-hand descriptions, scholarly interpretations and editorial analysis of religio-political, social and economic aspects. Several theories, hypothesis, turns, twists and trends related to political calls and movements, usually with religious *Teflon* coating, have also been detailed *ad nauseam* in the available print and cyber world. These accounts, some heartrending, some part fiction-part factual, pertain to how vested interests vitiated the atmosphere and how the *manufactured* situation was maneuvered, manipulated and built up, resulting in the Army operation- Bluestar- at the Golden Temple in 1984; and how the situation eventually spiraled out of control; the assassination of Ms Indira Gandhi and its aftermath etc.

As a journalist, while in the field, one got to have a ringside view of the oscillating and vacillating happenings in Punjab from mid-1970s to 1990s.Several of these were to change the very complexion of politics, some were to leave behind an indelible impact, as much on the psyche of the people, as on their socio-economic status.

Therefore, what is presented in the following passages and pages is neither a chronological listing of dated events or what all had happened nor even scholarly presentation of history of Punjab, across specific decades and time-frame. It is simply a recall, a recollection, a reflection of the images etched on the memory screen during the course of writer's journalism career. It is a view in the rear mirror; a kind of 'reverse writing'. The sentence on the rear mirror reads: *objects in the mirror are closer than they appear*. And, in a walk '*down memory lane*', as is attempted in this book, *objects* are also 'distorted' because one is expected to capture those *snapshots* of a time in *words*! That means applying a filter to make the recall: crisp, short, sweet, sour and bitter too, perhaps!

These images are presented here in no particular sequence or order, but as these appeared and flashed on the mind's radar, 36 years later, while sitting back and analyzing the situation, as it existed and unfolded in 1980s and thereafter.

In these random anecdotal narrations, peppered and interspersed with personal beliefs, opinions, thinking, perceptions and interpretations, an attempt has been made to link that time with the present times. The narration is devoid of either forward or backward linkages; in other words, there is no one continuous story; simply put, it is just: episodic.

*

Postscript: The journalist in me was a compelling factor to try and update some contemporary developments that took place in the region, as book's narrative was nearing the finishing line.

There is nothing like the *last word.* Therefore, it may seem somewhat incongruent to be commenting on some of the evolving developments in the present times. There were several issues that attracted my attention and provoked my journalistic instincts to take cognizance of those. Of these, however, I am mentioning just two here, while other developments find mention at appropriate places in the text.

The two issues are: One, exclusion of Sehjdhari Sikhs from right to vote in the SGPC: Shiromani Gurdwara Prabandhak Committee elections. After the passage of the *Sikh Gurdwaras {Amendment} Bill, 2016,* in the Rajya Sabha in March 2016, the Lok Sabha also passed the Bill without any discussion. The Congress did not oppose the Bill. The President has given his assent to the Bill. However, the case of Sehjdhari Sikh Party is still pending in the court despite the newly passed Act.

Two, developments in respect of sharing of Punjab river waters commensurate with the beginning of the hearing in the Supreme Court on February 20, 2016 on the Presidential reference to the *Punjab's Termination of Agreements Act, 2004*. The latter issue is of economic and emotional value to both states. The one pertaining river waters is also of life-line interest and importance to both Punjab and Haryana. These issues have compelled me to describe at same length the developments that have impacted the region with cascading effect. The effect continues.

*

It may be recalled that under tremendous political pressure, the union cabinet gave the green signal to the amendment of the Act to bar Sehjdhari Sikhs from voting in SGPC elections. Following the cabinet decision, the Union Home Minister Raj Nath Singh introduced the *Sikh Gurdwaras {Amendment} Bill, 2016*, to exclude Sehjdhari Sikhs from voting in the elections to the Sikh religious bodies in the Rajya Sabha, on March 15, 2016.

It is estimated there are about 55 lakh registered Sikh voters, who vote in SGPC elections. The Sehjdhari Sikh Party claims to have been enjoying voting rights since 1944 but was debarred by the home ministry notification to vote in 2003. This issue has political as well as Panthic overtones, given the fact that the state Assembly elections are due in 2017.

The SGPC general house elections are conducted and controlled by the Centre. There have been occasions when these have either been inordinately delayed or not held and, if held, not notified, much to the chagrin of the elected members. The SGPC elections were last held on September 18, 2011. However, the new body could not take charge following Punjab and Haryana High Court quashing the notification the union home ministry had issued on October 8, 2003. The court's decision came in December 2011, following a petition filed by the Sehjdhari Federation {now Sehjdhari Sikh Party.} In the absence of any general house, the court allowed the 15-member SGPC executive, elected in November 2010, to conduct day-to-day functioning of the religious body. It is by virtue of this ruling that Avtar Singh Makkar- SGPC President - and other office-bearers have continued to hold office since then. [With all encumbrances, including legal, removed, a new SGPC executive committee was constituted on November 04, 2016 with Kirpal Singh Badungar as its President; a known loyalist of Parkash Singh Badal.]

*

Also included in the book are the developments related to sharing of river waters in the Punjab and Haryana Vidhan Sabha, which were in session simultaneously in March 2016. Those developments were as unexpected as sudden: the unanimous passage of the *Sutlej-Yamuna Link Canal Land {Transfer of Property Rights} Bill, 2016* by Punjab House, thereby, de-notifying the entire land acquired for the purpose of supply of Ravi-Beas water to Haryana through SYL canal; return of Rs 192 crore by Punjab to Haryana, and the latter sending the cheque back with an acidic note; deployment of nearly 200 JCB machines to level the land and the symbolic filling up of the canal by 'farmer owners' of the acquired land and uprooting of thousands of trees, backed as they were by Punjab politicians, both Akali and Congress; Supreme Court's order on maintaining *status quo* following submission of interlocutory application by Haryana in the Apex court on such operations in the wake of Punjab's Bill; subsequent resolution by a defiant Punjab Assembly declaring not to accept any order on constructing a canal or on sharing water with other states, *come what may*; a beleaguered Haryana Assembly's resolution condemning Punjab's moves, its combative stand in the Apex Court; strident stand and the shrill of the political parties on either side of the SYL, and war of nerves between politicians of the two states etc.

It, however, goes without saying that the manner in which Punjab had acted and Haryana had reacted, such political posturing is bound to set bad precedents for other states, politicians and coming generations. Political leaders must remember that brazen behavioral actions and attitudes that to succeed one has to be '*unlawfully qualified'* is no way or a solution to sort out inter-state issues. Howsoever, emotive or vexing issues, problems and conflicts may be, these can and have to be sorted out and solutions found within the four corners of the Constitution and National framework without resorting to disruptive means. Mirror-image reactions do not serve any purpose or last long.

As I said, there is nothing like the *last word,* it can neither be ever written nor said, therefore, what may finally emerge is difficult to predict or anticipate.

1

Rewind

Date with journalism

That day, half a century ago, I had not gone to school; fever had held me back. As I lay in bed, tossing with nothing to do, I played with a serrated cycle spool. My mother would occasionally come into the room to check on me. Seeing me fiddle with the steel ring, she warned me against playing with it: *you will get hurt*. The next time she came in, I lay quiet with face to the wall; the steel spool lying besides the pillow. She turned me over and saw the swollen lip. The spool had done its bit. She laughed and caressing me said: *I'm your Mom. I can fore-see, what you cannot. Do listen to me!*

Changing the topic to divert my attention, she asked, *what you would like to be when you grow up.*

Patarkar! I shot back holding back the pain without even knowing what I had said or why. She guffawed!

Not long, thereafter, in August 1964, there was an inter-house debate on: *education is better than sports* in our school: Government Senior Model School, Sector 16 Chandigarh. Instinctively, I picked up a notebook and started taking short takes of what student speakers spoke, and later submitted the write-up to Pyare Lal, school librarian and in charge school magazine, *Symphony*. In a brief introductory paragraph he wrote, "…….*A new addition to our growing writers. He seems to have watched many other events in detail - a quality so essential for a successful reporter. Here is a specimen of his caliber as a writer"*. {Frankly, I hadn't watched *any*, what to say of *many* other events. That was the first-ever attempt made; spontaneous, as it were!} I went over to thank him for the encouraging words, and asked, what *does the word reporter mean*? He smilingly explained. That's how it was; later, as destiny had willed, I was to become a reporter: *Patarkar*; journalism became my profession!

*

I am reminded of my school days at Punjab Public School Nabha in mid 1960s. In the foyer of the main school building was placed the newspaper reading stand. In one corner were hung two blackboards - *Home News* printed on one; Foreign *News* printed on the other. Each morning a staff member would write *news headlines* of the day from the daily newspaper under the respective heads; at times the duty was assigned to students of the senior classes. On few occasions, I too had volunteered to scan the newspaper and write on the two boards; of course, with the help of a teacher. This assignment had twin purposes: one, inculcating in the students habit of reading newspaper; two, enabling students improve their handwriting on the blackboard! Little did I know of or even think then that such an exercise would, one day, land me in journalism!

*

After matriculation in 1965, I joined PAU: Punjab Agricultural University, Ludhiana, for a five-year B.Sc. {Agriculture and Animal Husbandry} degree course in the College of Agriculture. As an undergraduate, my interest developed in public speaking and writing. Thereafter, while pursuing M.Sc {Agricultural Journalism} in the College of Basic Sciences and Humanities, these two traits were to be chiseled and honed by our English teacher, Professor Amarjit Singh Hayer, who selected me as student editor of the English section of the university magazine; and also appointed me joint secretary of the speakers' union.

*

I owe a debt of gratitude to the visionary M S Randhawa, who was PAU Vice-Chancellor, when I was a student; and, later, when I worked for a brief period as PIA: Press Information Assistant in the Communication Centre, where I first cut my teeth in journalism under noted Punjabi short-story wizard, Kulwant Singh Virk. It was Randhawa's far-sight to start the M.Sc Journalism degree course. He had hand-picked me and had also asked me to get like-minded students, who had background in agriculture and a flair for writing to tell the world at large what agriculture and allied fields is all about. He wanted journalism students to highlight not only the success stories of progressive farmers but also focus on their hopes and despairs.

My introduction to visionary Randhawa was accidental. For this, all credit to Professor Hayer and Hockey Olympian Prithipal Singh, who was Director Students' welfare. This was, perhaps, because of my writing *Letters to the editor* to *The Tribune*; and participation in co-curricular activities at PAU. Encouragement for this interest came from both of them. The two were known to provide the required opportunities and atmosphere to every individual student to flower and flourish in the chosen fields. It was great learning experience: I owe a debt of gratitude to these two individuals and the institution: PAU.

It was at PAU that the eminent journalist couple Ms Promilla and D N Kalhan of *The Hindustan Times*, who taught us and prepared us to enter the portals of journalism. It was Ms Promilla, who as editor of '*Herpage'* in the HT, gave me the first break by carrying my first-ever article in a newspaper, that too in a National newspaper, under the headline: *She has a doctorate in chapatti-making*! {D N Kalhan was a former News Editor of *the Hindustan Times.*}

*

Having served as PIA, the first breakthrough to join a newspaper came in 1975, when *The Tribune* appointed me as its first-ever Staff Correspondent at Bathinda, a socio-economically backward region of Punjab. I got my application for the post vetted from the *Tribune's* Special Correspondent, the late, P D Mohindra, whom I had come to know, as PIA, during his visits to PAU. He was from village Lalton, had studied at Ludhiana, and would occasionally visit the university.

*

Let me share the first lesson that I learned even before I acquired the tag of a journalist: one afternoon, as Mohindra sat enjoying the winter sun in the company of his colleague B K Chum of the *Indian Express*, I walked into his house in Chandigarh. After formal greetings, I sat down and quite foolishly said *I came to discuss my application for the staffer's post: one each for Bathinda and Ludhiana that Tribune had advertised.* Chum left after few minutes; and then all hell and fury broke out. Mohindra shouted at me and said *you do not know who the other person is. Why should you speak out and reveal your purpose? If you want to become a journalist learn to be discreet, quiet and think what to say, what not to say, where to say, where not to say and when to say and when not to say.* He said it all in one breath! Then, as was his wont, which I later discovered during the course of our long equation and association, he changed his mood and tone and made me feel at home.

He corrected the application and assured to help, which I am sure he did; as I was selected.

Mohindra was a voracious reader. He encouraged others too to read. *One cannot be a good writer or journalist, if one is not a good reader,* he would often say. This advice was to become my cardinal principle. And, whenever we met, he would always say: *come home; every time you do, I will gift you a book*! I missed out on his lucrative offer.

Decades later, in a belated move the Punjab government honoured him for his services to Punjab and journalism. With the prize money, he purchased books and donated these to his village school library and other institutions. Thank you, Sir! {Mohindra, 85, died of cardiac arrest at his Chandigarh residence on May 09, 2015}.

*

And then came the interview day. *The Tribune* interview was an experience in itself. The Board of Trustees President was Ram Chandra, ICS. I remember Lt. Gen P S Gyani {Retd.}, not others present and, of course, the Editor, R Madhavn Nair. I do not remember all the questions put to me. However, I do remember that the interviewers were patient, soft and made one feel at ease. Leafing through my dossier, it was Nair who spoke first: *If what you have submitted is true, what is our man doing in Ludhiana*? He made this comment because I had submitted the clippings of the news items that had appeared in *The Tribune* alongside the original press notes that I had issued, as PIA. This was done to strengthen my claim for a staffer's post. The suggestion to do so had come from my senior colleague at the Communication Centre, Haqiqat Singh Mangat, who was in charge of the Centre's library and clipping section. In fact, he had prepared the dossier that I submitted along with my application. *What can I say, Sir,* I replied.

I was asked to wait outside.

The wait lasted till late evening. *The Tribune*, however, did offer lunch to all candidates. When I was called in later in the evening, Nair said: *You are new. You have no experience*; {honestly, I missed a heartbeat, thinking no luck}; t*herefore, you will spend two weeks at the Desk and get familiarized with the working of news operations in the field and in the newsroom. We have selected you for Bathinda. Good Luck!* In that very interview, K G Dutt was appointed staffer at Ludhiana, replacing K S Chawla, a non-staffer. Just as I was leaving, Gen. Gyani spoke; {now what! I wondered.} *Wait, are you married*? *No, Sir*. He smiled, *Good*! That, perhaps, was my first and the only major experience of appearing for an interview. The day was April 16, 1975.

*

Here, let me also share something, which may appear trivial to you, however, it has its own importance and value, at least for me, as I look back 40 years. After a few days, I received a *Khaki* envelop with my name and address written in capital letters; a real piece of calligraphy! Inside was the two-page appointment letter, dated April 21, 1975. As per appointment letter, I was to join duty at Bathinda before May 20, 1975. My basic pay scale was: Rs 375-30-525-45-975-75-1200!

And, 10 years earlier, while I awaited for the matriculation examination results to be declared, the employees of Panjab University went on a strike in support of their demands. That was in 1965. At that time, Panjab University used to conduct the matriculation examination. Not having much to do, I got a part-time job, on daily-wage- basis, in the secrecy branch of the University. My job was to reply to communications received from the examiners etc. and draft replies, which were vetted by the superintendent. I found the job interesting. I worked for 10 days. At the end, I received my first pay – or was it wages - Rs 40!

And, decades later, when I completed my five-year term as State Information Commissioner, in January 2012, my basic pay was Rs 80,000, same as that of the Chief Secretary! What a journey, it has been!

*

I reported at Chandigarh prior to proceeding to Bathinda. As a new comer to the world of news and newspaper, I learned that all action began in the newsroom: operational theatre of the organization; a kind of *news world* in an oyster. There used to be eerie silence inside the newsroom and in the corridors; and one did not come across more sanitized and cleaner toilets elsewhere than in *The Tribune*.

The realization of being part of a well-heeled and respected institution one swelled up with a feeling of pride. This also gave one a feeling of self-importance, as well as of nervousness! A sort of self-conscious air lifted one's morale! It was in the newsroom I learned how field copy from staffers, stringers and news agencies: wire services, as these are called, was handled, cut, dressed up and made *fit* for printing or literally *spiked* {on a steel needle mounted on a wooden base.} There was the *horseshoe-shaped* desk in the middle of the room and in the slot sat the chief-sub editor and around the rim of the huge table sat subs {sub-editors} working on the *copy* the man in the slot distributed to them. Things are different today; on-line!

Occasionally, one was gripped by anxiety neurosis: sometimes, the d*esk* made one feel as one of their own, and some other times, it made one feel like an alien! It was in such an etherized atmosphere that the sports master-editor, the late Samuel Banerjee, was the one who made me feel comfortable, giving small yet important tips on reporting. {And, it is a different matter, how in the evening one enjoyed the milk-and-*jalebis*, which were part of evening tea at the desk!}

*

Much later, when I was transferred from Amritsar and posted at Chandigarh, it further confirmed my belief how *important* and *powerful* the newsroom {read *desk*} was/is. The word itself connotes how the web of all the News Editor's men and women deal with and handle the *copy*, which pours into the newsroom 24x7; and, how perpetually and perennially, the reporters: chief of bureau down to stringers or part-time correspondents, were ever in running arguments, combat- and conflict-mode and mood with the d*esk*, which had/has its own ways to make or mar a reporter, when dealing with his/ her copy. The *wise* subs, constituting the majority in the newsroom, would often poke fun at and even ridicule reporters by flaunting their copy!

In my case, I learned that some of them would hold the copy high, and with a smirk, would ask if anyone was interested in making a shirt or a pair of trousers out of it! Those days, paper rolls were used for typing and in Teleprinters. The roll would be unrolled to display length of the story. Later, these rolls would be cut as story *takes* for easy handling of the copy. Sometimes news *gems* would be pinned on the newsroom display board to make or poke fun at reporters. Well, all part of the game!

*

Apprenticeship over, I joined at Bathinda on the stipulated date; on a hot May morning in 1975. {And, a month later, on June 25, emergency was imposed; it lasted till March 21, 1977!} My beat was the entire Ferozepur division, including Faridkot and Ferozepur districts, as well.

Finding rented accommodation was not easy. Having left the comforts of our home in Ludhiana's posh Sarabha Nagar, what came my way was an un-white-washed one-room set with a kitchen; and toilet a little distance away: in the backyard; minus the flush system. For water needs, there was the hand-pump!

*

Several months later, I visited Chandigarh and made a courtesy call on Nair. He inquired after my well being and then with a smile said, *I have read some of your stories. Good job. You have come from a village. I know Bathinda is very backward. Spend a day here and see city life!* That was his way of caring!

*

Unconfirmed reports were that it was on the asking of the then Chief Minister, the late Giani Zail Singh that *The Tribune* had created the post of a staff correspondent at Bathinda.

Soon after I had joined, he happened to visit for a function. The then District Public Relations Officer, Jagmohan Singh Brar, introduced me. *Yes, I know of his appointment*, Giani ji responded, putting his hand on my shoulder {those days security hassles were far less than what one faces today; unimaginable, unanticipated and unheard of then}; and asked: h*ave you got government house*? Before I could answer, the then Deputy Commissioner, R R Bhardwaj spoke up: *yes sir; he has been given a house.* I kept quiet. The very next day, the Deputy Commissioner's General Assistant, Inder Singh, sent for me and allotted a house. Who says silence does not pay? The lesson Mohindra had taught, paid off!

*

That was also the time when land phones were still a luxury and mobiles were unheard of. Even the transmission of press messages at the central telegraph office was done via Morse-code key system, as Bathinda did not have an automated telephone exchange. The new exchange came much later. It was inaugurated by the then union minister for communications, Shankar Dayal Sharma, who dialed Giani ji, sitting next to him. It is a different matter that due to a technical snag, at first dial the phone did not connect!

*

At that time, Congress had decided to have its session near Chandigarh; at Mataur village. That village now stands submerged in S A S: Sahibzada Ajit Singh Nagar or Mohali district, as it is better and more popularly known than even Ajitgarh!

The Tribune had planned a special supplement for the occasion; and in that, role of the *Praja Mandal* movement was to be one of the highlights. I was asked to do a piece on Zail Singh, who was an activist of that movement against the British. I did the assignment. Later, Giani ji had second thoughts and wanted to have another sitting with me, as he wanted to share more information on his role in the *Praja Mandal* movement.

In fact, when Giani ji wanted to speak to me about the write-up, I did not have a telephone. Therefore, the chief minister's office called up the Senior Superintendent of Police, P C Dogra, asking him to make me speak to the CM. When Giani ji came on the line, he asked, *you do not have a telephone*? I answered in the negative and also informed him that my office had applied to the General Manager Telephones, Ambala. But it had not been installed, yet. Within two days, a telephone was installed. He desired that I visit him at his residence at Chandigarh. I visited him at his official residence at Chandigarh and expanded the write-up. The article appeared in the special supplement of *The Tribune on* December 29, 1975. He was pleased with my work. That was his way of building bridges. We two had a long equation, even after he became the Union Home Minister and, later, the President of India.

As Home Minister, Giani ji at times would visit Faridkot, his home district: his village Sandhwan was a few kms from Faridkot. For these visits he would land at Bhisiana IAF: Indian Air Force station, Bathinda, and drive down to Faridkot. On several occasions, I travelled with him. He had an earthly sense of wit, wisdom and humor. A reporter once asked him how was the law and order situation in the country. Giani ji looked at him through his rimmed glasses and with a knowing smile remarked: law is with the law minister, order is with the prime minister; I am visiting my home. On one occasion, while waiting to take off for New Delhi, we got talking while strolling on the tarmac: walk the talk! After some time, I said other people, including Congress leaders Buta Singh and Kesho Ram, were waiting to meet and talk to him; I better take leave of him. He held my hand and said, *continue, I do not want to meet anyone.*

*

After he completed his term as the President, he was on pilgrimage to Takht Keshgarh Sahib in December 1994, when he met with a road accident near Ropar, which falls in the Anandpur assembly constituency that he had represented, as MLA: Member Legislative Assembly. He was rushed to the PGI: Post-graduate institute of medical education and research. And, there I was when he passed away, while still in the ICU: Intensive care unit, on December 25. His body was brought out of the PGI and taken to the union territory guest house and was kept overnight to enable people pay their last homage before it was flown to New Delhi. At the PGI, standing next to me was the then Professor of Nuero-surgery, V K Kak, who whispered to me: *in my entire medical career, I have not seen so much life-support system wired to anyone, as was provided to Giani ji* !

Incidentally, one of his daughters lived across the road in a government house opposite ours in Chandigarh. So, I was, sometimes, privy to what went on at PGI during his admission. After his death, there was a heated debate in the family whether cremation should be in New Delhi or at Sandhwan. Delhi was chosen over the native village because of political reasons.

*

Bathinda gave me an opportunity to practice what we were taught: *developmental journalism and positive reporting*. With the proclamation of the emergency and with not much of political reporting to do those days, one did not encounter much trouble with the censors. {Those days, the CID: Crime investigation department wing of the police acted as the censors in Bathinda!}

Those days we sent our dispatches either via the telegraph office, where they would be screened or by post. Censors would ask us to supply them a copy of reports sent through post, which we did not. One day, some of us approached police official in charge of censorship to request expeditious clearance, as our mail usually got delayed. Sheepishly, he admitted that he was *weak* in English and had to depend upon his college-going son, who was away for a few days. *Let him return you will have no problems*. Be that as it may, it was a different experience working during the emergency and with friendly censors! The two stints in Bathinda, including reporting on the adjoining Faridkot and Ferozepur districts, helped me learn and pick up myriad nuances of the profession.

*

And, 40 years later, when one looks back, much has changed in the *wild west* Punjab, as much on the ground in physical and infrastructure terms, as in its politics and economy. Also, across decades, much has changed even in the field of journalism, as a profession. The two entities have under gone a complete metamorphosis in every way. Journalism, in fact, is one of the world's oldest professions, anchored in: *truth, ethics, objectivity and facts;* it is also considered a *noble* profession! Many may agree to disagree with this hypothesis in present times!

*

My innings with *The Tribune* lasted till December 2004. It was a great learning experience having worked under the wings of R Madhavn Nair, Prem Bhatia, V N Narayanan, Hari Jai Singh and H K Dua.

How or why I opted for VRS: Voluntary retirement scheme, I will not discuss macro or micro details – publicly - given the fiduciary relationship between me and *The Tribune*; suffice to say it had to happen, it happened, and it happened for *good.* It is better to forget the bitter-sour memories of that time-frame and instead reflect only on sweet remembrances of the decades spent working there. As I reminisce, all I can say on the circumstances leading to taking VRS is: *thank you Dua Sahib, thank you A J Philip. And, I do hope The Tribune Trustee, Justice S S Sodhi {retired} remembers all the briefs I had shared with him of those episodes; thank you, Sir*!

After this rewind, let us fast-forward and turn the yellowing pages of my notebooks and revisit the ageing newspaper clippings from which ink too has begun to fade. Let me begin from the endpoint of my field {district} posting and reporting; and lead you to that hotspot – Amritsar.

*

When I look back, I can say that I have always held the view that in majority of cases, those on regular staff and with a pay band served an organization for long years, till retirement. Such of the appointees developed a commitment to the organization and worked with sincerity, devotion and passion; learning and giving their best all the time. But, across time, systems have changed. The new concept is of *contract* hiring and firing. The hop-step-jump syndrome has become a rule for professionals, who switch from one news establishment to another, whichever offers a better designation and better pay-packet. However, in this new system *that* commitment, devotion and passion, perhaps, is missing. Well, that's the way world goes!

Living, reporting and imbibing new experiences with a mix of smiles and tears, surprises and shocks; and being a participant with a degree of involvement, at times, and a witness, often helpless, to the unfolding developments, at other times, full of turns and twists, was a great learning lesson. And it is out of that lesson that I share some of the glimpses in this book.

What follows, therefore, are reminiscences of my reporting years, as also commentary on issues I strongly felt needed to be discussed and debated, not only from the two border districts: Amritsar, Gurdaspur; some vignettes are from my assignments in the Punjab Bureau, Chandigarh; some from my posting at Bathinda, Ambala and travels within India and abroad.

I do not claim to capture every whiff of wind and drift to recall all the ground realities and behind the scene developments. What I intend sharing, by and large, are first-hand experiences. And, given the circumstances at that time, one had to be circumspect, then; perhaps, not now.

It is everyone's right to agree to disagree with fellow humans, yet everyone has to have the patience and tolerance to hear, if not listen, to another person's views and opinions. In that sense, this book is based on my personal perceptions of what I had seen, experienced; and interpret those developments, when one looks at *that* period in retrospect.

2

Fast-forward

Hotspot

My first posting, as I have said, was at Bathinda in 1975, when the place was dubbed as the backwaters or the Wild West or Sharjha of Punjab, marked as it was with the shrubbery and sand dunes that go with the desert landscape; and as do gangs of dacoits. I had had a short-stint at Amritsar earlier too, in 1977, during 400 years celebrations of the founding of the city. Thereafter, I returned to Bathinda for the second stint. Soon, I was moved to Ambala in early 1981-82; and again posted to Amritsar, in mid-November, 1983.

In fact, it was during one of my routine visits to Chandigarh from Ambala, when I was asked to see the Editor-in-chief, Prem Bhatia. That was like asking someone to enter the lion's den and expect him to come out unscathed! *Speak in Punjabi, it will be better for you*, a sound advice came from an Associate editor, K P Sinha. Bhatia was all sweet and honey. He inquired after my family and then got up, put his arm around my shoulder, and paternally said: *I am transferring you to Amritsar, as a reward, and with high hopes. I expect balanced reporting. You will get orders in due course of time.* There were no ifs, no buts, no arguments, no counter-points; not with him!

*

At that period in its history, Amritsar, the politico- religious nerve-centre and commercial hub, was beginning to heat up, as was Punjab; Amritsar itself was the news: either making news or remaining in the news. To be posted at a hot news spot at that time was a crucial appointment from journalism's angle. Much had happened in the past few years in Punjab in general and in the 'holy' city in particular; more was happening day-in and day-out; and much of all that was happening was unsavoury, unanticipated, unimaginable, unthinkable, unpalatable and, perhaps, unpardonable.

*

In the wake of Akalis' agitation in 1982, as well as happenings in Punjab, when I was posted at Ambala, I had witnessed how Sikhs proceeding to National Capital during the Asian Games were subjected to humiliation, harassment; and shamed by the police at the bidding of the Haryana Congress government. That was in reaction to Akalis' announcement to "disrupt" the Games and hold demonstrations in support of their demands and against the Center's *step-motherly* and *discriminatory* attitude towards the Sikhs and the state. {Subsequently, it emerged that a News Agency had misquoted the Akali Dal which led to a virtual bar on the Sikhs to proceed to the National Capital as also the resultant humiliation of high and low Sikhs.}

Around mid-November, 1983, there I was on my way from Ambala to Amritsar, tumbling and tossing in a rumbling truck. I moved into the government house vacated by my predecessor, Jatinder Sharma, shortly before mid-night. A new dawn awaited, as did a new field of journalism to be discovered and covered, new experiences to be gained; newer lessons to be learned in reporting: as far as possible straight, objective, unemotional, uncolored and unbiased; in sync with the never told *Tribune* policy or the related cardinal principles; as also reporting in the larger *interest of the state*.

There were occasions and events that can be termed as adrenalin-pumping; and as then, so now, it is still difficult to decipher those developments or make either sense out of those occurrences or put that in proper perspective. What follows are, to put it simply, only kaleidoscopic patterns of those troubled times; a tryst with terrorism.

*

The Tribune sub-office in the middle of the famous Hall Bazaar was at a vantage point from where one had a clear view of the chaotic life down below from the second floor window, till the office was moved to the back quarters on the same floor. {Much later, the office was shifted elsewhere.} The road below was and still remains the main artery that leads to the Golden Temple from the Hall Gate {renamed Gandhi Gate}.

If the *Booklover's Retreat* shop below was a refreshing break from the routine, so was the aroma arising from the *Bhai Sahib*'s stamp-size non-veg shop at the entrance to the office. Even otherwise, the walled city is known for its mouth-watering eating joints from *Kesar- da-dhaba* to *Bhrawan-da-dhaba* to *Gyan- halwai-di- lassi*, and numerous other wayside eateries, rehriwalas and peddlers, all selling an assortment of palate-tickling delicacies, both veg and non-veg; typical trade-marks of *Amritsari* life: it is a gourmet's delight!

I am reminded of W B Yeats following opening lines from his famous poem:

The Second Coming:

Turning and turning in the widening gyre
the falcon cannot hear the falconer;
Things fall apart; the centre cannot hold;
Mere anarchy is loosed upon the world,
the blood-dimmed tide is loosed, and everywhere
the ceremony of innocence is drowned.
The best lack all conviction, while the worst
are full of passionate intensity.

I am inclined to get attracted to the last two lines: T*he best lack all conviction, while the worst are full of passionate intensity.* In that time period, particularly mid-1980s, and even in other times and on several other occasions, religion came up or was deliberately and intentionally brought with passionate *intensity* for political battles; not that this has seized to happen in the present times – it is still brought up! And, when it comes to - T*hings fall apart; the centre cannot hold* - perhaps, this seems true even today: the situation is out of control and tense!

*

Having rubbed shoulders with young *boys* bristling with automatics, as also with puritanical Sikh intelligentsia and having interacted with the trade-mark steel arrow holding Sant Jarnail Singh Bhinderanwale and his bête noir Sant Harchand Singh Longowal umpteen numbers of times alongside a battery of Akali and

Congress leaders, one can say that individually and collectively they all were/are guilty of putting to shame - Punjab, Punjabis and Punjabiat! They were not non-state actors but very much state-actors or villains?

And, when I last met Bhinderanwale at Akal Takht, hours before indefinite curfew became effective and operative on June 2, I cannot still forget the scene in that room, where he sat surrounded by his close confidants and there was a pile of arms and ammunition all over. As I left the premises, along with PTI: Press Trust of India staffer Gurdip Singh, I remember whispering to him: *this place will not be the same again, once the Army operation gets over*! {Gurdip Singh died after a brief illness on June 12, 2016 at Mohali.}

*

With the passage of time, sketchy details, in bits and pieces or *inside story*-type narrations came into public domain with a string of books penned by knowledgeable persons as to what all had happened in Punjab, particularly, at the Golden Temple complex in the wake of the Operation Bluestar, its operational details - how it was conducted and carried out - and who were the main characters etc. Magazines had also brought out special issues dissecting and vivisecting, analyzing and theorizing on the Punjab problem or the Sikh issues; each with its own hypothesis and sermonizing!

Whatever one may say or whichever way one may look at that single action the Centre or the Congress took: *Operation Bluestar,* one believes, it was a disaster, as were series of other man-made decisions, which can only be termed as missteps or calculated steps, which failed and faltered and left behind a burning, bruised, bleeding Punjab! While the debates, discussions and deliberations, the blame-games continue, so do continue the aftershocks and tremors that are still felt. The front-and fault-lines remain!

*

Before proceeding further, here, in brief, are two flashbacks: pre- and post-1984:

Pre-1984 scenario: Though, Punjab's tryst with destiny began soon after 1947, it got complicated with the first Census, 1951, when the Hindus logged Hindi, as their mother tongue, not Punjabi. The long-drawn agitation for Punjabi Suba, culminating in trifurcation of Punjab and carving out of it Himachal Pradesh and Haryana states in 1966, the subsequent Akali struggles, agitations over non-implementation of the *Reorganization Act, 1966,* the Akali Dal-led Morcha against the Emergency imposed by Indira Gandhi in 1975; the Sikh-Nirankari clash in 1978; desecration of religious places in the state; Akali-led Kapoori {Patiala district} Morcha against Sutlej-Yamuna Link Canal in 1982, when Ms Indira Gandhi laid the foundation-stone, and later the Morcha transformed into *Dharam Yudh Morcha* and the venue shifting from Patiala to Amritsar; advent of terrorism or militancy alongside etc. had a cumulative effect and impact on the evolving situation, ultimately resulting in government's questionable or calculated action in the form of Operation Bluestar in 1984.

Looking back, one remembers that the situation began to heat up in Amritsar sometimes in mid-April 1984 before the actual launch of the Operation Bluestar on June 3. Hectic efforts were underway for forging unity or for reconciliation of the two warring Sants: Longowal and Bhinderanwale at the level of the high priests: Giani Kirpal Singh, Jathedar, Akal Takht, Giani Harcharan Singh Mohallon, Jathedar Takht Keshgarh Sahib, Giani Lakha Singh, Jathedar Takht Damdama Sahib, Giani Pritam Singh, Head Priest of Akal Takht, Giani Sahib Singh, Head Priest of the Golden Temple and Giani Mohan Singh, a priest of the Golden Temple; besides some SGPC officials. Tension hung low over the complex through May. The peace efforts did not yield the expected dividends, as several other developments eclipsed the ever evolving situation.

If the CRPF deployed around the complex and elsewhere in the city seemed restive, the Akali leadership appeared restless, frustrated and even fuzzy over delay on the part of the Centre to concede their demands. It was a virtual war of nerves. Sensing hawkish posturing in Bhinderanwale camp, Longowal had convened a meeting of the party big-wigs and other office bearers. For the next few weeks there was frantic activity inside the complex: the most visible was the erecting of fortifications, digging of trenches and building of bunkers. Towards the end of May 1984, there were sporadic firing incidents in the complex vicinity. On June 1, the Akalis gave a call for *non-cooperation*, meaning stopping of all food grain movement outside Punjab, as well as a call to farmers not to pay any revenue or taxes. And, the *Dharam Yudh morcha* too had been an ongoing process since 1982.

What added to this *rebellious* call {non-co-operation}, as some analysts described the Akalis' decision; CRPF resorted to *indiscriminate* firing towards the Golden Temple. At least 10 persons were killed on June 1, 1984. There was tension in the city; the civil administration was helpless and hapless; totally demoralized. Deputy Commissioner Gurdev Singh Brar was seen seething with helpless anger, as he paced in and out of the office room of Superintendent of Police, CID Pandit Harjit Singh. And, standing there in the city Kotwali alongside some colleagues, police and civil officers, one could hear the firing. *This is totally a provocative act*! This was what several of the officers kept repeating, more to themselves than to the media. Later, it transpired, the firing was a well calculated and calibrated move to ascertain the positions of the militants/terrorists inside the complex; reliable sources said there was *no return* firing from inside the complex! In the next two days the Army units had moved in, curfew was clamped; rest, as we say, is history!

Post-1984 scenario: To salvage the situation, consequent to the damage caused to the Golden Temple complex, particularly Akal Takht, and to voice anguish of the Sikh *quom*, for once there appeared to be some kind of unity among warring Akali leaders and factions with high priests taking a strident stand on certain issues – *Panthic*! Desperate to salvage the damage, the Army, with Buta Singh at the centre-stage, worked out repair and re-construction plans inside the complex. And, to give the whole exercise a *Sikh effort and effect,* the Nihang Chief Baba Santa Singh was roped in. Simultaneously, as a security step and to secure the complex from future siege by any elements, a proposal was mooted for a *corridor* around the complex that would enable security forces to keep vigil. That proposal involved massive demolitions; already a large number of private properties, residential and commercial buildings and structures had been damaged due to the artillery shelling on localities – all once bustling Bazaars – behind Akal Takht.

With such proposals underway for a corridor around the complex, meanwhile, deputy commissioner Ramesh Inder Singh {he had succeeded Brar just before the Operation Bluestar} had constituted a committee to assess the losses civil population had suffered. Families that lost life or property were to be paid Rs 5,000 as ex gratia grant. As many as eight markets around the complex were hit, where 140 property units, involving 311 residential and commercial establishments, had been reduced to rubble. Some 40- odd properties on the Sultanwind Gate had been set on fire – victim of arson! The corridor plan was to involve dislocation of nearly 2,400 families and demolition of nearly 3,000 properties. The corridor, 60 ft wide, was to have a running length of 5,880 ft. When the actual operation demolition started, there was stiff resistance. {At present from Town Hall to the Golden Temple the entire stretch has been remodeled and named 'Heritage street' leading up to the Plaza in front of the Golden Temple to give the place a new approach; and a new look.}

*

Incidentally, in 1985, SGPC had moved an application in the Amritsar court, seeking Rs 1,000 crore, as compensation for the "damages" caused to the Golden Temple complex during the operation Bluestar, run by the Indian Army. That day I had also accompanied the then SGPC President, the late Gurcharan Singh Tohra to the district courts. The case kept pending for long; and later it was transferred to the Delhi High Court on January 17, 2013. The court directed the SGPC to submit court fee of Rs 10 crore, if it wanted to continue with the case. After the usual flip-flop, first the SGPC decided to withdraw the case and filed an affidavit to that effect. Under flak from intellectuals and others, later, it changed its mind and withdrew the affidavit; deposited the requisite fee to fight the case seeking Rs 1,000 crore as damages. This was in 2013. The case is still in the court. It has been more than 30 years!

*

To express anguish and to counter Santa Singh's *Sarbat Khalsa*, a Sikh convention was held at Gurdwara Shaheedan. On that rainy day, defying all restrictions the administration had put in place, a huge congregation had assembled on the call of the high priests on September 2, 1984. The Sikhs were asked to prepare for *liberation march* to the Golden Temple on October 1, as also, and more significantly, Giani Zail Singh was *excommunicated* from the Sikh Panth along with Buta Singh. The Sikhs were angry that as a Sikh and the supreme commander of the armed forces, the President had failed to avert the Army action. Thereafter, with time running out, work of repair and restoration of a semblance of *all is well,* MES: military engineering service personnel and Nihangs were deployed to expeditiously carry out repairs inside the complex.

Nihang chief Baba Santa Singh camped at the six-storey high *Burj* –tower – Phula Singh, near Ghee mandi Sheranwala Gate, close to the Amritsar International Hotel, which served as his *Kar Sewa* headquarters for the duration that he camped there; he would frequently try to throw spanners into the government-Akali/SGPC works! He was a stooge of the government mechanizations, thanks to Buta Singh, and even a *Sarbat Khalsa* was convened by him and Buta Singh prior to the one called by the high priests – the Sikh convention - at Gurdwara Shaheedan. Later, Santa Singh was also excommunicated from the Panth. Buta Singh sought pardon years later and appeared at Akal Takht to accept the punishment, *Tankha*, to return to the folds of the Sikh Panth.

Once the complex was handed over to the high priests albeit SGPC, the work of redoing after undoing what the government had done was entrusted to Baba Kharak Singh, who started the *Kar Sewa* with de-silting of the holy tank –the pool of nectar – on October 12. The Akal Takht was demolished and rebuilt. Also, behind the scene parleys were started to seek pardon for Zail Singh. His emissaries met the high priests several times and finally on September 26, Zail Singh was exonerated and taken back into the Sikh P*anth*. The very next day he landed in Amritsar and appeared before Akal Takht, where he spent 50 minutes with the high priests. Thereafter, he made an emotional speech addressing the Sikh sangat gathered in the courtyard between Akal Takht and *Darshani Deori* – main majestic entry point to the sanctum sanctorum; the army had labeled this open space as the *killer ground*!

*

Incidentally, the *Tribune* had deputed Satindra Singh, Delhi Chief to cover the visit of the President. He had travelled with the President. He left it to me and asked me to send my copy to him. The joint byline with him gave me confidence. In fact, he had earlier camped here for a fortnight to monitor my working. Later, he disclosed that he was sent following complaints against me that some professor at Guru Nanak Dev University wrote my copy! He reported to Prem Bhatia that such insinuations and allegations were *hollow and stupid*!

*

This was second visit of Zail Singh, when I met him. On his earlier visit on June 8, after the Operation Bluestar, media was not allowed anywhere near the complex, what to say of entry inside. Years later, Ramesh Inder Singh told me that since the programme was announced at a short notice, the Governor too rushed by air. However, due to President's flight, he had to wait before permission to land was given; the President had landed before him.

At the Golden Temple on June 8, he said, Zail Singh was accompanied by Tarlochan Singh and commentator Jasdev Singh besides many others. As the President started stepping into the *Parikarma*, one of his attendants opened an umbrella over him. As Zail Singh saw this, he ordered it be shut and removed. While proceeding towards the *sanctum sanctorum*, some shots were fired from the side of the two Bungas. The Army, however, assured the delegation that the place had been secured!

One can say fairly responsibly that Zail Singh, as President, fulfilled his crucial obligations, both as the supreme commander of the armed forces, as also as a devout Sikh with eerie poignancy and adroitly; allegations against him notwithstanding, including slogan-shouting outside the complex, while he addressed the Sikhs inside on September 27, when he submitted himself before Akal Takht. He had sought from the Almighty *forgiveness* to all those who had desecrated the holy precincts. His commitments and promises to the high priests of vacating of the complex by the security forces, handing it to the SGPC and pardon of innocent Sikhs taken into custody during Operation Bluestar and to follow up the cases of terrorists etc. were some of the points that had defused the situation and had resulted in his exoneration. Moreover, he explained the position of the President, who did not interfere in day-to-day affairs of the government.

*

It is equally pertinent to mention that Ms Indira Gandhi visited the Golden Temple on June 23, 1984, and spent half an hour inside. The media was not allowed. I along with Gurdip Singh had walked up to the Bhandari Bridge to go to the complex but was denied permission. As we stood at the foot of the Bridge, Ms Gandhi's cavalcade drove past us. She sat on the front seat of the Ambassador. Later, Giani Sahib Singh told us that Ms Gandhi made an offering at the Harimandir Sahib and listened to the kirtan for few minutes. In his brief talk with her, he had demanded withdrawal of the Army and that devotees are permitted inside to pay obeisance; even if for fixed hours.

*

To cut the long story short, with the passage of time, as normalcy seemingly began to creep back, in the following months, October on wards, with senior Akali leaders in jails and their respective protégés trying to occupy and reserve the space and vacuum in their absence, engaged themselves in the usual tussle, common among the Akali leaders, for up-man- ship started. The high priests made several attempts to forge peace and amity but without any tangible results. So much so that at one stage the frustrated high priests wanted the SGPC to define their role and not to burden them with every other issue.

And, even before blood had dried in the *Parikarma*, the warring, obstinate leaders and splinter groups would not listen and were at their old games once again; these factional leaders forgot the harrowing times of what the people, the state and above all the Golden Temple had been through in the past. Such was the nature and scale of veiled maneuvers, machinations being played out then for and by vested interests by wily politicians and such were the days and developments that have remained etched in my memory.

After 1984, the first Operation Black Thunder or Police action came in 1986. The second Operation Black Thunder was in 1988. The period between 1986 and 1988 was one of the worst in the history of the Golden Temple, as also for the state. Meanwhile, the security forces, led by the Army, had carried out Operation Woodrose in the countryside almost simultaneously with the Operation Bluestar to cleanse the villages of militants/terrorists; and restore peoples' sagging morale and waning confidence in the administration.

*

One has been at the centre-stage of much of action that took place in those unusual times. For instance, one had observed, standing on the zero-line, the then Prime Minister A B Vajpayee travel in a bus from Wagha to Lahore {February 1999}, signaling bus-diplomacy to normalize the relations between the two nations that separated in 1947. That late afternoon, February 19, setting sun scene, with a cool breeze blowing, came live 16 years later, when I saw on TV images of Prime Minister Narendra Modi alight from his special Indian Air Force Jet at Allama Iqbal International Airport, Lahore, on December 25, 2015, hug Nawaz Sharif, and fly in a helicopter to his palatial house. That planned or impromptu visit, whatever one may call it, should be seen and perceived as a small step to restore normalcy in the relations of the two countries, so closely knitted and yet so different and apart!

*

Incidentally, Punjab Chief Minister Parkash Singh Badal was among the group of persons who had accompanied the Prime Minister Vajpayee in that bus. Badal had returned the next day. At the Wagha border, as we waited for him to walk across the zero-line, we noticed that following him was his *Man Friday*, who held the strings of two animals. These were the two Dumba sheep that were gifted to him, on his demand. From the brochure I was given by a Pakistan veterinary doctor, and later, from literature available with the ICAR: Indian Council of Agricultural Research-Central Sheep and Wool Research Institute, Avikanagar in Rajasthan, I learned more about the Dumba sheep: Dumba are fat-tail, fat-rump breed of sheep found in and around Jaipur and Ajmer districts of Rajasthan. These are not indigenous and exact source of origin of these animals is not known. Main objective of rearing and keeping these animals by entrepreneurs or live animal traders is to fetch a huge sum of money during the Eid festival, as they have great aesthetic and religious value. Elite people spend huge money on purchasing these animals. The market price of these animals in Mumbai and other metropolitan cities is very high, as claimed by entrepreneurs. Adult males are sold at the rate of Rs 90,000 to Rs 150,000, female Rs 70, 000; and lambs Rs 15, 000-Rs 30,000 in the market. Pakistan has some of the best Dumba sheep!

3

A Parrot, Hawks and Doves

It took some time to get familiar with the geography of Amritsar city, its labyrinth of by-lanes and streets: quite a nightmare; and the district, as also with the religious, political and militant groups' line-up, groupings and ground situation obtaining and evolving at that point of time. In fact, one or two rounds of the Golden Temple complex were part of the daily *beat*; a routine. And, inside the SGPC: Shiromani Gurdwara Prabandhak Committee complex, housed in different buildings were powerful camps: one each of Sant Harchand Singh Longowal and Sant Jarnail Singh Bhinderanwale; one of Akhand Kirtani Jatha, led by Bibi Amarjit Kaur, widow of Fauja Singh, who was among the 13 killed in the Sikh-Nirankari clash in Amritsar in April 1978; and, of course, there were the Babbars, all armed, in the Akal Rest House. {It was the Babbars, who first made me taste *Bajre-di- roti* with *saag*. They would also, at times, show their prowess by riding Enfield motorcycles atop the adjoining Guru Ram Das Serai.}

All this occupation in the complex had happened, much to the consternation and chagrin of the SGPC. It was a potpourri of religion, politics and gun-totting militants; doves and hawks: radicals and moderates; and anti-social elements, which came in later - post Operation Bluestar! Thus, the complex did not just house the office of the SGPC alone in the Teja Singh Sammundari Hall. Besides, there were various self-invited guests-cum-residents, as well. There was the defunct office of the Shiromani Akali Dal {SAD} in the vacant Baradari, as also Bhai Ranjit Singh {allegedly involved in the killing of the Nirankari chief}, occupying a small part of the Teja Singh Sammundari Hall, away from Bhinderanwale camp followers; and protected by the Babbars.

Flanking the SGPC office was the Guru Nanak Niwas, where ensconced was Sant Jarnail Singh Bhinderanwale and his battery of armed men. {He, himself, later moved to the Akal Takht, a safe sanctuary inside the Golden Temple complex}; and in the other flank, Akal Guest House and Guru Ram Das Serai, were accommodated devotes coming to pay obeisance, apart from the Babbars. Activists of the All-India Sikh Students' Federation, owing allegiance to Sant Bhinderanwale, were also entrenched inside the complex; as were members of the Youth Akali Dal, next to Manji Sahib Dewan Hall; and, even the *Parikarma* {the marble path or the circumambulatory around the sanctum sanctorum} rooms were occupied by those whom SGPC had not permitted. The complex was, thus, a *City State*!

*

In due course of time, these very rooms began to be feared, as some of these were being used by elements, mostly unwanted and anti-social, who engaged in extortion, torture and killings in what was termed as trial by Kangaroo courts! A score of skeletons were to be later found from the debris in the square lawn, opposite Guru Ram Das Langar building, when SGPC launched a massive operation clean up. Here, I am reminded of an incident when, along with some others, including Prabhjot Singh, my colleague from Chandigarh, we were holed up in one of the rooms for close to two hours for no reason or rhyme. We were called for what was purported to be a news briefing! In fact, most of the underground organizations and outfits, including the dreaded five-member Panthic Committee, headed by Gurbachan Singh Manochahal, would also hold press conferences in those very Parikarma rooms or issue *diktats* from there: announcement of Khalistan, in respect of breaking, re-making, elimination, assimilation of established institutions; realigning of political parties, reconstituting of the SGPC, time-and-again replacement of the high priests etc. Later, these rooms were dismantled. That gave more depth to the corridor at the edge of the Parikarma.

*

At that time, SGPC was like a *caged parrot* {to borrow the term Supreme Court had used for the CBI} with wings clipped and clearly a hapless, helpless victim of connivance of circumstances; despite trying to put up a brave face and making tall claims of being autonomous, independent, sovereign and *in control* of the complex, as well as of the *situation* inside. Yet, the fact remained that it often found it difficult to resist the *diktats* given out by armed men from within. Perhaps, it had no choice but to oblige, willingly or unwillingly; and oblige it did!

The SGPC secretary Bhan Singh and SGPC President Gurcharan Singh Tohra's private assistant, Abnashi Singh, were, one may say, men with nerves of steel with abundant patience and perseverance, when it came to dealing with the ever demanding groups, which had forcibly entrenched themselves inside the complex or from the camp followers of the other self-styled leaders and, of course, the two Sants, who displayed debatable and disputable ideologies; not hiding their different approaches to what the Sikh *quom* desired and demanded and how to proceed to achieve those goals. {Abnashi Singh along with Dr Baldev Singh Brar was to disappear one day, never to return again; they were believed to have been tricked by the gun-totting boys and killed somewhere on the outskirts of the city. Even their bodies were never found!}

*

Much before the day I joined, SAD was already in the thick of its *Dharam Yudh Morcha* {launched to seek justice: political, social, economic and religious}; the entire SGPC complex was always and ever bustling with people, pilgrims, devotees, tourists and visitors. Every evening, the Manji Sahib Dewan Hall would reverberate with echo of *Bole- so-nihal* cries, as batches or jathas of volunteers were flagged off to court arrest at the city Kotwali. There, not only buses were parked to take them to different jails but were also served langar {community kitchen}. SAD workers and district/police officials would mark the presence- take a roll call- of those courting arrest; and off they would go reciting *shabad*- religious hymns- and brandishing *kesar*i-saffron- flags with bands tied across their turbans, while women wore saffron *siropas*-robes of honor- around their necks. This daily ritual had an aura of festivity, commitment and devotion to the Panth!

*

At the end of the day, as one analyses now, did the *Dharam Yudh Morcha* or for that matter all the *struggles* sponsored and launched by the Sikh {Akali} leadership, including raising of a corps of Marjeevare – who sacrifice anything and everything at the bidding of their masters - achieve for the Sikhs or the state what these were intended to: justice - political, religious, social, economic, linguistic, territorial, sharing of river waters etc.? Across the decades, the emotive issues to which the Sikh masses responded enthusiastically, more because of their religious *faith,* rather than *trust* in the leadership, has waned. How come the leadership has failed to deliver or achieve what it had set itself to achieve and for which it had mobilized mass support; and yet, faltered in not articulating the aspirations of the people with all the Sikh demands still remaining unmet; a distant dream; a great betrayal, indeed!

*

It was in such a complicated situation inside the complex that one had operated, observed and reported despite the professional hazards and risks, including having seen armed *boys* kill those whom they suspected to be government *agents*. Attending long-winded congregations, militants-organized *Sarbat Khalsa*, rubbing shoulders with gun-totting youth and attending monologue-laced press briefings convened by fire-spitting self-styled leaders had become a routine; often boring and at times scary! The reel of reminiscences plays on, over and over, even today. Whenever and every time, we, the old-timers meet, we talk of those Amritsar decades.

*

Years later, whenever one happened to visit the place for obeisance, old memories would flood the memory and pictures of a bygone era would appear on the mind-screen, as if those characters were still around and stalking; distracting from the notes of *Gurbani* that floated across the holy tank!

Of late, the façade of the main entrance to the Golden Temple: Ghanta Ghar or Clock Tower entrance facing the Jallianwala Bagh road has totally changed. The place has been morphed into a marble Plaza with fountains, benches and canopies at the corners and artistic-*Jali* panels atop high-rise walls cover the private buildings facing the Temple. The shops in front and ones that were part of the complex are gone and hectic construction activity is underway; in fact, it is all over the city, and the remnants of the past are being systematically and consciously erased, forever, and a concrete jungle built!

At present, neither the Amritsar city nor the periphery of the Golden Temple complex or life inside the SGPC perimeter is the same; everything, the very outlook of the place has changed: under construction infrastructure within and around the complex; and efforts to improve local transportation system have added more woes to the existing chaos that had been the city's hallmark {*trademark*?} all these decades! Modernization, gradually and surely, is beginning to cast a shadow over the traditional culture and flavour of the place. Is religious importance being overshadowed by ambitious grand tourism plans? Is history and geography being re-written? Sigh!

4

Media and Militants

Such were the times and such was the atmosphere inside the SGPC premises that it was ever surcharged and polarized, given the web of complex and curious mix of religion, politics and cult of militancy. Any sane talk or discussion or comment was considered a sin! In that action-reaction-over reaction ridden situation, getting to the root cause of what was happening or who were writing the script required *investigative* reporting. That was not to be. To do that was not only difficult but fraught with risks, as well, because the place was dominated by hot-headed religio-political and militant leaders {mostly self-styled} professing different ideologies, if any, and also idiosyncrasies.

*

Whatever one may say or whichever way one may look at it, back then, I have no hesitation in saying, when it came to getting to know the inside news, there existed an unwritten *give-and-take* between the journalists and the sources: security/intelligence agencies. The media, in fact, had neither choice nor discretion in this matter but to report what it was told at gun-point or with a tinge of intimidation either by different organizations: militant, political, religious or security/intelligence agencies or what was given out in government press handouts through the public relations office.

It was left to the wisdom and common sense of the individual news person to sieve facts from *plants* and decide how much to believe, how much to disbelieve, how much to retain, how much to discard and how much to report. The interpretation and final reporting of the available information also depended upon the individual's understanding of the situation or cross-checking with alternative sources and proper verification of the information in hand; something not without the anticipated and unanticipated risks!

The professional hazards the media fraternity faced were multi-dimensional. Among these was journalists' vulnerability to allegations by every side: police, militants, government, political and religious organizations with each claiming journalists were informers of one or the other side. Yet, despite being caught in the cross-fire, the media in Amritsar survived through the troubled times to report.

This decision- and choice- making tested one's nerves; after all, it was the question of professional credibility, personal reputation and also image of the organization one represented. And, of course, survival! Above all, reporting had to be in the overall interest of the people and the state. Frankly speaking, there were times when due to self-induced competition, the two news agencies, UNI: United News of India and PTI created confusion, given their different ways of interpreting a statement or situation. The two were located in the same row of government houses on the Taylor Road. It is a different story that because of misinformation and over zealousness, the state apparatus, on several occasions, searched the office-cum residential premises and also harassed the UNI staffers, for example Jaspal Sidhu and Kuldip S Arora; even the National Security Act was invoked and some journalists sent to jail. And, then there was stabbing of *Indian Express* staff correspondent, Sanjeev Gaur, besides, of course, gunning of several scribes in the state.

*

I soon discovered that in the then prevailing situation and circumstances, there was unique comradeship among the media persons. It could either be out of the fear of the known and the unknown or professional demands and desires. Whatever be the reasons, the truth is that barring some exceptions, it was either the mutual needs or, perhaps, compulsions and compunctions that created an ambience of sharing of news and caring for each other's safety and security. Exclusive stories, of course, individuals continued to file. The sharing of *spot* events and happenings was, perhaps, a convention among journalists.

Yet, one can say with a fair degree of responsibility that behind all this bonhomie in the journalists' fraternity, one could sense and feel the subterranean under currents of a division among the Sikh and the Hindu colleagues, who were seemingly further sub-divided into smaller groups, owing allegiance to different political leaders, parties and organizations; and espoused their causes, whatever these may have happened to be.

There were also whispers, one often heard, of some journalists working for the intelligence agencies, both central and state, as well as for various security outfits ranging from the Army to the CRPF: Central Reserve Police Force to the BSF: Border Security Force to RAW: Research and Analysis Wing to IB: Intelligence Bureau; and, of course, the state CID. These agencies, there were strong indications, had their own independent cells and moles, in the media, SGPC, as also within the religio-political and militant outfits operating from inside the complex.

Honestly, to be a Sikh and working in the then prevailing situation was a difficult, daunting and demanding task: while one's own community harbored high expectations, for the other community, one was ever a suspect! And on top of all this, there were persistent threats of being eliminated! These threats invariably accompanied every press note that militant organizations delivered, demanding full, verbatim coverage. So much so, the militants had even issued a code of conduct for the media; just as they had prescribed a dress code for the school-going children!

The attacks, the threats and the killing of several journalists, across the state, at the hands of the militants was a reality, just as were searches, intimidation and detention by the government instrumentalities that further complicated and compounded the working conditions. Thus, in that charged atmosphere, it was like walking on the razor's edge, particularly, for ones known for their honesty, integrity and truthful reporting! They were doubly unblessed!

For the battery of visiting journalists, including foreign correspondents, the destination was the two Sants, Longowal and Bhinderanwale; and *sources* were the Amritsar-based journalists {call them reliable, if you will}! Rarely did the visiting journalists {there were some exceptions} venture out into the field to study the mood or capture the fear-psychosis or anxiety neurosis that gripped the countryside. From the meetings with these visiting journalists, particularly those who came from New Delhi, it was apparent that they had had briefing from the powers that be or the security/intelligence agencies monitoring Punjab situation. Thus, invariably, they would try and fit the actual ground picture into the frame that was embedded in their mind. This, at times, distorted the real issues.

Also, there were several occasions when the local journalists were called for a press conference at a given point and then directed to some other place and sometimes taken to remote villages and fields for a briefing and later told to hang on till the militant leaders departed. On return, the journalists faced questioning by the security forces. It was a cat-and-mouse game! I was part of such hide-and-seek covert press meetings with some key militants of that time!

*

In the villages, militants' mid-night knocks were dreaded. The boys would demand, at gun-point, shelter, though temporary, and food. And, after they left, security forces would swoop down on the militants' unwilling hosts: *passive harbors*, as the security forces labeled them, and would whisk away some men-folk for interrogation and detention. In many such cases, these persons simply disappeared or were reported *missing*. Thus, these village folks were caught between the devil and the deep sea!

*

I remember a time, when a small booklet was in circulation inside the complex: it depicted a collage of newspapers and photographs with image of a parrot either to tease or chide or to describe the plight and helplessness of the media or to mock at the media, as mouth-piece of the government! The media was accused of *biases and prejudices*. More than the impression such a depiction would make on the minds of the ordinary people, it created a kind of fear-psychosis in the media, which, naturally, felt that any hot-head could accost and confront reporters inside the complex. With due humility one can look back and say that working in Amritsar then was like being caught in a pincer: threats from militants and demands from the state instrumentalities!

*

On a personal note, may I add that I had an added advantage then; my colleague and guide, Harbir Singh Bhanwer was an asset: he doubled up as SGPC official, as also *The Tribune* correspondent of standing. He was of immense help to understand and analyze the ever evolving situation, given his encyclopedic knowledge and understanding of the Sikh politics, history, religion and the Sikh *Rehat-Maryada*: code of Sikh conduct; and his insight into the pulls and pressures operating within the groups or factions housed inside the complex. He was not only very methodological in keeping track of and record of the happenings and available related literature and background material in a chronological order but was also adept and apt at retrieving whatever information was required for *padding* of stories or write-ups and in giving a make-over to the spot developments. He was ever liberal in sharing background material with his colleagues, if and whenever asked for!

His own books based on his deep and vast knowledge and experience of Amritsar reporting, as a journalist, have been well received. He lived in modest first floor accommodation the SGPC had provided him on the first floor of the rooms in the Parikarma facing the *sanctum sanctorum* to the right side of the Clock Tower: the main entrance to the *Harimandir Sahib,* above the Punjab and Sind Bank. As luck would have it, I was able to contact him in the nick of time, asking him to vacate his quarters and leave with whatever essentials he could grab, since the curfew had been announced in the wake of anticipated major security forces' offensive on the complex in the first week of June, 1984. He did exactly that and rushed to the residence of one of our colleagues, K S Tomar, a bachelor then, who represented *The Hindustan Times*. Tomar later became chairperson of the Himachal Pradesh public service commission, Shimla. These days one rarely comes across such journalists, as Bhanwer. After his appointment as *The Tribune* Staffer, he was transferred and posted at Shimla in February, 1987.

*

As mentioned earlier, this was my second posting at Amritsar. On both occasions, I had the good fortune to learn much, professionally. That learning came from G R Sethi, an octogenarian legend, who had been associated with *The Tribune* even before Partition, when the newspaper was published from Lahore, now in Pakistan. One day, he shared how, as correspondent, he would cycle between Amritsar and Lahore. He contributed to *The Statesman*, as well. *Sethi Sahib*, as we addressed him, had joined *The Tribune*, after a stint with the *Civil and Military Gazette* and worked for 70 years. Born on November 4, 1900, he died in December 1988. He was an institution in himself and much more. By nature, he did not believe in wasting paper. One would find a pile of invitation cards on his large desk, in the middle of a room walled by rows of book shelves. On the back of these cards he would jot down notes. Those days, news was transmitted over the Tele-printer and the sent copy rolls would be sent to Sethi Sahib. He used even the back of those rolls. He led a simple, frugal life; he was a walking encyclopedia.

*

After Bhanwer had left, four months later, one afternoon, June 2, 1987 to be precise, a tall young boy came into the office; perspiring and puffing; my teacher S S Dosanj at PAU had already spoken to me about him. He was Ramesh Vinayak, who too had graduated, as had I, from PAU's same department of Journalism, Languages and Culture. Believe me, for the next three years or so, we worked like the Siamese Twins, trying to give our best to the newspaper and its readers. The same day Ramesh had set foot, a journalist had been shot dead in Tarn Taran. He volunteered to go there and file his report. That was the beginning of a relationship, rarely seen in our profession. It has been now over 29 years. We still share much and bond well over personal and professional matters.

I remember, one day, he called up to say he wanted to come over. Soon, he arrived with a box of sweets. *What is the good news that you have brought sweets*, I enquired. His eyes became misty, he bent to show respect; we hugged: it was June 2, 2012; the day marked 25 years of our friendship and equation. There was silence and then we together went down the memory lane recalling events of that time. After my transfer to Chandigarh, Ramesh held the fort alone for over one year till he left Amritsar, in December 1991, and joined *India Today,* which took him globetrotting, both on sabbatical as well as professional assignments. Later, he switched to *The Hindustan Times*, where he is now Senior Resident Editor, Chandigarh. He has reached this slot by the dint of sheer diligence, hard work, sincerity, sobriety, patience and perseverance. He has made his mark in the profession, and yet, remains unpretentious!

*

There was, yet, another side of the media then, not at reporter's level. It was, more so, at higher level: perhaps, or may be, at either the level of proprietors or managements or editorial. One did not come across a level-reporting field in the media, broadly representing the language press and the English press. And, in the cacophonous SGPC complex too, it was a different atmosphere, when it came to media. On the one hand, there came a stage when some of the colleagues were hesitant to visit the place and preferred to share the spot news with those for who

SGPC was a must, regular professional beat. On the other hand, on one occasion, in the charged atmosphere, Hindu Shiv Sena office-bearers had called a press conference on the premises of the Durgiana Mandir. Some senior colleagues from the media were in the city from Chandigarh. We went there. Believe me, I was sweating and nervous. It was Gobind Thukral, who firmly held my hand and repeatedly assured me: *do not worry. I am with you*. Such were the times; thank you *Thukral Sahib*!

*

As part of professional duties, every day, one had also to rummage through scores of daily press notes, all in Punjabi and mostly hand-written, received from various militant organizations, political parties and government. In the press notes received from the militant outfits and other religio-political organizations, invariably there would be implicit and explicit warning signs that these press handouts be reported verbatim. One could discern the sadistic pleasure or the delight the senders must be getting in public disgrace of others. Condemnation and finding fault-lines in others was their pastime. In such a situation, while analyzing that period now, one can say that those who ruled the roost at gun-point then, in their zeal, had lost the capacity to see things rationally or objectively. All they saw and spoke and thrust on others around were -- indiscretions.

Besides, of course, the daily round of the SGPC complex, personal contacts with the SGPC officials and the two Sants: Longowal and Bhinderanwale, both different, as is chalk from cheese, in temperament, thinking, expression and mannerism, we had to ensure balance in reporting. I remember, how, with a faint smile, Longowal would often ask us-the reporters-if we have been to the Chambal valley: meaning, if we had met Bhinderanwale before coming over! On some occasions, with a smirk, Bhinderanwale would ask us if we have been to the *Sadh*, meaning Longowal!

*

I would be doing injustice were I not to remember and salute the indefatigable Kirpal Singh, who would deliver the press notes emanating from the complex, particularly, of the SGPC and the Akali Dal. He would cycle around the newspapers'/agencies' offices carrying the press *Dak* in a *Khak*i cloth bag. The Akali Dal press handouts were invariably drafted by Gurmeet Singh Cheema, Press

Secretary to Sant Longowal. Kirpal Singh remained active till the Operation Bluestar interrupted his rounds of the media offices.

*

In the very first fortnight of my arrival in Amritsar, I was surprised by the kind of attention given to me in the Bhinderanwale camp; this foxed me. It was much later that I learned the reason behind this attention: during one of our casual talks, *Akali Patrika* representative, the late Mohinder Singh, who was believed to be fairly close to the Bhinderanwale camp and supposedly knew what went on where inside the complex, explained to me the reason for the way Bhinderanwale and his men paid attention to me. He reminded me of my story on the arrest of Swaran Singh, an alleged accused in the murder of Lala Jagat Narain {head of *Hind Samachar* group of newspapers} in September 1981; and my deposition in the Session's Court at Ludhiana in that case. That reporting and court statement, I believe, was, perhaps, one of the reasons behind the acquittal of Swaran Singh; and consequent extra attention paid to me.

*

The following incident, perhaps or possibly, is the outcome of that unusual attention: one day, accompanied by my senior colleague, PTI staffer Gurdip Singh, we just climbed up the Akal Takht to meet Sant Bhinderanwale, who was strolling on the roof. We got talking, nothing in particular. Sant's *Gharvai*: closest attendant handed him a bowl of milk. As Sant sipped and talked, suddenly he stopped and handed over the bowl to me, indicating that I drink the rest of it. For a split second, I demurred; Gurdip and I locked eyes and he nodded- *take it*. I took the bowl and finished the milk. It was a new experience! Much later, I mentioned this to my mother, Gurbachan Kaur, who explained that this was a normal practice or a kind of ritual in which *such* saintly people indulged in to indicate their *closeness and fondness* for someone. It is O.K; I was left dumb and numb!

*

Flashback: Here, let me share my experience of reporting on Swaran Singh's arrest, interrogation and, later, my appearance in the court at Ludhiana for which summons were served on me at Ambala. That day, several other media persons had also been called in the same case: murder of Lala ji. For that court appearance, I did not get the expected support from my office. All that the News Editor told me was to *stick to your version.* Meantime, *Hind Samachar* group had also contacted me asking to dispose favorably. I simply and politely said *I will confine to what is stated in my report.* Arrest of Swaran Singh was a *breakthrough* for the Punjab police in the Lala Jagat Narain murder case. The controversy, however, was with regard to the place of his arrest: Muktsar or Bathinda. I had disputed police claim. After visiting the place, I had stated in my story that the arrest was made in Bathinda district. In fact, the night he was interrogated, I was present in the office of the Senior Superintendent of Police Faridkot. I sat as a passive listener and later filed my story. That night Swaran Singh had repeatedly stuck to his stand that he had never met Sant Jarnail Singh Bhinderanwale either before or after the killing and had acted because of his intense anguish over the writings in the *Hind Samachar* group of newspapers. I, however, did spot him in Guru Nanak Niwas and remembered the night he was interrogated in Faridkot SSP's office; he was wearing a light parrot-green *Kurta-pajama*!}

*

It seems much easier now to write, talk and share what went on in Amritsar at *that* time. It also amuses when one goes through 33-year old yellowing notes or when one flips through carefully preserved news clippings, some with fading ink, some brittle; and the related background material of *that* period. As one goes over the yesteryear papers, it refreshes the memories of what was seen and reported or what was not reported. Frankly, it was not that easy to work in those circumstances. What kept one going was *faith in God*, straight, sincere, balanced reporting {as far as possible} and regular dialogue with the Editor-in-chief. And, of course, the news displays and the bylines!

*

Admittedly, several stories were spiked at the instance of Prem Bhatia, like the one wherein I had reported on devotees and others who were squatting at the entrance to the Golden Temple with their hands tied behind their backs or similar groups being abused and kicked in the City Kotwali, immediately after Operation Bluestar. There was a kind of internal censorship in *The Tribune*. This was more than evident from the fact that several stories were spiked based as these were on the interviews with those who had had firsthand experience during Operation Bluestar since they were trapped inside the Complex and were later detained by the security forces for questioning after the operation. Such interviews were with SGPC officials and some priests.

In fact, when normal communication lines were restored after state-wide clamp down in the wake of the Operation Bluestar, I received a message on the Tele-printer from a very senior colleague in New Delhi *Tribune* Bureau, Satindra Singh, asking about my well being. My reply to him was put up to Prem Bhatia by someone in Chandigarh, who had the nerve to tear off my message from the Tele-printer room. Later, Prem Bhatia wrote a long letter to me expressing his concerns and justifying how he wanted to get in touch with me, when he was among the Editors/correspondents who were brought to Amritsar on a sponsored tour after the Army action but could not. It was a kind of in-house mischief by someone who wanted to earn some Brownie points and be seen in Bhatia's good books!

*

Every morning, around 8 am, the telephone would ring. On the line would be Ms Shakuntla Bhatia, who would very politely enquire after the family, say little niceties and then say, *Here, talk to Prem*. At that hour every morning, there would be silence in the house so as not to miss anything that the chief had to say or talk about. He would ask about day's upcoming developments, talk of outline of an editorial he planned to pen; and expect a summary of the possible developments, given the ever evolving and changing situation. The morning *conferences* kept me on my toes, alert and helped to be more indulgent and vigilant, professionally. Those daily 8 am briefings were like the Wednesday night 8 pm *Binaca Geetmala* that Amin Syani presented on AIR: All India Radio.

*

As to what it was like reporting or covering Punjab then, a detailed account is given in senior journalist Gobind Thukral's book: *Troubled Reflections: Reporting Violence*; published by Shimla-based Indian Institute of Advanced Study in 2009. As per the Institute's web site: The book offers a firsthand account of reporting violence in Punjab, once considered toughest assignments for journalists. During the peak of militancy in Punjab from April 1978 to 1995, the journalists were at the receiving end of the morbid State and the trigger-happy melancholic militants. These torturous years were marked by a real fear of the gun, as a large number of editors, reporters and their associates were prey to the marauders in different garbs. It was also a period when information was hard to obtain and write about as the police laced almost each news story with lies and the apathetic bureaucracy mired in corruption, indulged in subterfuge. The militants dictated their own terms for reporting which the journalists could ignore at the risk of their lives. The wily divided politicians played their crafty games, as did a few media houses.

In this scenario, journalists found themselves in a stifling and frightful situation. There was always that lurking fear of the gun. But much worse was the paucity of authentic information that could be weaved into convincing news stories and analyses. Information came in bits and pieces and, at times, there was no second line of source to cross check. Journalists were supposed to sniff and filter it, and they tried that. This book details how well they performed this difficult task. It also details various filters that allowed or stopped news from reaching the public and various players that decided all that found adequate space. There is discussion on prevention of deadly conflicts and the role of newspapers, particularly in resolving conflicts and bringing peace. And, finally what should be the role of media in general, particularly in reporting violence and tries to figure out why and how communalism infected it right from the beginning. Thus, reporting in that period taught many lessons, literally changing the perception about journalism and how media can and does impact and influence the public mind and opinion.

*

The years spent in Amritsar-Gurdaspur taught me many lessons and helped me gain better perspective, professionally. One could not have asked for more, when it came to reporting from the front-lines or fault-lines in a troubled state during tense times!

Reporting, thus, had its own up and down swings in those trying times. That experience, honestly, changed one's very perception of judging men and matters or interpreting and analyzing a given situation or its multiple ripple effects and consequences. Looking back, one realizes that there always remained an invisible angle to journalism that is both *human* and *humane*!

5

Ordered Disorder

Visits to the SGPC complex aside, there were other assignments, engagements and spots, as well, to be covered: the killings of or by militants/security forces across the district and or in the adjoining Gurdaspur; or visits of the VIPs; and, of course, normal *beat* stories. Given the daily long working hours and travels, the responsibilities of running the house and bringing up children was left to Wife. A combination of circumstances and factors: instigated or stage-managed, would change the given situation and influence political equations that continued to evolve and develop with the passage of time. Frequent assimilations and eliminations in the political arena, making and breaking of SGPC executive, quicksilver changes in the lineup of the high priests, mergers or dissolutions of militant and political outfits would further compound the confusion.

Talking of yesteryears, many of those operating from inside the complex, who claimed to be avowed followers or fans of a political leader, or a militant outfit, would have no qualms in changing loyalties, unhesitatingly and unabashedly! One day they would be in one camp, the next day they would line-up elsewhere. During my entire stay in Amritsar-Gurdaspur, one saw from close quarters how the very protagonists of Sikhism or espousing the Sikh cause vandalized the *Maryada* of the *Harimandir Sahib*, as also the reputations of those, who were trying to do some good to the community. These semi-literate elements or disparagers would make an issue where none existed and try to enforce it on the others. These fly by night knights have caused immense damage to the two principle communities – the Sikhs and the Hindus - and the state. Let us not feign ignorance or pretend that such elements do not exist at present or are not trying to queer the pitch; such elements do queer the pitch as and when is their wont and suits them.

Today, in retrospect, one finds there are more questions that remain unanswered. And, if answers are there, no one is willing to provide these! The continuous failure of the political, as well as religious leadership, even today, is too obvious. The credibility graph of the religio-political leaderships has dipped steeply and, unfortunately, it seems not to have learnt any lessons, what to expect answers to unanswered questions that still haunt the people and the state. Politics continues to dominate religion. There does not appear to be any transparent manner in the appointment of say SGPC President or the high priests. As then, so now, the ruling SAD holds the key to these crucial appointments. Regarding the SGPC general house and its elected members or *Sant Samaj,* less said the better.

And how much respect do the high priests command in the eyes of the powers that be: SGPC and SAD, is illustrated in the following incident: in those days, the high priests of Takht Keshgarh Sahib {Anandpur Sahib}, Takht Damdama Sahib {Talwandi Sabo, Bathinda} would often frequent the SGPC and meet with their counterparts, Jathedar of Akal Takht and head priests of Akal Takht and the Golden Temple.

I would meet the two visiting high priests, Harcharan Singh Mahalon {Takht Keshgarh Sahib} and Lakha Singh {Takht Damdama Sahib} in the SGPC offices or in the serais, where the two would be lodged. It was observed that they had no attendants, no proper facilitations during their stay; they had to literally beseech SGPC officials for their honorarium and for other sundry issues! I did a small story on the plight and neglect of the high priests, who were looked up to by the community for guidance. *The Tribune* had carried the news as a box item. This had the desired effect and impact. Soon, thereafter, the high priests were provided with permanent attendants, personal vehicles and other facilities commensurate with their position and the exalted offices they held. I vividly remember Jathedar Lakha Singh later telling me: *Saadi zindgi bana ti* {you have made our life!}

All along the high priests {*Jathedars*} have not only been perceived to be but have actually been treated as *mere employees* of the SGPC. This became more obvious in later years, when their appointment and removal became a recurring phenomenon; perhaps, a joke, with either the SGPC {read executive committee} or the militant organizations installing their own set of hand-picked persons at the high places! This practice, perhaps, continues even now. The political bosses {read SAD} have their way since Akali leaders treat SGPC as their pocket borough! What to say of the high priests, the SAD bosses' choice prevails even in the selection or election of the SGPC executive members and the President. Political analysts say that in these matters, during the time of Gurcharan Singh Tohra, as SGPC President, the SAD leadership had little or no role at all. What makes political leadership salivate is the *golak* {currency chest}; the cash collection that the SGPC makes from offerings at the Gurdwaras under its management and control, oils the political wheels!

Things have come to such a pass that on several occasions voices have been raised against Akal Takht's decisions and edicts, questioning whether these were taken independent of internal, external and extraneous influences or high priests had succumbed to political pressures. Or were the edicts issued on merit and in fairness. On one occasion, an Akal Takht Jathedar had issued a *Hukamnama* {religious edict} over fax while travelling in some other part of the country, much to the consternation of the SGPC, as well as the Sikh community, making a mockery of Akal Takht as an institution. More often than not, SGPC has courted more controversies than kudos!

*

The five high priests came into limelight following the Operation Bluestar and continued to hold sway for quite some time, till the SGPC found its feet and voice; and regained effective control after much secret back channel negotiations or at times open discussions with the district administration {read State government}, which concluded with a written understanding involving some dozen-odd dos and don'ts. That was sometime in 1988. In between, there were several dismissals and appointments of high priests with each influential set of politicians or self-styled religious leaders or an assortment of militants indulging in pick and chose policy to suit their ends or whims and fancies.

One can say with fairness that as a consequence of the Army action to flush out extremist elements, the process of erosion of credibility of the established Sikh institutions also set-in. This denigration, perhaps, continues and seems unstoppable, thereby, lowering the dignity, prestige, independence and autonomy of not only of the Akal Takht: seat of spiritual and temporal authority but also of other Sikh institutions. SGPC: mini-Parliament of the Sikhs, is considered to be a repository of Sikh religious matters, a protector of the Sikh rites, rituals and code of Sikh conduct: *Maryada*; yet, it must also be apportioned a fairly large portion of blame for failing in its assigned responsibilities and duties, when it comes to propagation of the Sikh religion or freeing the community from the clutches of *Babas*, *Deras, Sants and Mahants* or for not doing enough to check apostasy among the Sikhs or ensuring acceptance of a uniform code of conduct; what to say of having miserably failed to even to get enacted an All-India Gurdwara Act.

*

SGPC itself is an outcome of an Act of legislature. Elections to this are conducted, controlled and notified by the Centre: Ministry of Home Affairs. There have been occasions when these have either been inordinately delayed or not held at all for years and, if held, not notified, much to the chagrin of the elected members.

The Akalis were close to the Janta Dal government in 1977. As Amritsar was also celebrating its 400th anniversary of the founding of the city, the then Union Home Minister Chaudhary Charan Singh was chief guest at one of the functions at Ram Bagh. He had categorically declared that within one year an All-India Gurdwara Act would be enacted. Where is that Act, one may ask Parkash Singh Badal, who was present on that occasion along with other leaders. Drafts of the proposed All-India Act are gathering dust somewhere in Akali Dal's office or in government cupboards in Chandigarh and New Delhi. Also, in another case, the Supreme Court wants the government to say whether the Sikhs are a *minority*, when it comes to SGPC educational institutions, where major chunk or percentage of seats is reserved for the Sikhs!

*

Incidentally, the SGPC has, till-to-date, failed to retrieve the rich treasure trove of literature – religious, historical – that the Army reportedly took away and a large portion of that got burnt when the Central Sikh Reference Library was badly damaged and burnt. No one knows in whose custody is that literature.

I am reminded of visit of Marshal of the Skies, Arjan Singh {Retd.}, the late Lt. Gen Jagjit Singh Aurora {Retd.}, former Prime Minister, the late I K Gujral and the veteran journalist Kuldip Nayyar to the Golden Temple after the Operation Bluestar. Walking in the Parikarma, I happened to ask Arjan Singh, his reaction to what all has happened. Without hesitation, he paused, and whispered: I feel like picking up the gun and shooting those who have caused such incalculable and immense damage to the holy place.

*

The Army chief Dalbir Singh on a visit to the Golden Temple in March 2016, when asked and reminded about the unreturned library books had simply said he would "look into the matter". The matter, perhaps, has ended.

*

Analyzing the happenings, events and perpetually evolving unanticipated developments that took place three decades ago, one is reminded of what Rabbi Abraham Joshua Heschel once said: *in any free society where terrible wrongs exist, some are guilty; all are responsible.* {Abraham was a Polish-born American rabbi and one of the leading Jewish theologians and Jewish philosopher of the 20th century.}

I, for one, believe, though it is inconsequential, that we all are responsible for what Punjab, Punjabis and Punjabiat have suffered, may it be due to a decade of militancy or terrorism; or rabble rousing radicals/fundamentalists/fanatics/bigots; or a strong mix of divisive religion and politics {*together these two make a toxic nexus*} etc. Consequently, things went wrong and eventually went out of spiral. Yet, one wonders if anyone or someone is today willing to lead to correct the pathetic state of the state, which is in a shambles!

In ways more than one, opportunistic politics by all parties also fanned what had come to be termed as the *Punjab or the Sikh problem*. Unfortunately, the Akalis, who live in a cocoon of their own making, still believe that they are the *sole representatives* of all the Sikhs. For them time stands still! Sikh scriptures are a repository of wisdom and guidance, embracing all humanity with a universal message that repeatedly reminds us of: *oneness of humanity, wellbeing of one and all, and exhort us to fight against injustice, tyranny, inequality, discrimination, oppression, casteism; and social evils.* These scriptures expect and urge the Sikhs to act as the *protectors and saviors of the helpless and hapless; and contribute one-tenth of their earnings to charity*. And, yet, Sikhism remains at a crossroads!

*

Even in the present times, the Sikh leadership, both religious and political: read Akalis, has failed to respond or react to the happenings and developments that have shaken the rationalists, who find fellow humans at the receiving end: victim of what all that Sikhism stands for, including freedom of speech, expression and thought that has been repeatedly stifled, smeared and murdered. Height of intolerance to other's opinion! Who can forget the manner in which academics, authors, writers, film makers, artists and thinkers were silenced and killed in 2015?

Yet, the Sikh leadership - Badals - remained a mute witness and observed a stoic silence even when all this happened; and, more so, when other minorities were involved, across the country. Not once it crossed the mind of the Sikh leaders that they too are a significant and visible minority. What happened to others could happen to them too! Admittedly, Sikhs braved emergency in 1975. Led by political leaders thousands had courted arrest. That, perhaps, is the only occasion when Sikh leadership performed on the national stage, where main character actor was Jayparkash Narayan. Otherwise, the Sikh leadership has mostly remained immersed or confined to narrow politico-religious issues concerning the Sikhs alone; that too for narrow political interests and votes to retain and remain in power.

*

And when Prime Minister Narendra Modi compared Parkash Singh Badal to Nelson Mandela, the social media reacted the way it was expected to - ridiculing Modi, chiding Badal. In fact, writing in *The Tribune*, October 13, 2015, Sarbjit Dhaliwal in his essay: *Mandela's mantle does not sit easy on Badal*, had articulated the feelings of majority of the thinking and worried people, who felt anguished at the incalculable harm the ruling NDA, its own fringe outfits under the wings of the Rashtriya Swayamsevak Sangh, and its own ministers, MPs and MLAs were doing to human rights and human dignity; even Nation's respect.

Even the editorial of that day, *Writers speak up, free speech non-negotiable, control mob rule*, was also a telling comment on the growing intolerance in the country and how Sahitya Akademi awardees returned their honors/awards. It read: *It is perhaps for the first time in independent India that so many writers from such varied backgrounds have spoken in one voice in support of the freedom of speech and expression and against threats to social harmony and cultural diversity of the country.*

*

The point that is sought to be made is simple: there continues to be in Punjab, since mid-1970 and 1980s, *ordered disorder* - to paraphrase the title of Laurent

Gayer's book, the complete title of which is: *Karachi: Ordered disorder and the struggle for the city; published in 2014. {Gayer is a Research Fellow at SciencesPo, Centre De Recherches Internationales.}*

One wonders, if the situation obtaining three decades ago was, for the then *political rulers* of all hues, a source of power and mystique? Was it due to the omnipresent indifference of the power players and brokers of that time that Punjab tragedy erupted? My interaction, across the decades, with the Congress/Akali/Sikh political leaders and scholars, some are still around, has been that they remain wary of discussing and talking about that period. And, sadly, as one scans the political and religious landscape in Punjab today, one does not see, in terms of intellect and stature, anyone who can take on the mantle and lead the Sikh *quom*!

The Akali old war horses and their close relatives or protégées, across time, have within the party hierarchy become immune and intolerant of any disagreement, what to say of dissent; and expect unquestioned loyalty. Even the most well-thought, well-intentioned constructive criticism is viewed with suspicion; and construed as rebellion against the leader{s}. Those expressing independent views are looked upon with disdain and are gradually insulated and kept at a distance. There have been instances, quite often, when rambunctious elements close to the handful of senior Akali leaders effectively silence those who wish to express independent or different view on issues. This is true of even the Congress, where also a venal family and party hold sway!

*

For multiple reasons, Punjab has been on the boil; it continues to simmer and sizzle. Though, the virulent violence and rule of the gun had been contained by 1993/1995, new strains of that virus are in the air in Punjab. These strains, perhaps, have emerged from the political and religious fractions and fissures that have been created intentionally or accidentally or by design or otherwise, across time. Those bruises and crevices have left deep, indelible scars on the psyche of Punjab and Punjabis. These remain raw: these have only coagulated, not healed. It is divisive politics at its best. How long will Punjab continue to pay a hefty price for such dangerous games? Perhaps, as long as politicians of all hues, who believe only in moonlighting keep their stranglehold on politics and religion. The fact, however, is:

Punjab continues to live and walk on the razor's edge, sharpened as it is by multiple isms and schism!

And, there need not be an iota of doubt that if terrorism choked Punjab, so did competitive politics and religion, laced with acerbic insinuations, innuendoes, allegations and conspiracies; the polity had abandoned its indispensible equilibrium!

*

One may agree or agree to disagree with the political and police ways to bring the situation in Punjab back to normal after all the tribulations and troubles it had faced and vicissitudes of turmoil it had been through. However, there, perhaps, is some element of truth and some objectivity in what the former Punjab Director-General of Police K P S Gill has to say in his 1997 book: *Punjab: Knights of Falsehood.*

This is what the book is about:

The terror that swept Punjab through the Eighties and into the early Nineties was not created in a vacuum. The events of the early eighties were the spark that ignited the fire; but it was fuelled by the deliberate distortion of the message of Sikhism by those who had donned the mantle of Sikh leadership in this century. This leadership has seized control of the shrines, and set itself up as the final arbiter, of the Faith; contrary to the message of the Gurus, they have circumscribed the Faith in a meaningless litany of rituals and an obsession with communal identity.

This, however, was not sufficient to satisfy the power lust of these petty men. They have used the Gurdwaras as a stepping stone to an even more lucrative destination: the State legislature. For decades a vocabulary of hate cloaked political demands in religious garb, and at every turn in the political circus the Panth was 'imperiled'. It was this venomous rhetoric that was extended into action by the terrorists who eventually captured the communal plank.

When the time came to reap the whirlwind, the 'leaders of the faith' simply abdicated responsibility. Not only did they hand over the holiest of Sikh shrines to rapists and murderers, they even justified their most heinous actions in the name of an invented mythology of the 'oppression' of the Sikhs.

The murderers and rapists are now gone. But the leaders and the institutional structure that produced the malignancy of terror now occupy centre-stage in the politics of Punjab. Are we condemned to repeat the ruinous cycle of the past?

Is the collateral damage that has been done to the Sikh quom or the Sikh institutions reversible? Perhaps, it is. What is needed is sincerity and honesty of purpose, spirit of selflessness and, perhaps, sacrifices; besides a strong will to refurbish the scalded image of both - the quom and the institutions.

*

Elsewhere, I have commented on the Sikh institutions, which are at a crossroads. That write-up may be taken as a sort of sequel to this chapter. It is an idea, may be utopian; an idea whose time may well come, sooner than we expect! Sure enough, the need is to transform the Sikh institutions. For that to happen cleansing of the Sikh politics is imperative, so is consensus on the ways and means of making appointments on the matters- religious.

How long would the prevailing *ordered disorder* last in Punjab? My guess is as good as yours! Even the outcome of 2017 Assembly elections may not answer this question.

6

Mother

Among the many whom I met during the course of my professional pursuits, some memories remain evergreen. One such memory is of a chance meeting with Mother Teresa. The time spent with her way back on August 7, 1984 rekindled when the news of Mother Teresa being anointed *Saint* flashed across the TV screens in mid-December 2015 that she may be granted sainthood in 2016. Her beatification had been by Pope John Paul way back on October 31, 2003; and Pope Francis, on September 4, 2016, declared Mother Teresa a Saint of the Roman Catholic Church at a special Mass in St Peter's Square, Vatican City; a move that came after 19 years of her death. Pope Francis had approved her canonization [Sainthood}on March 15, 2016.

It was comparatively a quiet day, when the phone rang. My senior, PTI staffer Gurdip Singh was on the line: *why don't you come right away, if not much busy, I have a surprise and time is a constraint.* No questions asked I went over to his Taylor road residence-cum-office. Together we drove on his ageing Lambretta scooter. Over the noise of the rickety scooter's silencer he said we were to meet Mother Teresa, who was at Children's Home at Gumtala, on the outskirts of the city {Amritsar}. The news was not to be shared, he implored. Done!

It was for the first time that I was meeting her. Aware of the prevailing situation, she carefully avoided answering controversial questions. She emphasized and reiterated: *if Punjab wants peace that it deserved, it must have capacity to forget and forgive*! *Each one must give and share joy, love and happiness!*

On Operation Bluestar, she said: *there should not be any misuse of religious places: Church, Temple or Gurdwara.*

She would not comment on what went wrong where and who did what and why at the Golden Temple and maintained: *since God has made man, every man must be made to feel wanted. The real poverty is when a man feels rejected and unwanted.*

Mother Teresa was on a two-day visit to the home for children being set up. Asked if she would visit the Golden Temple, she held my hands in her frail hands and smilingly said: *I prefer to spend time with sisters and children and want to see how we can have accommodation for the sick, for the dying and for the destitute children.*

A recipient of Nobel Peace Prize, Bharat Ratna, Order of the Smile and much more, Mother Teresa, I found, was so humble, polite and ever smiling while talking in soft, soothing voice!

She was an Albanian Roman Catholic; her full name was Anjeze Gonxhe Bojaxhiu; she was born at Skopje, Macedonia on August 26, 1910; and passed away on September 5, in 1997 at Kolkata at the age of 87. I cherish that meeting to date!

7

Too Many C{r} ooks!

Looking back at the avalanche of events that took place, post-1984, the year of the Operation Bluestar at the Golden Temple, one's thoughts also go back to pre-1984 events and incidents which, probably, led to the Operation Bluestar; the consequences that followed have been chronicled *ad nauseam*.

These have been taken cognizance of and analyzed, including the circumstances and factors responsible for Punjab's tragedy: political, administrative, economic, social, religious et al; that contributed to and weighed on the minds of the perpetrators, on all sides, who master-minded the unanticipated mayhem, murders, lootings {of banks and police armories}, sacrilege of religious places, incidents of violence, including burning of railway stations; and played devious and divisive politics to avenge or defame or teach a lesson or two to one or the other community or to their own political and religious rivals and opponents or to settle personal scores or even to please their masters or the powers that be.

As one rummages through piles of papers, documents, notebooks, books, magazines and sundry files that one has preserved, as reference material, it emerges that Punjab in that period of its history {post-1947} had turned into a theatre of the absurd: internecine struggles within the Akali {Sikh} leadership did as much incalculable, irreparable and everlasting damage to the Sikh institutions {political--- the *original* Shiromani Akali dal; religious--- the SGPC and High Priests; the Sikh identity and entity, as did the usurping and rabble-raising by the indoctrinated youth and radicalized, fundamentalist, fanatic and fiendish militant outfits {self-styled guardians/protectors of the Sikh affairs, who, at will, either de-recognised or disbanded the Sikh institutions, both political and religious or re-constituted or re-habilitated these to serve their agenda}; and the rest of the damning damage {post-1966} being inflicted by the Congress leaders of the state and the Centre - the villains of the piece, given their vacuous personal egos and respective political rivalries or loyalties. One cannot absolve other political outfits: erstwhile Jan Sangh or BJP or the communist parties for having acted as spoil sports.

Together, this fractious scenario, both political and religious, gave a handle to several hands to fiddle with and burn Punjab; may these hands be of successive powers that be in Chandigarh, New Delhi; or either in or outside Punjab; or even abroad. In the two principal communities, the Sikhs and the Hindus, had emerged several self-styled leaders, who until the other day, were just no bodies and any bodies but had become some bodies, over night!

If blame is to be apportioned to any one for the miseries and hardships Punjab, Punjabis and Punjabiat faced for over a decade, let that be apportioned as much in full measure to the conniving, fickle and narrow-minded Akali leaders, as to the dubious, mischievous, Congress and other parties' leaders, who engaged in Machiavellian politics and created a hell of a mess in this border state, as also to the once domineering self-appointed Panthic Committee and trigger-happy ruffians masquerading as holier than thou *boys*, as they were referred to.

Much of the muck and debris left behind by these elements are yet to be cleared; there is, much to be done and lot to be undone on many fronts: political, religious, social, economic; community, communal, ethnic and at class-caste levels, given the clear divisions that have erupted in the once indivisible unity between the Sikhs and the Hindus; the coalition between the SAD and the BJP, notwithstanding. Why are the two communities shy of calling themselves Punjabis? A serious danger now lurks in the countryside with clear caste equations emerging, particularly in Doaba region; Malwa and Majha are not far behind.

*

A clear warning on conflicts, frictions and fractions in rural Punjab is presented in *Socio-economic development of rural Punjab:* two decades of *lost opportunities*. This is a slim 64-page June 2013 document that CRRID: Centre for research in rural and industrial development, Chandigarh, has prepared. It is a telling comment on Punjab's caste wars, though still in the shadows, and political dithering; call it turning a blind eye to ground swell or feigning ignorance about reality.

*

Remember, the large scale migration of the Hindus from villages and towns to outside Punjab because of fear psychosis and indiscriminate killings; and the incoming migrant Sikhs in the wake of attacks on them, post- Indira Gandhi assassination? The Sikh-Hindu division that had been deliberately engineered and orchestrated was quite obvious: knots that had been calculatedly tied with nimble fingers became difficult to unknot even with teeth, later! Otherwise, why *The Tribune* would start a series on inter-community marriages {between Hindus and Sikhs}, if not to bridge the man-made created divide, which further widened after the Operation Bluestar!

*

With the echo of Rajiv Gandhi statement that when a big tree falls, the earth shakes still reverberating in the Sikh psyche and at the peak of Hindu-Sikh cross-migration, I accompanied the then Deputy Commissioner, Ramesh Inder Singh Mander on the Gypsy wheel, to visit villages in Tarn Taran's Mand area, around Fetehabad: epicenter of first flight of Hindus. We saw the Hindus leaving their native places lock, stock and barrel for safe heavens in Haryana and elsewhere; efforts to try to persuade them not to leave proved futile. Understandably, piqued by the day-in, day-out happenings, several Sikh families had also left their villages and moved to safe places in urban settlements!

*

Too many c{r} ooks stirred the Punjab pot and kept it on the boil for too long! It is in this backdrop, I have attempted to recall some incidents, events and happenings that have left an indelible impression on my mind. There is no particular chronological order or any given sequence. These are the vignettes of the gory past, which, one may say with due humility, steered me to be objective in reporting, enabled me to analyze and interpret; and developed in me some abilities and capabilities to do so.

8

Gory Scenes

During my long journalistic career, I cannot forget three scenes, which I saw on June 6, 1984, when curfew was relaxed after four days for two hours from 2.00 pm to 4.00 pm; and I had managed to rush towards the Golden Temple complex. {PTI colleague Gurdip Singh had informed me of the relaxation in the curfew to enable people to re-stock their kitchens with the essentials, and had asked me to come over.} The scenes that I saw have left an indelible imprint on my mind. I recall what I saw and encountered in the vicinity of the city Kotwali that afternoon.

*

The following three scenes are only illustrative of what the author was witness to. Elsewhere in the book there are equally more appalling accounts, which too remain unforgettable, as to how innocents were done to death and precious life sniffed out of them at the dead of night in remote villages and towns, small and big. The picture in the mind is as clear even now, as if it all had happened only yesterday. Those killings were done by the mercenaries of death, who, perhaps, were no champions of any plausible political or religious cause they claimed to espouse.

*

Scene 1: As one rushed to the complex, one saw many young boys heading towards the Temple on roller-skates. It was also noticed that the Hindus were celebrating the Army action and offering *poori-chole* and sweets to mark the killing of Sant Jarnail Singh Bhinderanwale!

Just a few yards away from the Jallianwala Bagh, towards the Clock Tower-side, main entrance to the Golden Temple, there were Army men and vehicles all over; there was also a crowd of curious onlookers, jostling to see what was happening beyond a big roll of concertina wire roll that had been placed across the road to bar getting any closer to the complex. From that point, one saw plumes of smoke arising from the Akal Takht side and military vehicles ferrying casualties from the SGPC complex side. It was a curious mix of agony and ecstasy!

Scene 2: Inside the Kotwali premises, one saw men of all ages, with hands tied behind their backs with their own turbans, looking scared and famished, squatting on the hot road guarded by Army personnel, who occasionally barked orders or abused and kicked them. Looking on were some passersby and Punjab police personnel, who appeared to be helpless, frustrated, restive and agitated at what they saw, as if the captured were not civilians but POWs: prisoners of war! The senior police officers, sensing the anguish and mood of their men, were seen asking them to get inside the Kotwali; apparently to ward off any untoward incident between cops and the Army.

Scene 3: Outside the Kotwali was parked a civilian truck. The Deputy Superintendent of Police, headquarters, Apar Singh Bajwa, motioned me and said: *look inside the truck*. While he got talking to Gurdip Singh, nervously and hurriedly, I climbed up to see what was inside. In less than a minute, I had jumped off. What I saw is still vividly etched deep in the recess of my conscience. The truck was loaded with bodies of men and women, dumped as if it was a pile of linen that a washer-man had haphazardly gathered together for washing. There was stench of the putrefying bodies with flies, blood and sweat all over.

*

In the weeks that followed, municipal corporation vehicles loaded with human corpses extracted and removed from the complex were being taken to the civil hospital for post-mortem, a mere formality being performed mechanically, before cremation. Later, it emerged that in several identical post-mortem reports the doctors had recorded: *hands tied behind the back* as also *body bore bullet marks*!

The Sub-Divisional Magistrate S S Dhillon, an ex-Army Captain, was to later share with me that after Harcharan Singh Rode had identified the body of Sant Jarnail Singh Bhinderanwale, it was cremated, along with that of Bhai Amrik Singh and Baba Thara Singh, with all religious rituals observed in letter and spirit in the city's cremation ground. Also, that he – Dhillon - was assigned to take the mortal remains of the Sant to Kiratpur Sahib for emersion there.

These three bodies were taken for customary postmortem. The then Deputy Commissioner Ramesh Inder Singh Mander, much later, in a conversation with me corroborated what Dhillon had disclosed to me. This is what Mander had to say: along with the Superintendent of Police, CID, Pandit Harjit Singh, and the Civil Surgeon, Dr Dalbir Singh, they were waiting outside the postmortem building. An official of the office of the deputy commissioner, who happened to be staying nearby, spotted them and asked them to sit in his drawing room. The three obliged, given the hot June month. It was Harjit Singh, who said that Bhinderanwale and the other two must be cremated with due respect by observing all religious rituals. This was immediately agreed to.

However, the question arose where from to arrange the white cloth – coffin - to cover the bodies, as there was complete shutdown due to curfew. The wife of the official of the deputy commissioner's office solved the problem. She said, incidentally, she had the full roll of white cloth to serve as the coffin sheet. There was a sigh of relief in the room! Whereupon, necessary arrangements were made and a priest summoned to perform Antim *Ardas*: the last prayer. The bodies were taken to the Shaheedan cremation ground on the circular road towards Chattiwind Gate. As the pyres were lit, an Army Jawan standing on guard quipped: *with the last rites performed here, Bhinderanwale will get the status of a Shaheed – martyr*! He mistook the cremation ground name as one meant for only martyrs, whereas, in fact, it was so referred to because of its proximity to the Gurdwara Shaheedan, named after Baba Deep Singh, a great Sikh warrior and martyr!

Thereafter, urns containing the ashes of the three were taken, under heavy military escort, to Kiratpur Sahib for emersion. The task, as I said before, having been entrusted to Dhillon.

*

Thus, the fire, that had been calculatedly and consciously lit to burn Punjab, was to last for over a decade, engulfing the state and its two principal communities: the Sikhs and the Hindus. No one was left unscarred; if scare was all pervasive, political maturity and religious sagacity was nowhere evident. It was a man-made tragedy, all the way! Claims of the fire having been doused, notwithstanding, ambers continue to glow in the hearts and minds of those who lost their dear ones and their properties. Insidious campaigns were a common place occurrence to show Sikhs as terrorists/separatists; some feeble efforts were also made to conceal and underplay the communal divide in the state.

*

The question now is how to overcome, or more pertinently, will we ever overcome the immense damage caused by the virus of violence and bloodshed, perpetrated as it was by political cunning and religious bigots that engulfed Punjab. The continuous political prattle and rhetoric about *oppression of the Sikhs, discrimination against the Sikhs, the loss of the Sikh identity, step-motherly treatment of Punjab and Punjabis by the Centre, read Congress* etc. seemingly, is repeatedly fanned by vested leadership, more out of electoral and competitive politics, and whose only aim was/is to remain in power and retain power; perhaps, till eternity! Punjab has been sapped of its energy, vitality, dynamism and dignity, as a consequence of what the state has been through.

Besides the Bhinderanwale *factor*, some attribute Punjab or the Sikh problem to several other factors beginning with the language issue, the Sikh-Nirankari clash; as well as the demand for *Khalistan*, though not a very convincing argument or factor. Those who propagated *Khalistan* or raised pro-*Khalistan* slogans were dubbed as separatists. Yet, no one ever had the patience to either ask for or to explain its concept, its geophysical boundaries, and its religious composition, its political and economic set up etc. Till date, the debate rages on among the opponents and protagonists of that demand.

My belief remains that concept or slogan or idea of *Khalistan* did not impress or convince large sections of the Sikhs. And for want of any takers of that idea and in the absence of any mass support, it has died down; even today, it continues to remain more of a fashion-statement, a kind of call in despair to show resentment against the establishment, to arouse passions and to create a chasm between the two principal communities. The main ideologues or the script writers of the *Republic of Khalistan* were the USA-based Ganga Singh Dhillon and the UK-based Jagjit Singh Chauhan, who was at one-time minister for finance in Punjab.{Former staffer of the *Indian Express*, Jagtar Singh has produced a 516-page tome titled: *Khalistan Struggle: a non-movement*. It was published in February 2011. That is a lengthy essay on *Khalistan* and other aspects of Punjab problem.}

Such were the times and such was the scenario through which Punjab has been through. And, one hopes and prays, the evils that bedeviled Punjab would not revisit and the state would be cleansed of remnants!

9

Reflections

Bloody literature

Given the constraints of space, sources and resources, in the following passages only a bird's eye-view has been given of the kind of situation and circumstances that existed, prior to- and post- 1984, which proved to be the watershed year in the annals of country's history, in general and of the Sikhs in particular. I do not wish to either delve deep into or narrate the dated past history or chronologically list events to explain the manifold and myriad manifestations or recapitulate the vicissitudes of the rise, fulfillment and fall of the Punjabi nationalism, the Sikhs, the Sikh political and religious institutions or peaks and troughs of Punjab's economic situation encompassing, industry: manufacture and service sectors; and agriculture. However, a wide-angle brief random selective summarization of the events will be in order.

Even much prior to my joining at Amritsar in mid-November 1983, the same Punjab fields which once sprouted the green revolution were turning red with the blood of the innocents! Responsible for such acts of brigandage were militants, as well as the security forces - remember the encounters; mostly at Beas on National highway no.1? Fear- psychosis and anxiety neurosis, which had long ago begun to cast their shadow on the countryside, as also the urban settlements, was all pervasive. Such nightmare was to worsen after Operation Bluestar, when several people in the villages started hiring ruffians to settle personal or family scores; at times such an extra-constitutional *justice system* resulted in murders and extortions: {*Supari* system in the language of Mafia gangs!} And, in circulation were unconfirmed reports that this *justice system* had roots in several rooms around the Golden Temple *Parikarma* – the Kangaroo courts!

*

Yet, one observation that has remained etched in my mind all these decades is this: how the ordinary, average devotees, unmindful of the din, danger and lurking fear went about offering their prayers, taking a dip in the holy tank, paying obeisance at the sanctum sanctorum or at the Akal Takht or part-taking langar in the Guru Ram Das langar building, atop which Bhinderanwale held his daily religious discourses, heard grievances and gave sermons etc. Their devotional fervor was seen to be believed! This devotion continued even at the worst of times and despite omnipresence of gun-totting *boys* roaming around the complex or busy building sand-bag protection bunkers atop buildings or digging trenches in the complex. {Yet, admittedly, there were times when the scare and fear got better of devotion and there was perceptible dip in the number of devotees, visitors to the Temple. This also became obvious from the way the SGPC calculated and judged: in terms of offerings made in the sanctum sanctorum!}

*

Right from the time when Captain Joseph Davey Cunningham wrote the *History of the Sikhs* in 1849, to the present, enough literature is available on how beginning with the 15th century Guru Nanak initiated a religious movement and emphasized on what was common between the Hindus and the Muslims, and preached the unity of these two faiths practiced in Punjab. Nanak's movement crystallized by the beginning of the 17th century in the formation of a third religious community consisting of the disciples or the Sikhs of Guru Nanak and the succeeding teachers or gurus, culminating in a call to arms by the last guru, Gobind Singh, who created the *Khalsa* at Anandpur Sahib in 1699. The best of Sikh rule is attributed to Maharaja Ranjit Singh's period. Before that and thereafter the Sikhs have had skirmishes with history: the Mughals, the British, the establishment {post-1947} and, of course, among themselves!

I will stop here.

*

Those interested in understanding the nuances of the Sikhs, Sikhism, Sikh politics or why and how of all this and more or why all this is anchored in Sikh religion; the circumstances leading up to the June 1984 Operation Bluestar at the Golden Temple etc. and later happenings, may well go through Khushwant Singh's two-volume: *A History of the Sikhs* published by the Oxford University Press. The first volume is from 1469-1839; the second volume is from 1839 to 1988.

The later, in particular, gives a lucid account of happenings, behind the scene developments and how the stage came to be set for what Punjab has had to go through, endure and suffer; and how the physical wounds and psychological scars still remain raw and fresh. His other small book *My Bleeding Punjab*, published in 1992, and the one he co-authored with Kuldip Nayar, *Tragedy of Punjab: Story of Bluestar and after,* {1984} just to name two, throw ample light on the ways of the Sikhs and on the Punjab tragedy. There are several other books or anthologies or collective works by authors, columnists, writers, journalists, as well that encapsulate Punjab scenes frame- by- frame. Only an illustrative example has been given here.

*

There is a large treasure trove of literature related to pre-and post-Operation Bluestar Operation on the internet, as well, penned by bureaucrats, Army officers, SGPC officials; besides the two parallel *White Papers*: one of the SGPC and the other of the Government of India. Everyone has the right, and rightly so, to interpret the why and how of the entire course of events that were to change the course of Punjab and Punjabi life itself. In fact, several NGOs, human rights organizations: people's movements against state repression or people's movement for civil liberties, amnesty international etc., noted jurists and several other individuals, have also made significant contributions recording for posterity cold-blooded murder of youth in fake encounters by the security forces or of *missing* youths and on the Operation Bluestar itself; and its aftermath.

This vast literature with blood splattered pages also focuses on the role of the Army, political masters of that time; and what eventually led to the assassination of the Prime Minister Indira Gandhi, as also, the post- October 31, 1984 killings of the Sikhs; the festering physical, psychological wounds of the families, who lost their bread-winners, as well as their properties, are a gruesome reminder of those horrendous days! And, of course, the irony that persists: for the past 32 years, these victims of organized violence continue to wait for justice. Isn't justice delayed, justice denied? And, who can ignore and forget the way those in power ordered commissions of enquiry only to later or even mid-way scuttle these enquiries, so as to suppress the truth!

Punjab has been witness to and victim of enough of blood- and- thunder that has been captured in the flood of literature, post-June 1984 that makes the blood boil. Learned authors and commentators have also tried to identify and reach out to the root cause or give a genesis of the problems that beset Punjab and have recounted the circumstances and events prior to the build up to the Operation Bluestar or have portrayed graphic, eye-witness descriptions of that sordid Army action or massacre of the Sikhs, post-October, 1984 in the National capital and elsewhere. Therefore, for the present and the future generations, there are enough cuds to chew; and analyze.

In that sense, the book in hand is a humble contribution to the available rich literature. It is a recollection and a recall of what I had seen, observed and been through, as a journalist.

One shudders to think of once a 'leader' state: Punjab – the cradle of green revolution – reflecting blood drops on green crops, as also on writings in print and in cyberspace!

10

Akalis and Demands

As one looks back, several main actors and characters, which played major role on or behind the stage, have since departed from this earth. There are several still around, who can join the missing dots in the narrations of that period, as to what exactly happened, when, where, why, how and the role they played or did not play. The truth must be told, now. If not told now, it may never be told and be lost forever; it is already late.

The living actors and characters owe a debt to the present and future generations. They must leave behind for posterity the real picture of the actual happenings, so that Punjab and Punjabis do not ever again fall into such a trap. It is not just the question as to what lessons have been learnt or ought to have been learnt or what was intended to be achieved and what has actually been achieved or not achieved at the end of that painful saga with thousands of lives lost and families shattered, emotionally and economically. It is the question of recording factual and actual thinking processes and purposes behind what was staged. Such characters and actors include politicians, police personnel, intelligence agencies' officials, civil bureaucrats, judicial officers, journalists, academicians and others.

One has heard, in whispers, many a version of the behind the scene or back channel negotiations or clandestine talks/parleys the Akali leaders had with New Delhi and how Bhinderanwale and even some Akali leaders, as well, would warn against any bargain or sell-out of the Sikhs. On the Akali-government talks, there are multiple versions, interpretations and opinions afloat. However, there are no authentic, truly trust-worthy accounts available that one can depend or rely upon for fair analysis, understanding and unbiased conclusions.

Therefore, the Nation must also know about behind- the-scene talks and negotiations among the Sikh and the Congress leaders and the central government.

The knowledge that some of these parleys were held has been in public domain, much, however, has remained unknown. There have been only conjectures, as to who all participated and what transpired in those meetings. The minutes of those meetings must be put in public domain for the historians and analysts to examine. Files, minutes of meetings, notes, letters, charter of demands and other relevant papers must also be *de-classified*. Mere *White Papers*, either of the SGPC or the government, have not been enough! {In fact, there was a slim SGPC published White Paper after the Sikh-Nirankari clash, as well, in April 1978.} Why has not anyone thought of seeking de-classification of the information pertaining to that period or invoked the Right to Information Act, 2005, to solicit records and documents?

*

If papers and files on Netaji Subhas Chandra Bose can be put in public domain, why not files related to Punjab's sordid saga? For all that Punjab has been through, the Akalis have one word: d*iscrimination*, when they describe and define real or perceived sense of persecution and humiliation the community has had to face at the hands of the Centre, read Congress. Does this accusation absolve Akalis of their own role and part in the events that have today put Punjab on the brink of multiple crises?

*

Rather than cleansing the politics with the help of religion, it is the religion that the Akali leadership has politicized: cleverly, covertly, overtly, repeatedly and selectively used, abused and misused it for political gains all through the multiple Sikh struggles, across decades and time! Political expediency seemingly got the upper hand, whenever it came to invoking Akal Takht or the high priests.

*

When it comes to the role and responsibilities of the Jathedars of Akal Takht, one gets an impression of how vulnerable several of them have been, when it came to taking an appropriate stand, notwithstanding intimidation or pressures, internal, external and extraneous. Some Jathedars succumbed, some erred and some were forced to resign. A bird's eye-view is given here of some of the Jathedars, all SGPC appointees:

During my tenure Giani Kirpal Singh was the Jathedar of Akal Takht. He was into his second term; first was from 1963-1965; his reappointment was made in 1982; he lasted till 1986 – a crucial period of militancy in the state. He got mired in a controversy soon after the Operation Bluestar, when he was seen and heard on TV reading from a prepared text on the extent of damage caused to Akal Takht building.

After his exit, stepped in Professor Darshan Singh, a *Rag*i: singer of Gurus' hymns! His tenure during troubled post-Operation Bluestar was difficult. He enjoyed great respect in the Sikh community. Much later, he was also to become a controversial figure. His successor, Professor Manjit Singh courted controversy over his role in the World Sikh Council and development projects in Anandpur Sahib. He had to resign.

Bhai Ranjit Singh became Jathedar on his release from jail; he was behind bars for his connection with the assassination of Baba Gurbachan Singh, Head of the Nirankari sect. He served during the troubled period when self-centered Akali leaders vitiated the atmosphere and played dirty politics. He resigned in protest against such machinations! Then Giani Puran Singh was appointed. His irrational role is described in the following passages. Naturally, he was removed and his successor was Joginder Singh Vedanti, who stepped-in under unusual circumstances, when the three Jathedars of the Takhts were removed from their seats by his predecessor – Giani Puran Singh. Vedanti too had to quit on some curious and controversial issues, paving way for the present Jathedar, Giani Gurbachan Singh, who faced flak for his Dera Sucha Sauda flip-flop.

Therefore, as a brief reminder of how, in the past, as also at present, political leaders had/have misused the institution of Akal Takht, eroded its authority and misappropriated its independence, if ever it had one and enjoyed it, let me recall some instances and take you back to the year 2000. How can one forget those unfortunate developments?

The incident relates to the time when Giani Puran Singh was the Jathedar of Akal Takht. Giani Puran Singh, in his wisdom, issued a *Hukamnama* {edict} from a PCO: public call office at Guna, Madhya Pradesh on January 25, while on a tour, excommunicating SGPC President Bibi Jagir Kaur from the Sikh Panth. He had faxed the same to Amritsar. All hell broke out at this indiscretion since all canons of *Maryada* had been violated with impunity. Not just that, through another controversial *Hukamnama,* Giani Puran Singh, on March 12, excommunicated three High priests and two SGPC members, alleging that they had *violated* the January 25 *Hukamnama*. This created a crisis in the Sikh circles. That was the time when Parkash Singh Badal and Gurcharan Singh Tohra, were having a running feud over the question of supremacy and hegemony in matters - *Panthic.*

Days later, on March 28, SGPC executive *sacked* Giani Puran Singh and suspended him as Granthi {priest} of the Golden Temple and posted him to Muktsar. The same day, new Akal Takht Jathedar was appointed: Giani Joginder Singh Vedanti, who the very next day, March 29, *revoked* the *Hukamnamas* issued by Giani Puran Singh. Not only were this, all such edicts, declarations and directives issued by Giani Puran Singh also annulled. The three sacked Jathedars: Professor Manjit Singh, Giani Kewal Singh and Giani Bhagwan Singh; and five members of SGPC executive, who had been excommunicated by Giani Puran Singh, were rehabilitated and *Hukamnamas* against them revoked. That is how it was High priests vs High priests, who acted with remote held by politicians of that time.

Unfortunately, despite existence of a proper procedure for appointment and removal of the High priests, that has not been followed after 1984. Most of the appointments/removals done in the wake of 1984 were done at *gun-point*. It remains the responsibility of the SGPC to do the explaining for the continuation of such fluidity and fuzziness.

In fact, in view of the estranged relationship between the Chief Minister Parkash Singh Badal and SGPC President Gurcharan Singh Tohra, the Akal Takht intervened in January 1999, through a *Hukamnama* directing maintenance of status quo ensuring no action was taken against the latter till April 15, in view of the tercentenary celebrations, marking establishment of the *Khalsa Panth* slated for April that year. That *Hukamnama* was also viewed as a partisan step of Akal Takht favoring the SGPC chief. Opinions were sharply divided then, as were in 2015, over the role and functions of the three key Sikh institutions: Akal Takht, SGPC and SAD. The common refrain being that a politically strong leader{s}, who holds sway over SGPC, alone, calls the shots, including the way Akal Takht acts and reacts.

*

As an illustration, take the case of the Akal Takht flip-flop stances on a sensitive issue involving Dera Sacha Sauda. In 2007, taking offence to the manner in which the Dera chief, Gurmeet Ram Rahim Singh, had appeared dressed up, resembling the Tenth Master Guru Gobind Singh, at one of his congregations in Bathinda, the then Akal Takht Jathedar Joginder Singh Vedanti issued an edict, on May 13, asking the Sikhs to socially boycott the Dera and its followers and forbade them from having any *roti-beti* {bread-daughter} relationships with the Dera *Premis*. He was also to later reject the so-called apology of the Dera chief on May 20. In fact, in 2012 the case registered against Dera chief under IPC section 295, hurting religious sentiments, was also withdrawn: a political decision, yet again.

However, on September 24, 2015 Akal Takht and other high priests in their wisdom *exonerated* Gurmeet Ram Rahim Singh of the 2007 act of blasphemy, accepting his letter of apology. Even before the ink had dried on the edict, a fierce angry storm broke-out at home and abroad with ordinary Sikhs and radicalized organizations taking on the high priests and accusing them of having succumbed to political pressure sought to be exerted on them by the ruling Akali clique, read Badals, ostensibly with an eye on the 2017 Assembly general elections; given the fact that the mass following of the Dera sect in over 60 assembly constituencies, of 117 total in the state, in Malwa belt, would support SAD. Malwa is considered to be Akalis' strong vote base- its citadel!

Meantime, series of acts of sacrilege, across the state, further compounded the situation with the firestorm of anger and anguish spreading state-wide. The ire was directed against the government, for its failure to trace culprits. The first mischief was done, when the holy book: Guru Granth Sahib was stolen from a Gurdwara in village Jiwansinghwala, near Kotkapura, in Faridkot district in June, 2015. Later, with the discovery of torn pages of the holy book in the adjoining Bargari village and in villages in Ferozepur and Tarn Taran districts situation took turn for the worst. This led to widespread protests, road blockades and clashes between the police and the protestors. At least two persons were killed and 60 injured in the clashes and in police firing on the protesting Sikhs in Kotkapura.

Dramatically, 22 days later, in an unprecedented step, on October 16, 2015, Akal Takht Jathedar Giani Gurbachan Singh and other high priests *revoked* their own earlier edict of September, 24 arguing that the Sikhs had not accepted the same. The high priests also sought to make a difference between *Gurmata*: religious decree; and the *Hukamnama* -edict - in a bid to douse the charged up passions. Ironically, it was, perhaps, for the first time in the Sikh history, the criminally politicized SGPC issued *advertisements* to the media justifying the pardon – exoneration - given to Dera Sacha Sauda chief and appealing to the Sikhs to accept the verdict! This is something atrocious, said several analysts, who described such an ill-advised step as again *politically motivated* and, in ways more than one, lending, thereby, further credence to the people's perception that Akal Takht had blundered by issuing edict, dated September, 24.

The revoking of the edict again was attributed to political pressures and tactics, thereby, showing the institution of Akal Takht and high priests in bad light and exposing the ruling Badals, who were put on back foot. Such was the reaction that for the first time Badals realized the *anger* and *powe*r of the people, when even several SGPC members and SAD office bearers *loyal* to them began to quit in disgust and protest over the ways of the government; it was a sort of revolt that the Badals faced; an exceptional or an unanticipated development that the rulers, perhaps, never anticipated.

Political strategy to win votes by any means, including dragging in Akal Takht and the high priests to secure votes and placate the Sirsa-based Dera backfired on the Badals. Realizing the missteps and ill-advised actions the ruling political party had taken, Parkash Singh visited Akal Takht on October 17 to handover a personal letter of *remorse* to the Jathedar Giani Gurbachan Singh to *atone* for what had happened in the past few days. Not only this, the state issued large advertisements appealing to the Punjabis for peace, amity and communal harmony in the state, as also to guard religious places against reoccurrence of such unpardonable acts of sacrilege that have been committed under a conspiracy, given the similarity of patron involved. These tactics, as well as *Sadbhavana* rallies, backed-up by large-size newspaper advertisement issued by the state public relations department, in the name of the chief minister, appealing for peace and trying to set the record straight, were, as analysts had said, was more to deflect attention from the farmers' demands and agitations and invoke religion and the old war cry: *Panth in peril.* Therein lay the cunning and cleverness of the Akali patriarch leader, who had weathered many a storm in his chequered political career!

*

This is how politicians have treated Akal Takht, the high priests and made sovereignty of the Akal Takht questionable, and even that of the Sikh *Rehat*

Maryada {code of Sikh conduct}! Going by what one has seen and experienced, one wonders, if this institution - Akal Takht and of the high priests - has the requisite or desired independence and autonomy? This independence that is not like plasticine that politicians can mould it any which way, the way they have been doing across decades, time-and-again. Definitely, this calls for introspection. Is it not yet a moment for the Sikh political leadership not to denigrate the institutions, the moment of catharsis, of correction, of change?

*

See the irony of the situation. For the first time, one saw and read how even *Hazoori Ragis*, who perform inside the Sanctum sanctorum, and SGPC staff together protested, on October 20, 2015, against Akal Takht Jathedar Giani Gurbachan Singh continuing in his august position in the wake of wrong decisions taken by him and his colleagues on the issue of pardon of Dera Sacha Sauda chief, demanding why he should not be handed down *Tankha*. Showing of black flags and surcharged atmosphere on Dewali in the Golden Temple last year, November 11, was another reminder of how things have come to a pass; and how an acting Jathedar, Dhyan Singh Mand, appointed by the radical Sikhs at their congregation on November 10, 2015, read out a parallel address. All appointees, including new Jathedars, some organizers of that congregation were detained and first information reports lodged against them that included charges of *sedition*. After the November 10 congregation, the ruling Akalis have repeatedly accused the Congress for having patronized and sided with the radical elements to vitiate the atmosphere in the state.

*

When I landed in Amritsar, the state had been in constant turmoil for over a decade: political rivalry among the Congress leaders was as well pronounced and visible, as was division and factionalism discernible among the Akalis, who acted pretentious and agitated. They had given calls for many a programme {Rasta roko, Rail roko, Nehar roko, Kaam roko, non-co-operation movement by asking people not to pay revenue: land cess, water and electricity bills, preventing movement of food grains out of the state}; raising of *Marjeevare*: squads of persons, who would be ever ready to do or die for a cause at the command of their leaders, self-sacrificing type etc. All this had culminated in launching of the *Dharam Yudh Morcha* of which Sant Harchand Singh Longowal was the Dictator.

Though at the time of his appointment, as dictator of the morcha, Bhinderanwale was present and he had endorsed the resolution supporting the programme; subsequently, the two Sants were to part ways. However, prior to that the two Sants would jointly address the jathas before they marched out from the Manji Sahib Dewan Hall to court arrest. In fact, with a smirk, Bhinderanwale would often mock at the Akalis, who on their part, were/are ever wont to call their rivals, within and outside the party or *Panthic* fold, traitors or back-stabbers; what if these charges would remain unsubstantiated. And, across time, there have been departures and home comings of the same set of leaders: light, feather and heavy weights!

All these programmes or agitations were aimed at seeking *justice* for the *quom*; and for the fulfillment of the Sikh demands, including repeal of Article 25 of the Constitution of India that describes Sikhism, Jainism and Buddhism, as part of the Hindu religion. The Sikhs have long been seeking revoking of this Article and demanding to recognize Sikhism as an independent identity under the law. Akalis have also been asking the Centre for enactment of an All-India Sikh Gurdwara Act.

*

I have often wondered what exactly the Akalis had wanted and demanded from the Central government, given their oscillating and vacillating stand, and why had the Centre been dithering and delaying on the demands of the Sikhs, as the Akalis would have us believe. Were the Akalis clear on what they wanted or were they serious in putting forth the demands that they did from time to time? When one looks over the shoulder, one finds that the Akalis had been wavering on their demands: first drawing up a list, then adding more, later subtracting some, after an interval abandoning some and so on. There appears to be lack of consistency in their approach to the demands.

Nevertheless, to cut the long story short, and give a succinct background regarding Akalis and demands, here is a verbatim a passage from Khushwant Singh's book: *A History of the Sikhs,* Volume 2: 1839-1988; chapter, *The Anandpur Sahib resolution and other Akali demands;* page 342:

"In order to understand what made the Akalis and the government embarks on a collision course it is necessary to go back a few years and examine demands made by the Akalis from time to time and the central government's response to them. The Punjabi Suba had been conceded in 1966, but Chandigarh remained a Union

Territory shared as a capital by both Punjab and Haryana. Punjabi-speaking villages contiguous to Punjab still remained with the neighbouring States. The central government continued to control canal head works and made arbitrary allocations of water of the Sutlej, Ravi and Beas which had fallen to India's share by the Indus Waters Treaty of 1960. The government's tardiness in resolving these basic issues gave the Akalis grounds to charge it of being anti-Sikh. They assiduously cultivated a discrimination complex and kept adding to their list of demands. On its part, the central government, instead of conceding what was legitimately asked for, adopted delaying tactics, thus forcing the Akalis to launch a succession of passive resistance movements which often escalated into violence. Alongside the peaceful morchas grew terrorism which the police countered by brutal repression, often killing innocent people in staged encounters and torturing suspects. Police methods proved counter-productive and brought more recruits to terrorist groups.

The most comprehensive charter of demands made by the Akalis on behalf of the Sikhs was formulated in what came to be known as the Anandpur Sahib Resolution of 1973. There are at least three versions of the resolution in circulation which Akali leaders interpret differently...."

*

As to the Akalis' *Panthic* demands and espousing of the Sikh sentiments, the question is whether their concern was genuine or was it just a perceived sense of persecution. It seems difficult to identify even the starting point, as to where from did the Akalis exactly begin framing the demands. Their vacillation and oscillating postures have compounded the confusion. Some analysts go back in time to the 1950s, when the first boundary commission was set up to carve out states on linguistic basis or when the Punjabi Hindus disowned Punjabi and preferred to call Hindi as their mother tongue during the first census; some trace it to Punjabi Suba movement that the Akalis spearheaded that ended in the trifurcation of the state in 1966.

Many accuse New Delhi of playing a cunning fox while demarcating the boundaries at the time of reorganization of Punjab and playing truant: retaining Chandigarh, as the joint Capital of Punjab and Haryana; not handing over the control of head works; and acting in an unfair manner in distribution of the river waters.

Some attribute the situation spiraling out of control to Sikh-Nirankari clash of April 13, 1978; some to the fact that the Centre had been unfair in conceding Punjab's demands in respect of territory and sharing of river waters {the SYL: Sutlej-Yamuna Link canal}; and also not honoring the Rajiv-Longowal Punjab Accord {1985} etc. Akalis have always nursed a perceived sense of persecution, across the decades that it has all along been wronged and discriminated against by every commission and tribunal on territory and sharing of water the Centre or the Congress constituted. Why do the Akalis not introspect as to where did they go wrong or why and why did they not take any corrective steps to set their house in order and put up a united front? Always giving an impression of being a confrontationist or ever talking of making sacrifice does not always pay.

*

As mentioned in the Preface, the issue of SYL hogged the headlines in February-March 2016, when the Supreme Court began hearing on the Presidential reference made to it on the *Punjab Termination of Agreements Act, 2004* after 11 years. A five-member constitutional bench, headed by Justice A R Dave, was constituted for the purpose with Justices P C Ghose, Shiva Kirti Singh, Adarsh K Goel and Amitava Roy, as other members.

Since political stakes were high and worried over final outcome of the Apex Court hearing a worrisome feature, in a pre-emptive move, the SAD-BJP combine and the Congress came on the same page, despite shrill noises the two sides made over taking credit for protecting and safeguarding Punjab water. Thus, *a Punjab Sutlej-Yamuna Link Canal (Rehabilitation and Re-vesting of Proprietary Rights, Bill, 2016*, was unanimously passed in the Vidhan Sabha. The land, some 5376 hectares, that had been acquired for the construction of the contentious canal in 1977 was de- notified to be returned to the farmers. Separately, Punjab government returned the money, Rs 191.75 crore, to Haryana it had been given for land for digging the SYL canal. Expectedly, Haryana returned the cheque 'in original'.

Stung by the Punjab actions even before the Apex court had taken a final decision, Haryana too got into an aggressive battle-mode, legal and political. After an all-party meeting, which the Congress had boycotted, a delegation, led by the Chief Minister, Manohar Lal Khattar met the Governor Kaptan Singh Solanki and submitted a resolution requesting him not to give his assent to the Punjab Bill that sought to de-notify the SYL land. Khattar later wrote separately to the Governor to withhold his assent. Solanki had reportedly assured the Haryana delegation that he would get the Bill "legally" examined, and act as per the "constitutional" provisions. Reacting to Punjab Bill, Haryana assembly also passed a resolution condemning the Punjab move.

After the passage of the Bill, Punjab Chief Minister, Parkash Singh Badal, along with all 117 MLAs, called on the Governor requesting him to give his assent to the Bill at the earliest. {The delegation, however, forgot to submit a copy of the same to the Governor.} The Governor, reportedly, gave no assurance to Punjab leaders. {Incidentally, Kaptan Singh Solanki was Governor of Haryana, holding additional charge of Punjab, since S K Patil demitted office in Punjab Raj Bhawan in January 2015. V P Singh Badnore is the new Governor, who took oath of office in August 2016.}

Meanwhile, even as the hearing continued in the Supreme Court on validity of 2004 Act, and with the Governor not having given his assent to the 2016 Bill on re-vesting of property rights, in the game of one-up-man-ship, both the Akali and Congress leaders went into an overdrive, engaged around 200 JCB machines, and symbolically started filling-up the canal, uprooting thousands of trees.

Raising objections, Haryana moved an interlocutory application in the Apex Court, on March 17, 2016, which stepped in ordering status quo and directing Punjab not to return land meant for the SYL canal to farmers; and warned that Supreme Court authority should not be undermined by altering land use adding, "we cannot be a mute spectator when attempts are being made to let our order remain in-executable." The court also appointed Union Home Secretary, Punjab Chief Secretary and Director-General of Police as joint receivers of the land, till March 31. A central team also inspected the SYL areas and filmed them, where farmers and the Akalis {read government} had colluded to fill up parts of the Canal, uproot trees and level some land along the Canal banks. The Akalis also showed black flags to the team.

Meanwhile, in an unprecedented development, on the SYL issue, MLAs of the Indian National Lok Dal, Haryana and the Congress MLAs of Punjab tried to enter each other's chambers shouting slogans on March 17. Both state's Assemblies were in session, simultaneously. An ugly situation was warded off by the security men.

Later, Punjab Assembly passed yet another resolution, on March 18, 2016, which was defiant in tone. Inter alia it stated: the construction of the SYL canal will not be tolerated, and every stern step, if needed, will be taken to save the river waters of Punjab…..Punjab itself faces severe water crisis, and there is no drop to spare for other states. Therefore, there was no need of the SYL canal nor is there presently any need for it….

Without getting into the chequered history of 212 km SYL canal - 121 km in Punjab and 91 km in Haryana, suffice to say that it has already cost scores of precious lives of engineers and laborers; and hundreds of crores of rupees have gone down the drain. SYL had forced Akalis to launch the Kapoori Morcha in 1982, against the digging of the canal after Ms Indira Gandhi had laid the foundation stone of the SYL at Kapoori in Patiala. The Morcha was later shifted to Amritsar, and continued as *Dharam Yudh Morcha.* This emotive issue had, yet again, put the Beas and Ravi waters on the boil; and also triggered a political blame-game, leading to escalation of passions, estrangement and tensions among politicians and political parties within and without in the two neighbouring states.

*

Taking a rational look at the unfolding developments: SYL issue, CAG report on Punjab finances and state's last budget for 2016-17, *The Tribune* in its two editorials on March 17, 2016*: Checkmate: Badal closes a canal, opens constitutional wounds*; and *A Politician's Budget: high on populism, low on growth push,* cautioned as well as warned of consequences of such development.

In the editorial *Checkmate*, it concluded: "….That notwithstanding, his {Parkash Singh Badal}, and his predecessor Capt. Amarinder Singh's, actions have severely damaged our constitutional and federal arrangement. This has been virtually an act of secession, sponsored by the state Assembly, from commitments to the Union. Agonisingly, the demographic profile, history and geography of Punjab, all leave very difficult choices for any amends to be made."

In the second editorial, the parting lines were: " ….Attempts to pit Punjab's farmers against Haryana's may be beneficial to some political groups, these would certainly scare away private investment – whatever little the state might be hoping to attract."

In the wake of such a situation and developments, at this point of time, whichever way one may look at the pre-election evolving scenario, society at large, in both states, seemingly is headed towards deep waters!

Post-Script: The five-member Constitutional Bench delivered its verdict on November 10, 2016 invalidating the 2004 Act on Termination of Agreements. Also, it directed the Centre to complete construction of SYL at the earliest: this is the third time the Supreme Court gave such a direction. It had earlier done so in 2002 and 2004. The Court decision on the Presidential reference, as expected, led to a political and emotive storm in both Punjab and Haryana, particularly in Punjab since the Court decision had come barely months before the state went to the polls in early 2017. The ripple-effect of the judgment is too recent to be retold here. Nevertheless, going by the past experience, it is evident that the emotive water issue is going to be a long-drawn legal battle. Belligerent political posturing will not help. It is not a wise electoral plank.

Thereafter, in a special session of the Punjab Assembly on November 16, 2016, boycotted by the Congress whose MLAs had submitted their resignations to the Vidhan Sabha in the aftermath of the Supreme Court verdict against termination of water agreements, the House passed two resolutions: one, directing the government, cabinet and the government officers and officials to neither handover any land of any agency for the construction of SYL canal nor allow anyone to work on this project and give any sort of cooperation for this purpose; two, directs the government to immediately take up the matter with the Central government, Haryana, Rajasthan and Delhi, regarding securing cost/royalty in lieu of river water... so as to undo the injustice meted out to the state for decades by the Congress-led governments in the Punjab and at the Centre. Meanwhile, the Punjab revenue staff in the four districts, namely, Ropar, Fatehgarh Sahib, Mohali and Patiala through which the SYL canal passes, has completed required paper-work {records of mutations}to transfer land back to the original owners from whom land was acquired for the construction of the canal; or return to their descendents.

All this noise, rhetoric, blame-game and emotive out bursts of both the ruling combine, SAD-BJP and the Opposition parties, when the state is in election-mode, is nothing short of scoring brownie points. And, as *The Tribu*ne wrote in its November 17, 2016 balanced edit, '*Election-time itch'*: *Badal fishing for 'political martyrdom'*. ...And the acerbic debate continues....

*

These are some of the better known and talked of issues and factors that put the Akalis in a perpetual combative mode; ever ready for agitations, *morchas* and confrontation with the Centre: like Akalis' strong opposition to the imposition of the emergency in the country in 1975, mobilizing people and courting of mass arrests or their preparedness to be ever and always in an agitation-mode, as also their shifting stand on *Panthic* demands. These are also considered as possible factors for the suffering Punjab has had to undergo, since it irked the Congress/Centre.

The moot question, therefore, remains: with what issues {demands} the Akalis started and with what achievements the Akalis finally ended up with to show to their constituents, in the larger interest of the state or the Sikhs, who they claim to represent? Akalis also boast of articulating Sikhs' collective will, aspirations, frustrations and ambitions: political as well as religious; and socio-economic. Opinions within and outside the Sikh leadership vary on perceptions and interpretations of the events, as these unfolded across decades, as also on how far the Akalis succeeded in achieving what they had set to and sought to achieve all these decades, post-1947. Eventually, the Sikh demands raised by the Akalis were to spin out of hand and gun-culture took centre-stage.

I am deliberately not going into micro details on the issues involved, as enough material and matter on Akalis' performance in respect of demands and delivery, thereof, is available in scholarly literature; or, as we say, across the counter; splashed not only in ink, but also blood!

*

Therefore, without going into the details, merits or demerits of role of the Congress or the Akalis' way of thinking and pursuing the intended or identified objectives {goals or demands}, I would prefer to stop here but not without sharing a conversation that I had many years later with Parkash Singh Badal in this context, i.e. on the Akali Dal's prolonged struggles for fulfillment of their pending *Panthic* demands or redressal of the Sikh-centered socio-economic, politico-religious issues; identity crisis; and grievances, some, perhaps, genuine, several perceived that the party had/has always claimed to espouse.

This is the sum and substance of the conversation that, as *The Tribune* staffer, I had with Badal one day, while waiting for other colleagues to arrive for a press conference at Chandigarh, I asked him:

What have you gained, so far? What happened to all those demands for which you and the Akali Dal struggled and fought with all your might all these past decades with the Centre? And you had also gone to jail umpteen times, were witness to tragedy that struck Punjab resulting in spilling of blood of innocents that has drenched the land. Could you please list SAD's achievements, in real-terms, in the light of the grievances and demands, which have either been met or have remained unmet all these decades?

He looked askance, perhaps, not expecting such a question. Then he said, "*Kakaji, chadoji. Aj di gal karo. Asin Hor ki kar sakde si? Unha nu goli mar dende"?* {Leave it, boy! What more could we have done? Talk of present times. Could we have shot them?}

*

In this backdrop, I would not like to say anything more, any further on the demands the Akali leaders projected. However, it is fairly well-known that more harm, plausibly, has been caused to the Sikhs' way of life and Punjab from within the Akali folds than outside. When the Akali leaders accuse the Congress of triggering in-fighting among them or in their rank and file, one may turn around and ask these leaders: why do you fall an easy prey to the Congress' games and ploys? Are you so dumb? In fact, it is now fairly clear that whether it was the Congress or the Centre or the Akalis, all had in the past decades reacted sharply and inconsistently rather than thinking collectively, with calm and equanimity, as to where would their nefarious game plans lead the state and its people to! Failure to do so ultimately resulted in deep sarcasm.

At the end of the day, as one advances towards the sun-set of one's life and sits back to reminisce on what Punjab has become or has been witness to, one disturbing question refuses to fade away; it crops up time-and-again: what have we all achieved, as a state, as people? New Delhi has not conceded any of the demands for which the Akalis have agitated all their life: organizing agitations or filling jails. Yes, perhaps, one visible take-away Akalis may like to showcase: broadcasting of Gurbani from the Golden Temple at dawn and dusk; courtesy All India Radio, Jalandhar. {Now, of course, SGPC, on its own, has arrangements for live telecast of *kirtan*, which satiates the religious wants of Punjabis settled at home and abroad, at dawn and dusk. The telecasting monopoly is of the PTC News.}

*

Often, I compare Akalis to amoeba, which perpetually keeps splitting and reuniting! No wonder, at any given point of time, we have seen several claimants to be the real or true-blooded Akalis, representing the *original* Shiromani Akali Dal. Before moving on, just imagine how vexatious the Akalis have been on various issues, when it came to decision-making or preparing and projecting the *Panthic* agenda or grievances.

One sentence sums up what all the Akalis wanted and presented in their charter of demands: *Federal structure system of governance in the country*. Primarily, after Punjabi suba agitation, which culminated in the reorganization of the state in 1966, the Akalis put on the table their policy and program in the form of the Anandpur Sahib resolution, adopted at Takht Keshgarh Sahib on October 16-17, 1973. Then a revised list of 15 demands was put up to the government in New Delhi in October 1981. These demands ranged from religious to political to economic, linguistic and cultural. In between some demands were revised, some added, some deleted and some reiterated.

And, of the various versions {even interpretations} of the 1973 *original* Anandpur Sahib Resolution that were in circulation, one was adopted at All-India Akali conference at Ludhiana in October 1978, when Jagdev Singh Talwandi was the party president. {Incidentally, one day Talwandi called me aside and said; do not write the prefix *President* with my name. It is common-place word; write *Chief*. That sounds more impressive and powerful!} The last authentic version of that Resolution is believed to be the one that Sant Harchand Singh Longowal had sent to the members of the two houses of the Parliament; all along Sant Longowal had emphasised that the Sikhs were *not* for *Khalistan*; and it was also patently and blatantly wrong to dub the Sikhs as *separatists*.

The unimplemented Punjab Accord was like the last straw on the camel's back: the Akalis split vertically and horizontally, isolated Longowal, Balwant Singh and Surjit Singh Barnala. There started a bitter, long-lasting internecine war within the Akali leadership. And, as I have said, earlier, with the passage of time the leaders would make-up and unite, like the amoeba; only to split again.

Talking of the turbulent times, one finds similar opinion having been recorded by knowledgeable persons with regard to oscillating and vacillating stand of the

Akalis on the demands that they have so vociferously espoused all these decades and the manner in which man-made crises dominated Punjab, particularly, till the Operation Bluestar in 1984.

Take, for example, the second volume of Pranab Mukerjee's biography- *The Turbulent Years: 1980-96.* On Operation Bluestar and Akali demands, Mukerjee writes:

In 1981, the Akali Dal submitted a memorandum to Prime Minister Indira Gandhi *of 45 religious, political, economic and social demands and grievances, including the issue of sharing Punjab's river waters between Pu8n jab, Haryana and Rajasthan and the quest for the transfer of Chandigarh to Pun jab, and launched a virulent campaign around them.* It is further written that though *the 1973 Anandpur Sahib Resolution had called for a high degree of autonomy for Pun jab, the Akali Dal was not satisfied witgh it. In April 1981, Jathedar Jagdev Singh Talwandi, called for an autonomous state to be set up in North India forthwith, wherein Sikh interests would be recognized as of primary and special importance. This proposed state of Khalistan would have its own constitution.*

In November 1982, Sant Harchand Singh Longowal, in a new elucidation of the Anandpur Sahib Resolution, said a Sikh religious state with all Punjabi-speaking people should be created to preserve Sikh tradition and religion. Jarnail Singh Bhinderanwale started advocating the use of violence for a break-up of the Indian union and the creation of Khalistan.

The Akali Dal was constantly changing goalposts and was not clear about whether it wanted autonomy within Indian u ion or an independent state. The Akali Dal's organized effort to confront the government with its demands soon resulted in the rise of extremism. Taking advantage of the government's policy that the police would not enter any religious institution, the Golden Temple in Amritsar became a safe haven for their activities. Sadly, the Akali Dal never took a clear position regarding the hijacking of the movement by separatist elements. Instead, its leaders often used provocative language similar to that used by the militants.

After receiving the memorandum from the Akali Dal in September 1981, Indira Gandhi invited representatives for discussions. She sat with them not once but thrice, in October 1981, November 1981 and April 1982. However, all these efforts failed because of the Akali Dal's rigid stance. Even a few days before Operation Bluestar, an attempt was made to find a solution by holding meeting with the Akali Dal leaders, who were brought from jail to the lounge of Chandigarh airport at midnight. PV Narsimha Rao, cabinet secretary Krishnaswamy Rao and I {Pranab Mukerjee} represented the government at that meeting. Unfortunately, the talks remained unsuccessful.....

*

Any which way one may think, one fails to understand as to why the Congress or the Centre played games, dillydallied and remained ambivalent on decision-making with regard to the Akali Dal? Was it accidental, deliberate or part of Machiavellian script to paint the Akalis black? Can the Akali leaders, past and present, be absolved of what Punjab has been through?

The point that one wishes to stress, as stressed earlier, is: it is high time to reveal the whole truth and declassify all files pertaining to Punjab situation; how it evolved culminating in Operation Bluestar in 1984, and related police actions in 1986, 1988, as also in respect of Akali Dal's demands and talks between its leaders and the Centre. The Akali leaders who were deeply involved, and some of them who are still around, must speak out and record their memoirs, if for nothing else, at least from the academic point of view for people to analyze and judge the troubled times that Punjab has seen and, perhaps, continues to feel! Politics and academics go hand in hand!

*

Interestingly, despite all the infighting in the Akali politics, one thing is interesting: there have been and there are instances that when someone revolts or leaves the SAD or is expelled from the parent organization after being dubbed as anti-*Panthic*, he/she would continue to float around, like an autumn leaf, and disappear into oblivion or, if fortunate, would or could return to the *Panthic* flock and fold. This is how it was/is done:

In the religio- political see-saw, invariably, Akal Takht intervention was invoked: Akal Takht would pronounce *Tankha* {punishment for religious misconduct: usually cleaning shoes of the devotees or washing utensils in a Gurdwara or reciting a particular gurbani a given number of times every day for a given period. All this while, a slate is hung from the neck of the *Tankhaiya*, indicating his/her *sin* for which he/she had been punished for}. After the guilty person accepted this and completed the pronounced *Tankha*, he/she, was/is pardoned and accepted back in the *Panthic* fold.

*

In the present times, Punjab is again caught in a vortex of crises due to failure of the successive political leaderships to provide either good governance or maintain constant connect with the people. Any political party or coalition that assumes power after the Assembly elections in 2017, must promise to: govern impartially; bridge the trust deficit and deliver social justice; curtail corruption; maintain law and order and preserve communal amity/harmony. Also needed is to: stop politicization of bureaucracy and criminalization of police; provide job avenues to restless youths; caress poverty-stricken farmers, salvage farming by thinking of long-term measures to end tendencies among farmers to commit suicide due to debt burden and other reasons.

And, for sustainable agriculture and holistic rural development, next incumbent government will have to attend to: industry and service sector; improve urban and rural infrastructure; provide quality, affordable and universal education and health delivery systems in villages and better civic amenities; deliver with efficiency and efficacy all government services; free society from menace of drugs and substance abuse..

The Akalis seem to have forgotten the promised and much touted slogan of *Halimi Raj*, as announced at their mega Moga rally when for the first time they talked of Punjab, Punjabis and Punjabiat; not just the Sikhs alone! However, the economic and financial health of Punjab is so precarious and fragile that any government that assumes office in March 2017 will face a daunting, uphill task to pull the state out of the quagmire. Unless Chandigarh and New Delhi co-operate and Punjab's political parties work in lock-step, future appears bleak.

*

The ambivalence of the Akalis in mid-1980s is discernible from their muted comments when incidents of killings took place of the Hindu bus passengers, militants, journalists, academicians, religious preachers, ragis, police officials, political leaders etc. When it came to attending bhog ceremonies of slain militants or civilians or security personnel, the clash of political interests and communal divisions became more obvious. If, a killed person was a *martyr* for one section of the society, he was a *terrorist* for the other section of the society. Such were the times, when Akalis were caught in a dilemma: to condole or to condemn, to attend or not to attend the *Bhog* ceremonies of militants and or victims! {In fact, government censors were put on duty even on publishing *objectionable Bhog* advertisements for militants/terrorists in the language press.}

Faced with threats from the militants and radicalized Sikhs, the Akalis even dithered on many occasions, for example, whether to participate or not to participate in the negotiations or in the elections to the Parliament or state assembly. And, given the Centre's overtures and maneuvers, either in holding these elections or postponing these elections barely 24 hours before the poll time; or rigging these elections, it robbed the Congress {the Centre} too of credibility; and Akalis of courage of conviction!

For much of what was happening in Punjab then, blame must, therefore, be apportioned to the Congress/central agencies for keeping the ambers of the Punjab fire glowing and making every effort to disgrace the Sikh leadership. In the process, Congress also got somewhat alienated from the people, as it showed no concern! No wonder, because of long spell{s} of the President's Rule in the state, Punjab not only saw a procession of Governors come and go but also frequent reshuffling of their advisors; all at the whims and fancies of the Centre.

*

Punjab is one state that remained under the President's Rule for four years and eight months: 1987-92; in fact, the state has had President's Rule eight times, so far! And such has been the political vicious cycle that successive political parties in power at the centre have been dismissing state governments of the opposition parties without qualms. Remember Janata government dismissing nine congress-ruled governments in 1977; that included Punjab.

*

And, in my humble opinion, such has been the role and conduct of the Akalis, that one can barely name an Akali, who has remained unscathed, when it comes to self-aggrandizement, political gains and promoting self- or family interests. For them to call a fellow Akali, now a friend, now a foe, and give the ultimate shot of accusing he/she of being a Congress *agent* and discarding and dumping them to the dustbin of history is a common practice!

*

Interestingly, as if more by design than accident, beginning with Operation Bluestar in 1984, every two years, the complex was the theatre of security forces' action: in 1986 and again in 1988; both operations were called Black Thunder {officially, the State called 1986 -a police action; and between 1984 and 1986 there was the Operation Woodrose in the countryside}; in the Operation Black Thunder-2, as many as 146 militants had surrendered and several people were killed. In that operation, under a new strategy, those holed up inside the complex were *tired out*! These operations, in 1986 and 1988, were open to the media, which saw the action first hand.

The Operation Woodrose in the countryside that followed Operation Bluestar and the way security forces went after *passive harbors* in the villages after second Operation Black Thunder {1988}, it rekindled and re-fueled militancy that put the state on the boil. This was to last till mid-1995, according to some observers and analysts. Some, however, maintain that normalcy was vastly and visibly getting restored by 1993. The Operation Woodrose or the field- combing exercise resulted in wide-spread apostasy among the Sikh youth, on the one hand, and made many Sikh youth to run away to Pakistan, which played a significant role in imparting them weapon training, brain-washing and launching them into Punjab, after keeping them in *safe-houses*, on the other hand! {Though, the fencing of the 553 km Punjab border with Pakistan came later, narco-terrorism had been injected.}

*

And who can forget the way the Centre cleverly used Chief Minister Surjit Singh Barnala to *raid* the SGPC complex and re-enact Operation Bluestar under a different name: *police action* or Operation Black Thunder-I in 1986; necessitated because the Panthic committee had declared *Khalistan* on April 29. The announcement was made from Golden Temple complex room no. 46. {The day Khalistan was declared, Bhanwer had gone to attend the press conference; the five-members of the Panthic committee had called. The members were Dhanna Singh, Gurdev Singh, Gurbachan Singh, Aroor Singh and Wassan Singh. A 10-page background note on the justification of declaring Khalistan and calling upon foreign countries to give due recognition was also issued. Following this development, the security forces acted swiftly and cleared the place of anti-India elements. Thereafter, having achieved its sinister designs, the Centre sacked Barnala!}

Operation Black Thunder-2, in 1988, was essentially to cleanse the premises of unwanted occupants, since the complex was under siege of Jasbir Singh Rode, a former Akal Takht Jathedar. This Operation was triggered by an incident on May 9, when DIG S S Virk was fired at and seriously injured in the jaw, cracking his mandible while on a routine check of the CRPF force's pickets in the by-lanes around the complex. {Incidentally, on May 9, I was with the Governor S S Ray at Batala, when the word reached that Virk had been shot at and injured. Ramesh Vinayak was alone handling the story, when I returned, Ramesh seemed pretty shaken. Yet, he did a good piece.} After an indefinite curfew was clamped in the walled city localities, security forces lay siege to the complex.

*

The Operation Black Thunder-2 was a battle of nerves, wits and bullets that lasted 10 days before the ones who had voluntarily incarcerated inside raised their hands, waived white napkins and shirts; and surrendered. Among them were Jagir Singh and Nirwair Singh, who had called the shots all the while since the entry of Jasbir Singh Rode and his followers; including splinter factions of militants and AISSF {Gurjit Singh}. It was after that operation the *Parikarma* rooms were demolished, as those were used as the typical extortion and torture chambers! Those were harrowing days.

*

I am intentionally not getting into the history or details or nitty-gritty of numerous other key dated events and circumstances obtaining prior to mid-November 1983 or post-1984, as some of these have been cited in the above passages and much has also been written in the available literature. Suffice to say, as a consequence of what has gone-by; Punjab, Punjabis and Punjabiat received a severe body blow, as did polity and political economy, development and growth in this sensitive border state. Aftershocks are still being felt! Punjab is still not out of the woods, not yet. Physical and psychological wounds that have been inflicted on the body, soul and psyche of Punjab, both by design and accident, have only coagulated, not healed!

Those were unhappy times. Are these over and gone? Troubled, turbulent times are ahead.

11

Berserk Police, Life in Disarray

While situation went out of spiral post-1984 with multiple militant, political and religious groups and factions engaged in intense internecine war and armed conflicts; tinkering with the established institutions like the SGPC or that of the high priests was also common place occurrence. It was utter chaos. And, one also vividly remembers the number of restrictions, ban orders and prohibitory orders that the government pronounced from time-to-time and how meekly, the people of Amritsar obeyed those; of course, they had no other choice. These orders ranged from regulating opening/closing time of shops to ban on pillion riding by two males to night curfew in border areas, particularly, in Patti and Tarn Taran sub-divisions et al.

*

On top of such doctored and regimented life-styles, the people faced yet another grave blow: barely a month after the June, 1984 Operation Bluestar, a detailed development plan for beautification of areas around the periphery of the complex was submitted to the Centre. The idea was to create at least a 60 meter wide corridor to ward of any future unwanted and unwarranted activities inside the complex and to enable security agencies to patrol the vicinity.

Sooner than later, preparations started for action and undertaking demolition works on buildings, commercial and residential. The Rs 1,700 crore projects were to be completed in three phases. There was stiff resistance. Over 3,000 structures faced the hammer. Yes, demolition did take place in several pockets and along with the debris was carted away and buried forever the age-old, traditional culture that thrived in the by-lanes surrounding the complex. In fact, across decades, these buildings and the complex had existed cheek by jowl!

*

And, what further compounded the stifling situation and the daily life-styles of the people, even in rural settlements, was wide-spread news of use of civilians as *human shields* by security forces during raids and searches, as also the plight of *passive harbors*, accused of giving food and shelter to the militants roaming the countryside; militants would get, at gun-point, what they wanted, demanded and desired. The security forces took full advantage of the hapless and helpless people, who became either easy target of police encounters or of militants' AK-47s. Thus, doubly unblessed, as these vulnerable village people were, their harrowing tales sent a chill down the spine!

The security forces, thus, had a field day; a free run, literally going berserk with no questions asked. No doubt, that was the situation, then. Yet, there were reports of differences among the senior police officers on operational strategies or handling of emerging situations with political and religious connotations. Occasionally, these differences would surface and became obvious; in fact the accepted chain of command in disciplined police had broken with individual officers at the lower rung of the ladder having direct access to the top officers, thus, bypassing their immediate seniors.

*

Here is an illustration, as to how serious the situation was within the security instrumentalities: the incident relates to the government's decision to permit Jasbir Singh Rode to undertake his 10-day march, all the way from Takht Damdama Sahib in Bathinda to Amritsar, in October, 1987. As the march neared Amritsar, on October 10, standing alongside border range I-G Chaman Lal at the *Samadh* of Baba Naudh Singh, on the outskirts of the city on Amritsar-Tarn Taran road, I casually happened to ask Chaman Lal, w*hy you appear so tense*! The Deputy Commissioner, Sarabjit Singh, who was nearby, smiled. Both of them looked at me and said, *wait for an important development, later in the evening*. They did not elaborate beyond that. A newsman's instinct rang a bell: *he may be quitting*. Curious, I asked, *are you quitting as I-G*? Chaman Lal kept quiet. And, after Rode and his men entered the Golden Temple complex, the first thing he did was to declare his *goal* - *Khalistan*!

*

It was widely speculated that Jasbir Singh Rode had been propped up by the intelligence agencies, for whatever reasons, but such things were/are difficult to either confirm or disbelieve! The same way, it was said that when Giani Zail Singh was the Union Home Minister, he had signalled Jarnail Singh Bhinderanwale be given a *free passage* all the way from Bombay {Mumbai} to Chowk Mehta in Amritsar! Such impressions only further confirmed that whatever was happening then in the state was stage-managed and politically choreographed with a definite script! The result of such sinister designs and games is before us.

*

Later, *in* the evening, Chaman Lal called a press conference in the City Kotwali and announced his decision to *proceed on leave*, as he was opposed to such a step {allowing Jasbir Singh Rode a free run and entry into the Golden Temple complex, along with his armed companions} since the premises had been cleared with great efforts earlier, in 1986. Chaman Lal had the guts to stand up against *wrong* orders, instructions and illogical handling of a sensitive situation, which he cautioned could rupture into serious situation with grave ramifications.

In fact, Chaman Lal was one of the finest police officers that I have ever come across and from whom one learned much. He was border range, Amritsar, Inspector-General of Police. Earlier, he was the D I-G: Deputy Inspector-General with the BSF: Border Security Force, at Gurdaspur. One day, sitting in the circuit house, he shared this piece of information: he had summoned a police officer, Rajinder Singh, and asked him to release all old people, who were languishing in jails or in police stations at his bidding and were, in fact, innocent! He was also told not to harass *passive harbors*. Sensing and seeing the officer's body language, Chaman Lal tersely remarked: *do remember that the release of old, innocent people, is the only good thing you would have done in your entire police career*!

The going away of Chaman Lal at that crucial point of time was just a tip of the ice-berg, which exposed the nefarious designs of the powers that be that prevailed then.

*

Today, even more dangerous, deadly and menacing is the web of drug or substance abuse that has wrapped Punjab after a decade or so of terrorism. This will serve a far more deadly blow to the future of the state, even deadlier than the irreparable damage the AK-47s did. The need now, more than ever before and anything else, is to save the youth from drug or substance abuse; and to draw lessons from the past, make course corrections in the present for a better future.

*

The security forces then were seemingly beyond control and command, occasionally going berserk! One living example of how security forces went berserk is the conduct of the CRPF: Central Reserve Police Force that ran amuck in village Brahmpura on the cold night of December 27, 1987, breaking into almost all houses, dragging men folk out, beating them up; and molesting women. When I visited the village the following morning, I came across families which refused to share any information because of the humiliation they had faced and the way their daughters, sisters and wives were insulted. Later, the CRPF company commander Mukhram Yadav was suspended, an enquiry ordered. But not before a large congregation was held in Brahmpura and the same was addressed by Akal Takht Jathedar, Professor Darshan Singh - it was a mass protest against men in *Khaki*!

*

Wrap-up: Even at the cost of some repetition and in no particular chronological order, let us skim the surface on the way circumstances evolved and influenced the ever changing situation, prior to mid-November 1983 or post-1984:

After the Punjabi Suba agitation ended with trifurcation of Punjab in 1966, the Akalis launched a *morcha* against the emergency in 1975; in between there were small or medium agitations on one or the other issue. Jarnail Singh Bhinderanwale had become head of the Damdami Taksal – a Sikh seminary- in 1977 with headquarters at Chowk Mehta {Amritsar}. To begin with, he engaged in *Amrit Parchar* campaign: baptizing the Sikhs. Then there was a clash between Sikhs {mostly followers of Akhand Kirtani Jatha} and Nirankaris in Amritsar on Baisakhi day in 1978.

*

Amarjit Kaur, widow of Fauja Singh, who was among those killed in that clash, put up in a building in the Parikarma and had accused Sant Jarnail Singh Bhinderanwale for betraying the Jatha after instigating the Sangat to take Nirankaris head-on at their *Sammelan* in the city. She had shared her agony and sentiments with me in a long interview that I did for *The Tribune*.

*

And, two years later, in 1980, Nirankari chief Baba Gurbachan Singh was shot dead at New Delhi. The following year, *New Republic of Khalistan* flag was hoisted at Anandpur Sahib {1981}. The same year, head of the *Hind Samachar* group of newspapers, Lala Jagat Narain, was slain and in that connection Bhinderanwale was arrested from Chowk Mehta, amidst bloody clashes between Bhinderanwale supporters, radicals and the police. In August 1982, Akalis had intensified their *Dharam Yudh Morcha*. In April 1983, Punjab Deputy Inspector-General of Police, A S Atwal, was shot dead at the entrance to the Golden Temple complex.

Thereafter, Akalis tore Article 25 of the Indian Constitution in 1984, and in May, the same year, Longowal announced the *non-co-operation* programme. Operation Bluestar was launched in June 1984, almost simultaneously followed Operation Woodrose in the countryside; and again there were two Operations, both named Black Thunder-1, 2: one in 1986, the second in 1988 at the Golden Temple. Almost four months after Operation Bluestar, Indira Gandhi was shot dead on October 31, 1984. The following year, Rajiv Gandhi and Sant Harchand Singh Longowal signed the Punjab Accord: July 1985; Longowal was shot dead the following month, in August.

*

And, all along, there was a kind of musical chair game on between the SGPC and the militants {with government stepping in on and off}, when it came to either appointing of officiating/acting SGPC President{s}, since Gurcharan Singh Tohra was in jail; or in respect of dismissal and appointment of one or the other set of five High priests, who were central players in some of the decision-making processes and were giving directions, as the situation demanded and as long as someone lent them their ears and listened. Given the vicissitudes the SGPC had been through, the Army handed over the control of the complex to the five High priests in September 1984. And, with the passage of time, the High priests were heard, not listened to!

*

After the second Operation Black Thunder in 1988, SGPC was ultimately handed over the control of the complex. Though a belated realization, yet, the government did accept and recognize the importance and relevance of the SGPC. After 1988, the SGPC held sway over the complex, co-operated with the administration; and appointed high priests of its own choice. Isn't it strange that at one point of time, the SGPC would succumb to the diktats of the militants and appoint high priests at their bidding and of their choice; and, later, it would flex its muscles and sack them, appointing high priests of its own choice! How time changes! To better secure the complex, SGPC accepted the 10 steps the administration had proposed to ensure peace, tranquility and M*aryada* for times to come in the complex.

*

And, who can forget the parallel *Sarbat Khalsa* meets: one organized at the instance of the then Union Minister Buta Singh through Nihang chief Baba Santa Singh at Burj Akali Phoola Singh; and, later, the one the five High priests had called, *Sikh Convention*, at Gurdwara Shaheedan; or for that matter All-India Sikh students' federation-sponsored Sikh convention- virtual *Sarbat Khalsa*, as AISSF would have us believe- at Akal Takht, which disbanded the SGPC, the Akali Dal{s} and the High priests. The two *Kar Sewa*: one carried out under Baba Santa Singh, read central government, which repaired Akal Takht; and the second that Baba Kharak Singh organized, beginning with de-silting of the holy tank and then re-doing Akal Takht, all over again.

The de-silting operation was a spectacle that CRPF personnel had never seen before or, perhaps, anticipated. Such was the enthusiasm and religious fervor that the task was completed much ahead of schedule, as people would converge in large numbers every day, round the clock! A CRPF Jawan, on duty near the entrance to the temple towards the Clock Tower side expressed his disbelief when he told me: *Sahib, yours is a strange community. Rich people, dressed in best of clothes, come in expensive vehicles, and carry silt smearing their dresses. Also, they serve free food – Langar – to everyone, including us. This is strange!*

*

Incidentally, when Tohra was isolated and moved to Khalra and lodged in a Canal rest house, across a drain and pretty close to the Pakistan border, it set the rumor mills working overtime, as to the motive behind such a move. And, when Tohra complained of ophthalmology problems, he was brought to PWD Rest House in Amritsar, adjoining the Circuit House. The media was not allowed to meet Tohra either at Khlara or in Amritsar, such were the instructions. I remember having met him by playing *assistant* to world-famous ophthalmologist Dr Daljeet Singh, who was deputed to examine Tohra in the PWD Rest House. I succeeded in sneaking in incognito carrying Dr's bag, I was able to pass on a questionnaire to Tohra. That is how it was then.

*

In between, as violence and killings continued, so did talks and negotiations between the Centre and the Akalis. Punjab remained under the President's Rule; elections were announced {for Parliament} and later for the state assembly: these elections were held under the shadow of the gun; some militants had also won; some elections were boycotted; and some were postponed at the last minute {all at the will of the Centre}!

New Delhi witnessed a host of prime ministers; in June 1991 Rajiv Gandhi was killed; and in February 1992, Congress came to power in Punjab with Beant Singh as chief minister {the party had secured less than 20 per cent votes}; but not before the Centre had stage-managed a win, in 1986, for the Akalis, who were nevertheless, feeling cheated, disgruntled, disgraced and were also fractured. Surjit Singh Barnala became the chief minister, only to be dismissed later, when he had, wittingly or unwittingly, served the cause and purpose of the Centre with *police action* or *Operation Black Thunder* -1 at the Golden Temple in 1986; at that point of time, militancy too was seemingly on the ascent.

*

This wide-angle background and a bird's eye-view of the events, episodes and developments {pre-mid-November 1983 and post- June 1984}, has been given to re-encapsulate and refresh memories of that time, as also to describe the atmosphere prevailing then in the life of Amritsar, as well of Punjab, Punjabis and Punjabiat.

This is the broad spectrum in which I worked in Amritsar and Gurdaspur from November 1983 to 1990; and a brief stop-gap posting in 1999, when our staffer, Varinder Walia was on medical leave. After this overview of the Punjab landscape then, in the following passages and pages are presented some impressionable memoirs, travelogues, reportage, analysis, genesis of events and moments that have left an indelible imprint on the mind, as if all this had happened only yesterday. Besides sharing notes from a reporter's note-book, I have also shared my comments on how I looked or look at Punjab.

12

Sikhs and Salt

A foreign correspondent was visiting Amritsar some weeks prior to the Army action at the Golden Temple. On a word from my Chandigarh office, I was escorting him and answering his questions to the best of my knowledge and understanding. When we met Sant Harchand Singh Longowal, the visiting foreign correspondent asked him: *what will you do and how will you stand up to the huge security apparatus of the State, if the prime minister were to act against you? The Sikhs are a small community.* As interpreter, I explained the question.

Sant ji smiled. After a brief pause he told me in Punjabi to tell *Shriman*: *Subzi vich loon di mikdar zara jahi hundi hai, par eh swad vigaar ke rakh denda hai. Sanu koi ched ke ta vekhey, pata lag jayega;* meaning: *proportion of salt in the vegetable is very small; yet, it changes the very taste of the dish. We may be, numerically, a small community, try anyone provoke or challenge us, you will see the result. We will change the taste {of the Nation}*! When I told him of the reply, he smiled, amused! He closed his notebook and sipped his tea in silence.

Sant ji seemed mighty pleased looking at him; perhaps, he seemed to be in agreement with the reply!

13

Unholy Acts

It was several months later that stench of putrefied bodies and flesh evaporated from the complex after the Operation Bluestar. The June heat had precipitated the situation. It took a while before the place was cleaned up. Much has been written about the physical damage caused to the structures inside the complex and photographs published and circulated. There are also emotional descriptions about the psychological scars and wounds on the Sikh psyche left by the Army action. One did not get to see much of that Operation at first hand, till the place was thrown open to the public albeit with a rider: restricted hours and with *out of bounds* areas identified and demarcated-with the Big Brother, the Army, watching! Still, one could imagine and visualize the situation when the Army action was on.

However, it was different after the first and second Operations Black Thunder in 1986 and 1988, which one had seen from the beginning to the end. {The media had watched the siege of the Temple premises and ensuing operation in 1988 from atop the Brahmbuta Akhara from where the *Darbar Sahib* precincts present a picturesque view.}

*

The following passages amply reflect both the state of things inside the Golden Temple premises, as well as one's own state of mind/feelings, at that time - 1988. Once the complex had been cleared of the unwanted elements and before the place was spruced up, the administration decided to let in the media to see the ground realities, as these appeared and looked immediately after the operation by the security forces was over and inmates had surrendered. Even if it was a conscious decision, so as to spread the word around as to who had committed a sacrilege and who had defiled the holiest of the holy places, the eye-witness accounts and visuals amply and effectively conveyed the message, which was very succinct, telling, loud and forceful.

As I stepped on the sun-baked marble *Parikarma*, littered with glass splinters and ammunition shrapnel; the eerie silence and emptiness of the Temple greeted me. To the right was the charred *Ghanta Ghar* {Clock Tower}, pock-marked with bullets. The visit was totally different from the ones in the past after similar actions by the security forces - in 1984 and 1986. This time, it was not the physical damage to parts of the Golden Temple and other buildings, which mattered, but a moral and spiritual damage done to the holy precincts by those, who had made a small township in the *Parikarma* rooms with torture chambers, ration stores, offices for holding parallel courts and extortion of money; and even a medical room.

The damage-moral and spiritual- was, in fact, caused the day the *Parikarma* rooms were allowed to be re-occupied by those wanted by the law and feared by the common people. The place of veneration and worship bore marks of sacrilege; a strong stench of urine, faeces, stale food and dirty clothes filled the air. Such filth in tins, bowls and canisters was inside the sanctum sanctorum. Dirty linen lay strewn on the first floor and the staircases leading to it. A can full of night-soil and urine lay next to *Har-ki-Pauri*, where one could not stand; a place considered very sacred, where the devotees fill a cupped palm with water from the holy tank to drink and sprinkle over their head; after paying obeisance inside the *Darbar Sahib*.

The holy book lay wrapped in the dark room. The flowers too had wilted and withered. The shattered masonry and brickwork, on the first floor, stood as mute testimony to what had happened during the 10-day siege of the complex after the CRFP DIG Virk was shot and injured on May 9.

*

Should such a place become a sanctuary for the unholy militants and the lawless? How did they smuggle in arms and later building material for fortifications and partitions in the rooms? Who should be apportioned the blame, the SGPC, the security forces present all around manning some 20-odd entry points, the Sikh leadership? Perhaps, all, including political parties and their machinations, were responsible for defiling the sanctity of the Temple. Official sources told me that the interrogation of the arrested militants, who were residing in the *Parikarma* rooms, had revealed that they were extracting approximately Rs 35 lakh per month from helpless and scared shopkeepers settled along the periphery of the complex.

*

Inside every room in the *Parikarma*, it was the same story- smelling beddings and personal clothing, utensils full of leftover *langar* food, lots of ration, photographs of the Gurus; and the terrorists killed by the security forces, torture equipment, blood, urine, weapons, ammunition, letter-pads, pieces of human flesh, hair etc. Also, there were tape-recorders, cameras, steel almirahs, swords, and refrigerators, unstitched rolls of cloth, imported perfumes and toiletries.

One striking feature of the place this time was that *Harimandir Sahib* was not touched by the security forces, who scrupulously avoided firing at the shrine.

*

However, during the 10-day firing, only two stray bullets hit *Harimandir Sahib*-one just at the entrance to the sanctum sanctorum and the other had ricocheted and kissed a *rumala* - cloth in which the holy book is wrapped with veneration - covering the handwritten holy book, which was kept on the first floor above *Har-ki-Pauri*. The bullet had hit a glass panel and the deep red carpet was full of glass splinters. Another bullet had shattered the glass show-window of Shaheed Baba Deep Singh ancillary shrine in the Parikarma.

*

In fact, the commandos and others had conducted the operation from outside the *Parikarma*, entry into which was simply barred. The empty chambers around the forlorn *Darbar Sahib* seemed to pose more questions than provide answers: one was bewildered by the immensity of what had been permitted or what had happened inside and for so long.

I wondered if all the washing of the *Parikarma* underway with hosepipes brought in by the Municipal Corporation on that day and the fire brigade men would also wash the sins of those, who contributed to its sacrilege or allowed that to happen? Of what use was the bathing of Darbar Sahib with milk and water drawn from the holy tank, a daily ritual, from which bodies had been fished out, when Sikhs themselves were responsible for what had happened?

The symbol of dynamic authority-*Darbar Sahib*- stood silent and aloof! It made one's mood sullen. One craved for forgiveness and better wisdom. The shell-shocked Temple had become a favourite rendezvous for the media-men, who were allowed free access to see for themselves, who the real culprits were: the so-called militants inside or the government or, perhaps, both.

While parts of the teeming and confused walled city had remained locked in a curfew since May 9, and petrified people yearned for a break, inside the Temple the stench was choking. Beneath the bullet-riddled model of Akal Takht were pools of dried blood, as elsewhere in the *Parikarma* or in rooms like No. 14, the office of *Khalistan*, where the stink was sky-high!

*

Those very persons, who had accused Sant Harchand Singh Longowal and the former High priests'-appointees of SGPC of *surrendering* to the authorities/security forces, at the time of Operation Bluestar, and had vowed to fight to the finish, were themselves seen meekly walking out of the *Parikarma* with hands raised, crestfallen and nervous. They sat on the benches in the Guru Ram Das Langar building compound receiving first aid or eating bananas; and avoiding eye-contact with the media with whom they would interact on a daily basis; giving diktats!

*

It was a nauseating experience: even the pigeons lay dead, all over. Later, volunteers of the Sri Guru Singh Sabha and the Seva Society, *Harimandir Sahib*, mopped up the entire premises: cleaned, washed; and honor restored!

14

A Night in Parikarma

After the shootout on May 9, 1988, in which CRPF D-IG S S Virk was seriously injured with a bullet piercing his jaw, the security forces lay siege to the complex and followed *tire them out* policy to neutralize gun-totting persons. Simultaneously, there were prolonged negotiations between the SGPC and the district administration on ensuring permanent peace and tranquility inside the Golden Temple complex and upholding the *Maryada* in future. The SGPC insisted that it was for the government to ensure no arms and ammunition were allowed inside the complex. Under those circumstances, it was virtually a battle of wits between the two sides coupled with trust deficit. Ultimately, once a broad consensus was reached, work on restoring the *Maryada* began. The hitch was that the priests, who performed the daily rituals, were behind the bars. Their immediate release was a contentious issue. The choice zeroed on Giani Mohan Singh, who was in Patiala jail.

I remember it was Saturday night. To be present there that night, witness negotiations between SGPC and officials and later ceremonies at dawn, was exciting and exhilarating experience: the sparsely lighted *Parikarma*, the cool breeze and the shimmering lights dancing in the *Saro*war further added to the serenity of the place, which had, not long ago, been riddled with the bullets!

Much before dawn, around 2.30 am, the usual preliminary preparations had to begin. Along with other colleagues, I reached the Golden Temple, shortly before mid-night. A small number of devotees had gathered together close to the Brahmbuta Akhara. These were the persons who performed the preliminaries, like washing and cleaning up the *sanctum sanctorum* with milk and water drawn from the holy tank's *Har-ki-Pauri* and took care of other sundry activities: lighting incense sticks, spraying perfumes, putting fresh cut-flowers in vases etc.; before the Ragis started *Kirtan* {singing of religious hymns} and only, thereafter, the holy book Guru Granth Sahib would be brought in by the head priest. This journey from Akal Takht, where the holy book is kept at night, is marked by a small procession with the devotees vying to lend their hand at carrying the palanquin in which the holy book is placed. It is quite a spectacle of religious festivity, devotion with singing of religious hymns and chanting of *Waheguru*.

Security and civil personnel and officers were at hand that night to ensure smooth operations for restoration of *Maryada*. There were anxious moments as to when Giani Mohan Singh would reach or if he had been released or whether he is on his way. {It may be mentioned here that Giani Mohan Singh was part of 51-member Jatha that had courted arrest at Ludhiana on May 18. He was segregated and shifted to Patiala.} In the wee hours, Giani Mohan Singh entered the *Parikarma*. One could sense his apprehensions then. To a question, he had simply said: w*hatever had happened was bad.* On the acts of sacrilege committed in the past 72 hours or so, he first wanted to have a word with Giani Puran Singh. He was also ambivalent as to how *boys* would react to his restoring of *Maryada*. Yet, he smiled and said he was only doing his duty in the interest of the Sikh religion and the Panth. SGPC officials backed him and assured him that all was well! He was unhappy that his other colleagues were still in jails.

Giani Mohan Singh offered prayers at *Kotha Sahib*: the temporary abode where Guru Granth Sahib is kept for the night at Akal Takht; he placed the holy book on his head and walked a few steps before placing it in the palanquin to be taken to *Harimandir Sahib*. At 4.40 am he had stepped inside the *sanctum sanctorum*. As he unwrapped each of the silken sheets: *Roomalas*, it was brushed with cotton and sprayed with perfume. The book was opened and he read out the morning *Vaak*: *the order of the day*. The hymn was of third Guru Ran Das, who had actually found the Pool of Nectar: *Amrit Sarowar*. The *Maryada* had been restored. The Kirtan started earlier by Bhai Kirpal Singh resumed, so did the broadcast over the AIR: All-India Radio.

*

In fact, once restoration of *Maryada* was confirmed, I took a calculated risk that night: I went to the Brahmbuta Akhara, manned by the CRPF, and made a call to my office giving the *Desk* the latest up dates. That was around 1.30 am or so. The night-shift Chief-sub, Gurinder Singh asked me if the banner lead, *Maryada restored at the Golden Temple* could be given, I replied in affirmation. *The Tribune* was the only paper to break the news in its May 12 edition. It was a risk worth taking and it paid off. It was an unforgettable night spent in the *Parikarma*. And, as if it was a reward, after the night long vigil, a liberal helping of K*rah Parshad* was served that morning, making it difficult to even hold it in the cupped palms of both hands, what to say of making the pretty hot and sweet *Parshad* difficult to even eat!

*

15

When Pigeons Flew Away

In a reporter's life, there come moments and occasions, which get fixed in the grey matter. Those unforgettable memories with the passage of time become part of a kind of one's life. And, there are quite a number of such stories, which are stored in the memory disk. These are easily retrievable. Here, let me share two such stories:

One: after the Operation Bluestar, the Golden Temple had been partially opened to the public with fixed hours and with a host of restrictions; one was - photography prohibited, another was taking of *Amrit*: water from the Pool of Nectar - the holy tank - in bottles and small containers; the latter because of the apprehensions that the water was polluted and contaminated, given the possible mix of gun powder and drowning of humans.

In the initial weeks, the administration closely watched and monitored the situation on the opening of the Temple, particularly, public reactions and emotions. There was no certainty, as to when visitors or devotees would be permitted or not permitted or how many would be permitted or at what time. The situation was fluid and in a flux! On the slightest of pretexts, curfew would be imposed in the immediate vicinity of the complex and or movement - human and vehicular - restricted.

My old friend and senior colleague O N Garg, who worked for the *Indian Express,* was temporarily posted to Amritsar. We had earlier worked together in Ambala. He had reached Amritsar a day earlier, after a strenuous six-hour journey from Ambala. He had accompanied me to the Golden Temple on July 5, 1984. This was the second day, when devotees were being allowed to enter the Temple. I had not been there for over a week, after the Temple was thrown open to the devotees for limited periods every day. I still remember it was a hot, humid day with my sweat-soaked shirt sticking to my body. We stood side-by-side near the Jallianwala Bagh waiting for the clock to strike 4 pm, when the Army men would allow devotees and curious visitors to proceed to the Temple.

Reluctantly, a breeze would strike, kiss and disappear saying goodbye, as quickly it had come, leaving us gritting our teeth! As the time passed, the number of devotees swelled and soon there were more than a thousand-odd waiting to surge forward to pay obeisance. The time of opening of the Golden Temple also coincided with the three-hour power cut, adding to the miseries of the people! As the power went off, worshippers, who had entered some of the shops to be under the fan, started trooping out.

As the barriers were removed, old women stood up. The crowd surged forward; jostling and pushing, the young and the old, Hindus and Sikhs, quickened their steps to go in first; a kind of mini marathon! The clock at the *Ghanta Ghar* entrance was not ticking; it hands stood still, motionless at 7.45! The temple presented a different look: the ugly scars of shells and bullets had been either repaired or erased; there was smell of fresh paint; the burnt and charred wood-work and broken glass panes had been replaced.

In the *Parikarma* a large labour force was replacing marble slabs damaged during the Operation Bluestar. About 50 of the labour had arrived from Delhi four days ago. We saw people examine bullet marks in the corridor around the *Parikarma*, while a chief engineer was camping inside the complex. The work of repair was in the hands of the MES: Military engineering service. Garg's observation was sharp and valid: *there seem to be more curious visitors than devotees; and those hurrying along may not have ever visited the Temple even prior to the Army action.*

*

The exit from the Temple was from another point: a circuitous route, which opened into the business hub, Katra Ahluwalia, opposite the *Ghanta Ghar* entrance. As we walked down the bustling Bazaar, one could feel and sense a spirit of *amity and harmony* between the two principal communities, the Hindus and the Sikhs, who were in an estranged relationship; not seen to be engaged, any more! Down the Bazaar we saw CRPF personnel posted on either side; ostensibly relaxed! That July late afternoon was suffocating with heat and dust hanging low.

Inside the shops sat typical *Amritsari* businessmen in *banyan and dhoti*, fanning themselves with the traditional *Pakh*i: hand-held fan; their gold chains dangling from their necks! The buzz and drone of the generators added to the usual chaos and confusion at that hour. We saw a small group of people jostling with arms raised. They held currency notes in their hands. Curious to know what was happening, we too went closer only to discover that the favourite *Jalebis*- maker was doing brisk business. The crowd of both the Hindus and Sikhs was, yet another proof, if one was required, that old amity had not completely vanished; signs of that relationship were returning, howsoever gradually!

We too helped ourselves to the syrupy sweets! Close-by; there was an old Sikh with a soiled shirt and sweat trickling down his face. His colleague, a Hindu, held the *Jalebis*. They had their fill, licked their juicy, sticky fingers, wiped and rubbed their hands behind their backs and were ready to once again together pull their cart, loaded with blankets! They had been together, as partners in toil, for over a decade; the much talked chasm between the two communities had not separated them. Garg smiled. With his earthly wisdom, he said: *yes, good days are ahead! Amity is not over!*

We hoped, as Garg kept thinking and talking, that having seen so much fighting, death and destruction, still people continued to share sighs and smiles. And, perhaps, age-old ties between the two communities will remain strong and intact, lasting till eternity! Even in *that* difficult period, life flowed on, as another day passed; normalcy seemed on the city's threshold. *Guru-ki-Nagri* was stirring with life, yet again!

*

Two: one afternoon, on an impulse, I thought of venturing inside the Golden Temple in the off hours. Why not take a chance? I convinced and cajoled myself. I approached an Army officer at the picket outside *Chowk Ghanta Ghar*. The nameplate on his uniform kindled a bright ray of hope that I may be permitted inside. *Yes*, he snapped. I said, *Sir, were you the Prefect of the Beas House at Punjab Public School, Nabha*? He seemed relaxed: *Yes*. I introduced myself as *The Tribune* Staff Correspondent and quickly added, *I'm B-39*; that was my house number. We shook hands and talked for a while. He let me go inside with instructions to remain visible in the *Parikarma;* accordingly, a word over the wireless was sent to the troops about a visitor entering. The officer was O P Nandrajog! He retired as a Lt-General!

It was around 2 pm, when I entered: the white marble *Parikarma* reflected the bright sun, a blinding glare! I took my own time to walk to the *sanctum sanctorum*, taking a shortcut rather than the usual full round of *Parikarma*. I would look around a bit nervously. There was eerie silence. I could hear my own heart-beat. Honestly, the overwhelming nagging thought then was: *why did I take such a risk*! As I walked into the *sanctum sanctorum*, I found no Granthi {priest}, who sits at the head of the holy book or the *ragis*, who sing hymns to the accompaniment of musical instruments.

The stillness, the deafening silence was unanticipated in a place, which on normal days reverberates with the singing of hymns from the *Gurbani*; and given the rush and crush of the devotees, one patiently waits for the turn to enter the *sanctum sanctorum*; and once inside, one jostles to pay obeisance! One SGPC *Sewadar* lay in a corner, resting. He sat up. I asked him: *Bahut chup-chap hai, ki gal?* {It is very still! What is the matter?} He said he had been there all alone since morning. I went out from the side door towards the *Har-ki-Pauri*, where a *Jawan* was washing his clothes; nearby was his stove with a kettle on it! He was making tea, perhaps! I walked away without making any eye-contact with him!

That day, there was no P*arshad*. Even the pigeons had flown away! I made my exit, thanked my past House Prefect, "O P", as his class-mates and teachers called him; and sighed - what man has made of the *Harimandi*r!

16

The killing fields

Mercenaries

The three essentials: pen, notebook and torch were kept every night on the side table before going to bed. While people normally say their prayers before going to bed, we journalists, as a ritual, would call up colleagues, intelligence and security agencies to find out if there were any new or fresh incidents, anywhere! Of course, we too went to bed with a prayer on our lips: m*ay the night end peacefully*!

During the period spent in Amritsar and Gurdaspur, I saw much bloodshed and human tragedy that it wrenches the heart even today! On several occasions, we journalists would start at dawn, travelling over broken village link-roads and dust tracks to visit the *spots*, where AK-47s had done their job the previous night, leaving behind a tale and a trail of death, destruction and misery. At times only one community, the Hindus, were the target; at other times, a whole family or majority of its male members, the Sikhs, would be wiped out.

One shudders to think of scores of chilling incidents of brutal killings in 1988: say on the night intervening March 31 and April 1, when as many as 36 people were shot dead in Punjab; out of them 26 were shot dead in Amritsar alone! Or when eight members of a family were shot dead in Khalehra, four Km from Jandiala on the Grand Trunk Road-National Highway No.1- on the night intervening February 5 and 6; or, when 10 out of 17 members of a family were killed in Kaura-Wajhun on the intervening night of March 27 and 28. And, who can forget the gruesome killing of 18 members, including children, in the age bracket of six months and 15 years, of a family of four brothers in Theh Ravjja village.

Day-after-day and village-after-village, one would hear tales of horror, sorrow and gather gory details of how killings were done; sometimes people were lined up against walls and shot at point-blank range! {The marauders, people would say in hushed tones, came at the dead of night, climbed over the walls, pulled out the targeted members, mostly male, shot them dead and fled!}

These are just illustrative examples; on some of these I wish to share some details in the following passages. One would see bodies lined up on string cots, wailing relatives, shell-shocked and numbed fellow villagers standing in small groups talking in whispers. Often, it became difficult to approach them and ask questions- requesting them to recall what all had happened or how it had happened, the night before. And despite all talk of division and distance between the Hindus and the Sikhs, it was during such common grief and tragic occasions that one saw a semblance of the age-old bond between the two communities still remaining intact: one saw the pall-bearers from both communities carrying their near, dear and fellow residents to the cremation ground!

*

Invariably, the security forces would attribute the brutal killings to either Bhinderanwale Tiger Force of Khalistan or Khalistan Command Force et al. Whatever are the names of these killings squads and gangs, one wonders whose or what cause and at whose calling were these killers serving? Certainly, not of the Sikhs or the *Panth*; and definitely not of *humanity!*

To call them militants or terrorists is a mild term. *Mercenaries* is more apt a word to describe them! As to some of the unforgettable gruesome incidents, those haunt me even today, 28 years later. Even one death, say a farmer committing suicide, is sad and unfortunate. And, here were trigger-happy squads gone berserk indulging in wanton killings of men, women and children without mercy or distinction.

*

House of widows

An unforgettable incident relates to a visit to Chhabal. In this small town, close to the Pakistan border, lived Youth Akali Dal leader, Harjit Singh. On one Saturday night in June 1987, militants struck with vengeance at his house and they shot dead Harjit and his two brothers. In fact, father of one of the widows was visiting his daughter and he too was shot dead. He had been cremated at his village, Sarhali. At the time of the killings, Harjit's wife, Balwinder Kaur was expecting a baby; the couple already had a one-year-old daughter. The other two widows in the house also had small children, when the gun-totting marauders struck, in 40 minutes everything was over: three lives had been snuffed out, leaving the three widows behind to lead a long, lonely life!

When I reached the place, one heard heart-rending cries. The three widows were leading a 600-strong procession of mourners and villagers to collect the ashes of the slain brothers. I remember a touching scene when the sisters of the three killed brothers lay on the spot where the cremation had taken place. There were moist eyes all around and people stood with folded hands, quivering lips and praying!

What had happened that night, I enquired from Sukhwant Kaur, widow of the youngest of the three brothers, Parwinderjit Singh; couple had two teen-aged daughters. *That fateful night, past mid-night, there was a knock. The visitors said they wanted food. As the women got busy preparing the meal, the three brothers got talking to them, after they had pulled a cot close to them. At least two of the visitors went to the roof-top to keep vigil. One of them asked for bullets and Harjit said what type and caliber. Harjit was willing to pay if these were not available with him, she heard them talk. After the food was ready to be served, Sukhwant went to fetch water. And the shooting started. All three were killed. Then the visitors poured kerosene on them and set the bodies on fire. A jeep was also torched. Before jumping over the walls, after 40 minutes, one of them told my elder daughter, Bhago, Beta, we will not kill you and your mother.* The women spent the night with the neighbors and returned when the police arrived at day-break. A former Punjab minister, Major Singh Uboke, whom I met at the house, said he had received an anonymous call to say, *we have broken your arms by killing these brothers*!

*

The twins

It was a cold morning. The sun was still struggling to spread its rays of warmth, when I reached Khalehra, where eight members of a family had been shot dead. And, whose lives had been spared; hold your breath, three small kids, 15-day-old twins and their two-year old sister! Villagers said before fleeing the three kids were left in the custody of the neighbors, who were warned to take good care of them. Though this gruesome incident had taken place around 8 pm the previous night, the police had arrived next morning around 8 am. The killers, believed to be of Bhinderanwale Tigers Force of Khalistan had torched the house, a tractor and a truck; a new dimension had been added to their way of killings and attacks. A short note, handwritten in Punjabi was left behind, signed by self-styled *Lt.-Gen* Surjit Singh *Pinta*; he was nephew, sister's son, of detained terrorist Harjinder Singh Jinda. The note held Kundan Singh, whose family had been targeted, responsible for the killing of three terrorists: Lakha Singh, Sahib Singh and Avtar Singh *Pahra*; Kundan Singh was father-in-law of *Pahra* of the Babbar Khalsa gang. {*Pinta* consumed cyanide and committed suicide after he had surrendered in the second Operation Black Thunder in 1988.}

Police listed three factors for the killing: sex motive, land dispute and inter-gang rivalry. CRPF DIG Virk and senior superintendent of police Izhar Alam told us on the spot that the killers suspected the owner, Kundan Singh to be a *police informer*. {Just as we were leaving, I asked my colleague Avinash Singh, Staffer of *The Hindustan Times,* to click a picture of the 15-day old twins. That was widely published.}

*

Baby and bullet

At Theh Ravjja, 55 kms from Amritsar on Harike road, 18 members of the Hindu Rajput family of four brothers were shot dead, including women and children. The incident had taken place in mud hamlets. Going around the shattered place, I saw a woman, her face covered with a veil, sitting on a bare string-cot with a small baby lying in her lap. Frankly, I could not muster courage to ask her any questions. Just as I was about to move ahead, a police officer asked me to talk to her and see the baby. Hesitantly, I stood close to her to ask for details. Between sobs and sighs, she gave some details of the shootout. When I asked, *this is your baby*? She nodded and simply lifted the *dupata* covering the baby. A bullet had pierced the baby's heart; the mother, Kamaljit Kaur sat dazed, statue-like, with her six-month old Raj Kaur in her lap!

Of the 26 killed in the past 24 hours, 18 were at Theh Ravjja alone! What does one make of such butchery?

*

Why youth went astray

The point I wish to make and reiterate is who should be held responsible for such carnage on such a wide canvas and scale for over a decade and to what intent and purpose? The blame for spilling so much blood and extinguishing thousands of innocent lives has to be apportioned to the state, as well as state and non-state actors: the foreign powers inimical to the Indian state trying to wreck its integrity and sovereignty. At home, politicians, religious leaders, the establishment were equally responsible for what Punjab went through. They cannot be absolved of the blame.

How or why did the youth of Punjab go astray? What allured them: adventure or love for the gun! One has not come across any study on this aspect of the phase of militancy that had engulfed and singed the state or on the socio-economic background of the youth, who had entered the fray then. Interestingly, even at *that* time, despite all the attributions of violation of human rights, encounters, extortions, mid-night raids, torture and harassment of *passive harbors* in villages, all at the hands of the Punjab police, still the rural youth wanted to join the police. It is a paradox!

*

One day, Amritsar Senior Superintendent of Police, Suresh Arora {he is now Director-General of Police} gave me an insight into this issue: *why youths went astray*! This is what emerged: who is a terrorist, a religious fundamentalist? Or one who subscribes to the *Khalistan* ideology? Or one who is a Pakistan-trained mercenary? Or one who is a saboteur? Well, he can be one of these or a combination, thereof. The moot question was what motivated youths to take to the gun. Could these youths, who were in their teens, be weaned away from the gun or the ruinous path they had set out on and indulged in killings and extortions? Why such youth had fallen prey to *sheer adventurism*! They were the ones who had been swept away from home by the currents of that undefined, uncharted *wave*!

Suresh shared with me the story of four youths, all students belonging to respectable families, who had strayed from home and were saved from getting caught in the vortex of terrorism and restored to their parents in the presence of the village panchayats. While two of them had appeared in the 10-plus one examination, the other two had taken matriculation examination, as private candidates.

The four were: Maninder Singh--17, Satnam Singh--18, Avtar Singh--18 and Gurpal Singh—18. The four had met at the city bus stop and had developed friendship. Later, they ganged up to have some fun. They bought toy weapons, plastic pistols and a Sten-gun. These were enough to rob a person of his scooter and later snatch a .38-bore real revolver, made in the USA, and a .32-bore pistol made in Czechoslovakia. This happened on April 30, 1988. As luck would have it, two of them, Maninder and Satnam were stopped for checking. While former managed to run away, Satnam Singh was caught. It was his sustained interrogation that led to the arrest of the other three. It emerged that they had no knowledge about the weapons or about the *Khalistan* movement etc. While two of them wanted to join the police, third, wanted to be an *engineer* {skilled worker}, since he was working in a fan-manufacturing unit earning about Rs 350 per month, and the fourth wanted to have a white collar job. They disclosed to the police that they tried to join the All-India Sikh Students' Federation and had visited its office in the Golden Temple. However, they were asked to return after Baisakhi.

There were two options before the SSP: one, to *plant* weapons and detain them under the TADA: Terrorist and disruptive activities {preventive} Act; two, to deal with them through psychological counselling and restore them to their respective parents allowing the young boys to return to the mainstream and give up the mad path they had embarked on. Suresh chose the second option. As a witness to the way the four were dealt with, I had nothing but admiration for the efforts being put in under the new police strategy to *save* young boys going astray!

Once their handcuffs were removed and they were seated across SSP's table, they were taken aback with the hospitality, rather than the usual police hostility. They could be seen exchanging smiles albeit sheepishly! Suresh implored with them to take pity on their parents, brothers and sisters; and not spoil their life. Once they started talking and opened up, their reason for *adventurism* was straight lift from a Bollywood movie! What made them take to the arms was their burning desire for self-defence, as they had a quarrel with some college students; and they also harbored the feeling of revenge because two of them had been falsely implicated by some villagers in a case for having written a letter to a girl of the village. And, two of them had been admonished by the village elders for this act. That was the beginning of their going astray!

It was an emotive scene as they were handed over to their parents and families! Suresh was able to save many such adventurist youths. {Senior Superintendent of Police Izhar Alam too had restored some boys to their parents, thereby, preventing them from becoming terrorists or militants.}

*

In fact, ideal thing to do is to commit to writing for future, not re-writing the past. Or, as George Bernard Shaw once said: *we are made wise not by the recollection of our past, but by the responsibility for our future.* It is with such thoughts that I wish to briefly state how youths had gone astray. This is not an afterthought. Concern over youth taking to crime or joining one or the other militant gang or outfit would occasionally be topic of discussion even then. Now youths go astray because of joblessness and drugs!

*

While keeping a tab on rehabilitated militants, the police did learn that most of the gun-totting youth were from: poor families had low socio-economic status, were deprived of love, care and concern during their formative years; and were, by and large, victims of perceived injustice! Also, it was the *romantic appeal* that attracted them to terrorism! And, some of them were also of criminal bent of mind, indulged in robbery and obtained a sort of *respectability* under the cloak of terrorism. Interestingly, some of them had been motivated to terrorism due to *family disputes* or feeling of being genuinely *wronged* by the police or were *frustrated* at being unemployed and a *burden* on their family.

*

It was also observed during sustained interrogation that some of the surrendered terrorists neither repented their crimes nor regretted their involvement in terrorist activities, the only way to deal with such elements was to let them face trial in courts before they could be *reformed.* In fact, these *boys* had scant respect for law, did not fear law and never thought that the law was a deterrent. For the youth to go astray, interrogators blamed some sarpanches and panches and opinion leaders, who acted as *middlemen.* It was a complex, complicated issue at hand, which required intelligent and sensitive planning to draw up a long-term plan to save youths going astray, as well as for a safe and secure future for Punjab. Much still remains to be done even now for the youth, given their ways and having gone astray.

*

Image makeover

Post-Operation Black Thunder, 1988, the government had realized the need to change track and go in for an image-makeover. This was part of the changing scenario- urgency to restore normalcy to win over the people and end their feeling of *alienation*; refurbish the damaged image of the security forces: the only visible face of the several government instrumentalities; and to instill in the public a sense of security. As part of that strategy were: *Operation Bird, Shakti Samagams;* setting up of *designated courts* by replacing *special courts*; better coordination and working relationship among security forces, thereby, ensuring engaged not estranged relationship among them; and also improving coordination between the police and the judiciary; involving people to restore normalcy through *collective community* efforts through participative assimilation and elimination of trouble-shooters; recruiting *special police officers*; holding of public-Police meetings and so on and so forth.

Another step taken for close and effective policing, as well as for winning over the people and ending their alienation, three new *police districts* were created within the two border districts, Amritsar and Gurdaspur. These new districts were Batala, Majitha and Tarn Taran. One can say that for much of these efforts credit can be apportioned to I-G Chaman Lal, who wanted a *transformation* in the image of the security forces, both the police and the paramilitary. He found full support and endorsement in ample measure for these efforts in Amritsar's SSP Suresh Arora. With the two having zero tolerance for those police officers, mostly at the level of the SHO: Station house officer, who indulged in *coercive and corrupt practices*; several of them were either warned or shuffled or shown the door.

*

As stated earlier about the paradox of the situation and having observed that despite all the shortcomings and criticism heaped on the Punjab police, there still existed a craze and keenness among the rural youth to join the police. I gathered, there were, primarily two reasons for this keenness: *status symbol and economic necessity*. The youth were also doubly unblessed and frustrated: a large number of them did not want to stay in the village because the farm size was small and shrinking, thus, making farming uneconomical, unviable and unattractive; also, in the absence of proper education, qualification and skill, they were aware that they had no future in cities either.

This craze became evident when applications were invited for Majitha police district: against 150-odd posts, there were 4,000 applicants, including graduates! From interviews with a cross-section of candidates it emerged that they had little or no interest in rural or traditional sports; majority of them had barely managed to pass matriculation examination; and those who had, did so on the strength of *copying*! That recruitment drive was also a part of *image make-over* of the police. The aspiring candidates, who were trying their luck for a slot in police, had no god-fathers: political or bureaucratic to see them through the selection process! Unbelievably, recruiters had no choice but to reduce the physical fitness parameters even for the candidates belonging to the reserved categories to accommodate them.

Of the 680-odd candidates shortlisted, 114 were from backward classes, 79 were scheduled castes, 48 ex-servicemen and rest belonged to the general category.

Even now, when the air is thick with *make in India* and *skill development* programs, one wonders where is the wherewithal to provide to the youth in Punjab, even rudimentary training in skill development in the absence of industrial training institutes! Moreover, given the standards of education, particularly in rural areas, students are not even provided *information*, what to say of *knowledge;* imparting of *skills* in the absence of the two basics: information and knowledge, remains a distant dream, a far cry; such is the pitiable situation in the state.

Since then, things have only gone from bad to worse in the countryside in the past 28 years, when it comes to finding jobs, even self-employment; it is a gigantic task. As then, even today, the financial crunch is too much for the rural youth to survive! Where would these youths go, if not go astray with many taking to drug or substance abuse! I have always held the view that *abject poverty and low standards of living* in a prosperous state like Punjab, particularly in the Majha belt, should serve as an eye opener to the government. This has not been taken cognizance of by the decision-makers! Yes, faced with this acute and serious problem, since then, the successive governments instead have further shut their eyes—tight. Villages in Punjab are a living example of disquiet, disparity and disgust!

*

Operation Bird

With the passage of time and reports of people feeling alienated, the administration had no choice but to re-think its strategies and policies of tackling the situation, which was becoming emotive and seemingly slipping out of hand, given the growing high-handedness of the security forces. If, public-police interactive sessions in villages, involving panchayats and village elders, was among the new strategies, the other was to protect and sympathize with the *passive harbors* of militants.

At the same time, there emerged reports that ordinary criminals, who had no ideological commitment to any cause, were fast joining one or the other militant outfit or were simply using their names/letter pads to indulge in extortions, kidnappings for ransom and killings. To neutralize these criminals, masquerading as militants, particularly in the three new police districts: Batala, Majitha and Tarn Taran, besides, of course, Gurdaspur and Amritsar districts also became a priority for the police.

In fact, the need to change from the old *police ways* to new strategies and change of track became a necessity in the wake of growing unease and unrest among the common people in the countryside. The interrogations and revelations the surrendered terrorists had made after the Operation Black Thunder at the Golden Temple in May 1988, also played major part in forcing police to adopt changed tactics to win over common people, deal with militants and/or criminals, who were having a field day.

The security forces were also at their wits end as to what to do with a large number of *passive harbors* behind bars. In fact, under the aegis of *Lok Shakti Samagams* some were picked up for recruitment into the security forces. On the other hand, talk of normalcy proved deceptive under this program. Desperation in people became discernible. Consequently, information flow from informers had dried up.

It was in such a scenario that *Operation Bird* was thought of, as also for dealing with terrorists and criminal gangs. It was brain-child of the BSF and the strategy was thus code-named. It was, therefore, yet, another strategic shift in dealing with situation in the border belt. Ultimately, if this succeeded, it was only because senior security officers were obliged to closely monitor, guard and guide the operations, which involved taking help of either arrested extremists or their harbors. Indeed, *Operation Bird* was carefully worked out, given its sensitivity and purposefulness; and it proved helpful, as security forces realized that capturing of terrorists or militants was more useful than their elimination. Information began to pour in!

Based on the revelations of arrested terrorists, the information obtained was documented, cross-checked and mapped out on the ground tracing which groups were operating in which areas, their supporters, both active and passive. The area of operation of this strategy stretched beyond Amritsar to other districts, as well. Only thereafter, operations would be meticulously carried out; involving even creating inter-gang-rivalries. It paid dividends. As a result of this strategy, some families of known extremists were also wiped out. *{For example in Cheema Bath and Khalehra, where both families were the in-laws of two Babbar Khalsa activists: Sukhdev Singh alias Hira Singh of Padhri and Avtar Singh Pinta.}*

The interrogations, as part of the Operation Bird, in fact, gave an insight into the making of a terrorist, role of the community, weaknesses of the administration and the judiciary and the need to involve the people in fighting militancy or terrorism. Their inputs were crucial and important to devise new strategies and policies. For the success of the new operational thinking, each surrendered terrorist's case was taken up individually and separately with panchayats and boy's parents in their respective villages in the five border districts. It was followed up through sustained research to establish their antecedents and excepting the hard cases, the rest were let off; proving that a lot could be done through normal course of law, if cases were properly linked to crime.

*

IPS Probationers speak-up

A word about people feeling *alienated*. The feedback that people were feeling *alienated* was conveyed to then BSF DIG, Chaman Lal, by 20-odd IPS probationers, who were attached to Gurdaspur, as part of their training and orientation course. This aspect emerged in response to a questionnaire that the probationers filled-up after assessing the field situation, as part of their practical assignment and training. The two main reasons for such a feeling, IPS probationers said, were: *corruption and non-responsive attitude of the government functionaries, both civil and in uniform*. These police officers held the administration responsible for the growing *alienation* of the people, as there was no inter-action between the people and the powers that be. A brief report, based on the feedback, was later submitted to the Punjab Director-general of Police, J F Ribeiro.

Interestingly, these probationers, coming as they did from different states of the country, changed their own perception of the Punjab situation after the visit. To them life appeared to be normal and no communal tensions, contrary to a kind of impression the media had created. While the Sikhs were opposed to the presence of the CRPF, the Hindus welcomed their presence. For the IPS officers, dream of *Khalistan* was neither realistic nor achievable, given the background of the Sikh history and psyche. Their succinct observation was that *the Sikhs are fiercely self-respecting and believed in democracy*. The Sikhs favoured a *firm and determined government, which could deliver the goods and ensure security to the people*.

The IPS probationers suggested making available to them printed material on Operation Bluestar, as well as on the assassination of Ms Indira Gandhi. While they had been given briefing about the operational details undertaken by the security forces and the laws, including the National Security Act and the Terrorist Disruptive Activities {Preventive} Act; probationers wondered why there was lack of adequate number of trained *dog squads* for the aid in crime detection.

17

Did Law Block Justice?

All state instrumentalities were under stress and strain in that period, judiciary was no exception. All kinds of stories, some exaggerated, some half true, some humorous, as to how judiciary acted and reacted to cases pertaining to militants were afloat then; apart from the fact that judicial officers were of the considered opinion that no number of harsh laws or even an emergency-like measure would make any dent, what to say of a dimple, in the situation in Punjab. The reason given was that the judiciary itself stood *dislocated*!

The common refrain among the judicial officers was that the police was taking undue advantage of the obtaining laws and instead of tackling terrorism and dealing with terrorists were misusing the prevalent laws to frame cases in such a manner that even petty, ordinary cases of crimes, family disputes and discords, individual offences - which had no evidence of terrorism- were being brought to the courts for trial under the then draconian laws.

I remember, after the special courts were folded up in 1985, a new system of designated courts was introduced to deal with cases under the Terrorists and Disruptive Activities {Prevention} Act. The most common section invoked to book a person was Section ¾ of TADA {P} Act. This only showed, according to the judicial officers handling such cases, that the police lacked experience and invariably failed to frame proper cases under the said Act. So much so, the courts found that in 90 per cent cases, the police theory did not hold water and such cases were not even admissible under the Act to be proceeded in the court. Result? Those acquitted or bailed out were usually again picked up by the police.

This syndrome meant that for an accused person to remain *free* he had to *buy* that freedom after striking a *bargain*; a common practice then. The judiciary knew this but was helpless, such was the law! Some judicial officers of that time confided that in the eyes of the law such bargains were no less heinous a crime than the extortion of money by the extremists, whom the police claim to be fighting. In this backdrop, one met police officers who were wont to put the blame on the judiciary alleging that since accused, who were let off, again took to the arms and joined underground gangs, thereby, resulting in spurt in violence. The judiciary did not subscribe to this.

Were the designated courts a success? The experience of these courts was that in 80 per cent cases the police had fabricated the facts, including, even the actual date of arrest of an accused person. Police could not produce witnesses to support its claims. In most of the cases, the courts observed that even if all allegations the police had made against the accused were to be believed, even then the case did not qualify to be tried under section ¾ of the TADA {P} Act because no offence corroborated or qualified the police story.

Thus, a battle of wits or estrangement between the judiciary and the police was often evident. For every argument the police put forth, the courts had a counter-point: the police would say that even if a terrorist killed someone before his father, the latter would be unwilling to become a witness. The judiciary countered this saying this was so because the father was not sure if he would get the requisite protection from the police, were he to become an eye-witness! Courts found another fault with the police: the police verdict of *guilt* was not based on evidence but suspicion, which could never take the place of proof in the court.

No doubt, *speedy trial* is an acknowledged fundamental right of the citizens. Did this happen then? Does it happen now? Either those involved in court cases can answer these questions or the courts! This fundamental right was being negated through manipulation then, as it is done now. Day-to-day hearings in any case appear to be a thing of the past.

It was observed that often the accused were not produced in the courts for want of adequate security personnel to escort them from jails to courts and back. This also happened because an accused was also booked under National Security Act besides TADA {P} Act. Also, the police had obtained orders to prevent production of accused from the jails to courts under Section 268 and intentional snapping of the link between the trial court and the jail authorities. To overcome the excuse of shortage of manpower, the government in its wisdom declared the central jail, Amritsar, as a *high security risk jail* on the pattern of Nabha and Sangrur jails. At that time, in March 1988, there were at least 800 persons waiting trial under the designated courts.

In that period of trial and tribulation, one remained on one's toes. It was no different for either the law enforcing agencies or justice imparting instrumentalities of the government. The judiciary, as well as the bar members were unanimous that the existing laws and the IPC: Indian Penal Code covered all offences - sedition, waging war against the state and acts of terrorism. It was, therefore, no good trying to convince the public about the guilt of a person unless the guilt was established before a court of law. But who cared? In this battle of wits, the judiciary and police were often at logger heads. For instance, one heard in the court corridors that when the police collected insufficient evidence, which failed in the court, it prompted the police to look for *loopholes* in the judicial process. In fact, in an ideal situation also the police should be equally committed to secure the verdict of guilt, as is the prosecution. One can say with a sense of reasonable responsibility that at that time, this link and co-operation between the investigator and the prosecutor had also disappeared!

Undoubtedly, one fact could not be ignored in such a scenario: there persisted a sense of fear psychosis and insecurity among the members of the bench as well as the bar because of the prevailing law and order situation, where the state, it was widely alleged, had failed to provide security and protection. The security measures in the courts remained porous. Despite rolls of barbed or concertina wires placed around certain courts, there were incidents of shoot-outs and escapes of extremists from the court premises!

The question often asked then was: what do the courts do when witnesses are not produced despite production warrants being issued? This was so, despite numerous opportunities. The prosecution witness was closed, even where witnesses were well-known to the police and where these witnesses refused to support the prosecution. Most important, the accused had no opportunity to defend their self in the investigations, which were one-sided. However, the accused had a right to be produced before a Magistrate within 24-hours of his arrest and, thereafter, the detention came under the direct supervision of a judicial officer but not so the investigation against him, which right up to the time of presentation of the final report remained in the hands of the police investigators. Such run-ins between the police and the judiciary added yet another important dimension to the prevailing situation and justice delivery mechanism.

18

Reminiscences

Fear factor

Lurking danger: When looking back at the yesteryears, one reminisces about the kind of situations one had had to face: some awkward, some expected, some unexpected; some anticipated, many unanticipated. Though working then in that area: Amritsar and Gurdaspur, professionally speaking, was a kind of reward or prize posting, as much for the civil and police officers as for the press persons. Yet, undeniably, there was always a lurking fear, a danger of the known and the unknown even among the common people.

*

Finding faults with the past now is much easier, rather than imagining how persons on duty then dealt with critical situations that they had to often face. Just take the case of police officers. Not that the civil officers or press persons or ordinary people in the streets did not fear or suffer. Here is a scenario: a CRPF patrol party in a vehicle or on foot was ambushed by terrorists and some jawans killed to avenge *fake encounters*; a cop was slain because he had interrogated certain terrorists; a police officer's only son was shot dead on the campus of Guru Nanak Dev University because his father had pursued the militants, relentlessly; another official was high on the terrorists hit list just because he happened to be holding a sensitive post.

*

Occurrence of such incidents was a routine here, there, everywhere. But on a closer look, even today one shudders to think of or realize the indelible scars these incidents left on the near and dear ones. Security men, then, as now, are supposed to guard one and all, high and low. But who is to guard the security guards? As now, even then, through a process of trial and error, those performing high-risk jobs devised their own security mechanisms and requisite measures. And as one officer always used to say: *anonymity is the best security*!

Men in uniform are known {or supposed} to work long hours under a variety of constraints. Tension becomes a part of their life. Then, the senior officers would carry weapons in their hands despite pilot and escort gypsies. Fear haunted them, as well! On one occasion, during a high security meeting in the Circuit House at Amritsar, this writer saw three identical white Ambassadors with tainted glasses, red lights and no flags. All had curtains drawn. Another common feature of these three cars was the same registration number. That was one way to hide the identity of the back-seat officer or the VIP!

*

Mobbed!

When Harbans Lal Khanna, a prominent BJP leader in Amritsar, was shot dead, one was witness to one of the worst Hindu backlashes unleashed in the city. Not realizing the gravity of the situation, along with another colleague, I rushed to the Guru Teg Bahadur hospital. An angry, agitated, unruly crowd of party workers and supporters ran helter-skelter looking for doctors. A friendly BJP face advised us to go away, *just disappear*. We hurried to reach the *Tribune* office in the Hall Bazar. Slogan-shouting and stone-throwing groups were converging from all sides on the Bhandari Bridge to go to the hospital. The vegetable market at the foot of the bridge emptied out. Breathless and seeing the rampaging crowds surge, we dashed to the Hall Gate, where our *Hind Samachar* group of newspapers colleagues, Sonis, took us under their wings; literally hiding us and advised that we better climb up the stairs, where they stored old newspapers, so as not to be seen!

It was a strange experience. More than the fear we felt in the Golden Temple *Parikarma* room *lock-up* much earlier, we realized what fear was like with mobs on the rampage! As police and BSF arrived to control the situation, we climbed down and came out. The police chief P S Bhinder was there. That gave some confidence and a sense of security. When angry crowds did not relent and one of them even pushed a cycle cart hitting Bhinder; we were scared. Even as the mob was being dispersed, some shops in the vicinity of the Hall Gate had already been damaged. Once the crowds melted, BSF escorted us to the office.

I remember the parting shot of the BSF officer: *till you are here, change routes and timings of travel frequently while coming to office or returning home; at least as a psychological satisfaction!* That precisely was what the security and civil officers were doing. It was almost a taboo to ask or tell one's location or where one was going or when one would return. In fact, the unwritten understanding was: you do not ask, I do not reply! In fact, then, there was hardly any social life; schooling of children was also a problem. On occasions one lost appetite as well due to work pressure and persistent, constant stress and strain.

*

On the flip side

One day, DSP: Deputy Superintendent of police, Narinderpal Singh, who was posted in Tarn Taran, told me the following incident: while returning home after a long day, he stopped at a relatively deserted stretch and asked his boys {security personnel} to fire a round each. The idea was to test the functionality of their weapons. His experiment failed miserably, as none of the weapons fired! The weapons were jammed, needing servicing! *That literally gave me goose bumps*! His very next step was to check the entire cache of arms and ammunition under his command. In fact, as the word spread, special teams fanned out throughout the districts to ensure the weapons were operational and in working order!

After this incident became public, the state agency entrusted with the task of inspecting arms and ammunition in the districts was pressed into service. To its surprise and dismay, arms with the policemen were poorly maintained and those who carried rifles, Sten-guns and revolvers had not had any firing practice for a long period of time. This was a rude shock, particularly, when it came to border districts' police personnel.

The agency also observed that the policemen seldom bothered to clean and oil their weapons. This sorry state of affairs was at all levels in the police. This poor upkeep was beyond the comprehension of the agency concerned. One wondered if firing efficiency and up keep of arms was part of police drill and mandatory, why firing efficiency and accuracy, could not be made an essential entry column in the annual confidential reports of the personnel - all ranks?

Those issued Sten-guns did not inter-change the magazine of their weapon, as they were required to. Interestingly, even the number of bullets in a magazine was more than the prescribed number. This, naturally, put undue strain on the spring inside, rendering it useless in an emergency. When it came to inspecting armouries and *Malkhanas,* the agency was surprised that those in charge did not maintain proper records, as to when a particular rifle had been issued to whom and where that individual was posted.

It was amusing to see militants equipped with AK rifles, while policemen had obsolete .303 rifles chained to their waists, a bit unwieldy. Some weapons were also found to be jammed! In that period, one saw officers carrying their weapons without holsters. Besides, the police were not undergoing any physical fitness drill, periodically, as stipulated. One wonders what the situation is like now, decades later. Police sources admit shortage of ammunition for practice in the firing ranges, as also long duty hours and over-work!

*

Off course flight!

It was a cold February morning in 1985. I had just scanned through the newspapers and was folding them when I heard the sound of a motorcycle making its way to my residence in Amritsar. The man in uniform parked his bike and walked in smiling. As we shook hands, with a twinkle in his eyes and in a gruff voice, he said he was on *official duty for an inquiry*! For a moment I was taken aback; what inquiry, I muttered. Relax! He motioned me to sit, as he made himself comfortable.

He began by asking a question that he knew would not be answered; who gave you the helicopter news that *The Tribune* has carried? I gave an expressionless look, and kept quiet. What had happened that had made this officer drive over to my place was this: the Union Home Secretary R D Pradhan was visiting Amritsar. At hand were the state Chief Secretary S S Dhanoa and BSF Director-General, M C Misra. They were to discuss the problems and requirements of the BSF; and inspect the border, right from Ajnala in Amritsar to Dera Baba Nanak –DBN- in Gurdaspur.

As the three flew in a helicopter, the pilot had strayed into the Pakistan air space near D B N. He had gone over one km inside when he received a warning signal from Pakistan of the *intrusion*. It was an inadvertent mistake and the pilot right away changed course to return to Indian space. My report was considered as an *embarrassment*! The officer sitting next to me wanted to know my source, who had given me that news.

Let me share now, after 31 years, who the *source* of that news was! Normally, this is not done in our profession. The *source* was the same officer, who sat next to me making an inquiry; he had been appointed by his seniors to find the *source*! Yes, information giver was information enquirer! Such was the rapport and mutual confidence and trust between the individual media persons and their sources then. The trust was respected. Neither side betrayed the trust!

19

Governors

During the troubled times, when decision-making was fuzzy and flawed, the powers that be: politicians, who mattered, politicians who were sidelined but wanted to make their presence felt; extra-constitutional authorities: power-seekers and power-brokers, including bureaucrats, both in Chandigarh and in New Delhi, were working out various permutations and combinations either to sort out the deliberately tangled mess in Punjab or to knowingly compound the then prevailing situation. In the process, one saw a succession of Governors come and go: some made a mark, some made a mess; some courted controversies, some just faded out; some left behind certain logical legacies upholding the dignity of the office, as also their self-respect and some not even remembered by anyone today!

*

Between November 1983 and till my departure from Amritsar to Chandigarh, where too I was assigned Punjab beat when Beant Singh government took office, from close quarters I had seen a procession of Governors come and go: B D Pande, K T Satarawala, Arjun Singh, H Sema, S D Sharma, S S Ray, Nirmal Mukarji, Virendra Verma, Gen. O P Malhotra, Surendra Nath, S P Kurdukar, Lt.-Gen. B K N Chhibber, Lt.-Gen J F R Jacob, Gen. S F Rodrigues and Shiv Raj Patil. They all had short-to-medium terms, barring some exceptions; who lasted a little longer.

*

There was a time, when CRPF acted in a berserk manner and either refused to honor the curfew passes, issued by the district magistrate to the Press or officials of the essential services, and occasionally tore those off. At this act of the CRPF, then Deputy Commissioner, Gurdev Singh Brar, was livid; and he conveyed his anguish to the Governor Pande in the Circuit House using, as he did, the choicest Punjabi invectives to describe CRPF behaviour.

*

I found Gen. Malhotra straight-forward, honest and sincere. He wasted not a minute to quit when 1991 elections were called off at the last minute. As true soldier, he had even held the Independence Day function at Tarn Taran. He passed away at Gurgaon on December 29, 2015; at the age of 93. I had first met him when he had visited Bathinda, as chief of the Army staff to inaugurate the Army cantonment there.

*

Surendra Nath, a typical policeman, had his own style; and media in Amritsar did not find him very cordial. Before occupying Raj Bhawan, he was an Advisor to a Governor! I remember how he lost his cool when *Indian Express* staffer Dinesh Kumar had asked him at a press conference in Circuit House at Amritsar; if carrying of *trishuls* in scabbards by certain radical Hindus was justified, since they did so as a copy-cat; the same way as the baptized Sikhs carried sheathed small swords, as a religious symbol; and if that was permitted. Surendra Nath lost his cool and was left seething with anger and annoyance!

In fact, on occasions Ray would land up in Amritsar with his set of tennis gear and play the game in the clubs. After one such game, when he reached the Circuit house for an interface with the media and talked of having won the games, Dinesh Kumar asked Ray, ostensibly, with the tongue in the cheek, whether he had won or the opponent had lost! Ray caught the point and ignored the comment with a knowing smile! Such a gesture, playing tennis, was in a way Ray's way to send feelers and a message that situation was on the mend. Dinesh now works with *The Tribune* at Chandigarh.

*

Arjun Singh, perhaps, had the task cut out before him. He was keen to hammer out a solution and take credit for paving the way for peace, communal harmony and putting Punjab on road to normalcy. He will be long remembered for the Rajiv-Longowal Accord that was never honored by the Centre; and which proved to be the Achilles' heel, resulting in divisions within the Akali Dal; in the process isolating Harchand Singh Longowal, Surjit Singh Barnala and Balwant Singh with Badal, Tohra, Talwandi and the like going after them with all guns blazing. The killing of Longowal, not long thereafter, and cascading effect on Punjab's politico-religious landscape is still fresh to be given in detail here.

*

During the period of my posting at Chandigarh one had occasions to meet Chhibber, Jacob, Rodrigues and Shiv Raj Patil. Jacob was a good listener but stuck to rule book. Some of the meetings were in connection with retention of government houses by journalists and framing of appropriate rules. He was a Jew; his full name was Jack Farj Rafel Jacob. He died on January 13, 2016. He was the last of the illustrious Army officers of the Bangladesh War of 1971. His book *Surrender at Dacca – birth of a Nation*, had created some controversies. He had a point of view of his own.

*

Chhibber had a streak of arrogance; Rodrigues is the one who had administered the oath of office and secrecy to me, as State Information Commissioner. He was jovial and communicative; while, Patil had an attitude: I found him learned, inquisitive and sophisticated, during an interface when he visited the State Information Commission office in Sector 17, Chandigarh, in connection with formal launch of video-conferencing facility the commission had set up, and he asked many probing questions about the RTI Act.

With others one did not have much occasion for interaction. Satarawala was shifted even before he could find his feet. He tried to understand the intricate situation but seemed lost in the maze! Most of bureaucracy prefers to keep the mouth shut rather than comment on Virendra Verma.

Interestingly, Ray seemed to be either in a hurry to leave or was aware of growing opposition to his stay. He was the one who would hold meetings with field officers either in their respective districts of posting or at Chandigarh. For instance, as Ramesh Inder Singh Mander recalled: he would send government aircraft to Amritsar to pick him up – he was the Deputy Commissioner- where Gurdaspur incumbent would also come; and the two would then fly to Ferozepur to pick up their third border district colleague and reach Chandigarh. After the meeting, the same the trio would be dropped back, in reverse order!

*

Nevertheless, here is a fond remembrance: during the short tenure {less than six months} of Punjab Governor Nirmal Mukarji, I had the opportunity of meeting him twice. Once for an interview, after which he asked me to see him more often; and the second time when I wanted to confirm something that I had casually overheard while coming out of a press conference. What I overheard was then rumored to be only a rumor! Newsman's instinct and intuition told me to explore; explore I did; and this is what it turned out to be:

I called up Raj Bhawan and sought to speak to the Governor. I was immediately put through. When I requested Mukarji that I wanted to meet him and that if I could drive down straight away, he spontaneously said: *Sure, come over, I will leave a word at the reception.* That was the type of equation that I had with him; granting an appointment at short notice speaks volumes of the man. At the reception, the security staff was telling some visitors that *Sahib* was out of station. I gulped; only few minutes back I had spoken to him!! When my turn came, the receptionist said: *you have not heard*? *Sahib* is *not in*. I identified myself. He was a different man. I was escorted inside the Raj Bhawan.

I came straight to the point after brief curtseys: *Sir, have you resigned*? *May I have the details, please?* He had written his resignation by hand and sent it through a special messenger to the President, who was then at Shimla. News of his resignation was taken as the lead story; an exclusive. Eventually, I gathered more information on him, since I adored and admired him. Here are some facts:

Nirmal Kumar Mukarji - January 9, 1921 – August 29, 2002 - was the last member of the ICS: Indian Civil Service for part of the 19th century officially known as the Imperial Civil Service**,** was the élite higher civil service of the British Empire in British India during British rule in the period between 1858 and 1947. In the course of a long career Mukarji had been Home Secretary, Cabinet Secretary and eventually Governor of Punjab. When the *Khalistan* movement burst into prominence in Punjab, the Centre had first sent law-and-order hard-liners to the troubled state; Arjun Singh and then Siddhartha Shankar Ray, when the state was under the President's Rule. When the V P Singh government came into power in 1989, it chose to change the approach to the insurgency that the state government should take; and so appointed Mukarji. He reduced the intensity of counter-insurgency operations and put into place a timetable that would see the end of President's Rule and fresh elections. This approach paid off within a few years.

On Mukerjee's passing away, in a write-up, R K Kaushik, *Hindustan Times, April 17, 2012,* recalled the bygone era that evoked mixed feelings. It reminded of the glorious past and the gleeful memories, on one hand; it made you melancholic because the time gone by could not be retrieved or relived, on the other hand. It was 32 years ago during these days that Nirmal Kumar Mukherjee, ICS, demitted office as cabinet secretary of India. One evening in April 1980, Mukherjee came down the steps of Rashtrapati Bhawan from his office in the cabinet secretariat. It was curtains on the steel frame of the British Raj on that day; he was the last ICS officer to retire.

He was the junior most officer of the Punjab Commission and had joined as ICS on October 25, 1944. The last batch of ICS; this was called the *heaven born service* during the Raj days. It was started in 1855; the first batch had joined in 1856. After leaving the Raj Bhavan in Chandigarh, Mukarji continued to write on issues related to Punjab; his last major public appearance was as the keynote speaker and chief guest at the Indian Administrative Service's 50th Anniversary celebrations in Mussoorie in 1997, where he shocked the assembly by calling, in his speech, for an end to the all-India tenured services, and their replacement by specialized professional

*

Samosas!

Whatever one may say about the role of S S Ray, as Punjab Governor, whatever opinion one may have about his way of functioning, whatever one may say of the net-working of three *Rs*: Rajiv-Ribeiro-Ray, the fact remains that Ray was different from his predecessors as well as successors.

Of all the Governors, Ray seemed to enjoy his tenure the most, as he appeared relaxed. Ray was, invariably accompanied by his wife, Maya, wherever he went. The two were frequent and regular visitors to Amritsar those days. On several occasion, I traveled with him in his car with Maya seated between us. She would admire the verdant green fields stretched out for miles on either sides of the village link roads or praise the link roads saying *back in our state, West Bengal, even state highways are not that good.* {The situation is now different in Punjab: *village link roads are worst off. One may find patches of road amidst pot-holes and broken or missing stretches!*}

It so happened, Ray was visiting a slum area in Amritsar: *Bhadhar Kali* {Shaheed Udham Singh Nagar} locality, where terrorists had killed seven persons. That place was full of filth and stink there would go up to the high heavens! While crisscrossing the open drains in the narrow lanes of the locality, he stepped into a puddle of sullage and cow dung. The splash soiled his white pair of trousers; and his *Desi Jutti* got stuck. It was fished out and later, when he returned to the Circuit House was washed and left to dry. People waiting to see him were surprised to see him walk-in barefoot! Unmindful of the stares all around, he went about meeting visitors, briefing officials and interacting with the media. With his usual charm, he asked the corporation commissioner D S Kapoor to develop a park in that locality and focus on sanitation. There was complete *Bandh* in the city that day. Thus, finding alternate footwear was difficult, as the then Deputy Commissioner, Sarbjit Singh learnt to his dismay!

Waiting for the press conference to start, I sat chatting with Maya at the back of the reception hall. Suddenly, she got up, stood on her toes, looked over the heads of the small crowd surrounding Ray. *What's up*, I asked! She sighed, *Oh! No! Not again! Look, I am sitting away from him. And he has launched a full assault on samosas, which he is not supposed to eat.* In fact, while interacting with the members of the district peace and communal harmony committee, Ray had enquired if tea was being served. On getting *yes* as answer, he had asked if there was anything to eat, as he had skipped his lunch. *Samosas*, said Sarbjit Singh. And Ray's face lit up! Maya Ray looked at me and said *why don't you stop him from eating so many samosas? He is taking advantage of my not being beside him.*

*

Around that time, doctors and staff at the hospital had gone on strike. He heard slogans when he went to see some injured persons in the hospital. He smiled and turning to me said: *such agitations were signs of return of normalcy; a positive sign. But patients should not suffer*! That was Ray. He was good narrator of anecdotes; and at times did give news bites, whenever we happened to travel together. Yet, his three-year period was not without controversies, criticism and cynicism!

*

Punjab Governor was made Administrator of Chandigarh union territory shortly before launch of Operation Bluestar at the Golden Temple in 1984. The state was declared a *disturbed area.* Though, that tag is no longer there, the system of Punjab Governor continuing as Administrator of Chandigarh union territory persists and continues. With Beant Singh becoming the Chief Minister and with normalcy returning, active role and state-wide activities of the Punjab Governor have diminished. However, he is actively involved in Chandigarh's affairs, as an Administrator. At times, voices are heard demanding that Chandigarh reverts to *Chief Commissioner* System.

20

City of Myriad Hues

Amritsar is an enigma. It is a symbiosis of religion, commerce, agriculture and much more. Despite its close proximity to the international border, unlike Ferozepur, it has neither languished nor has it ever felt ignored or left behind in any way, across centuries. Its two distinguished marks are the Golden Temple and the Jallianwala Bagh, its next door neighbour; one symbolizes spirituality, humility, oneness of mankind; the other spirit of sacrifice, nationalism and integration with its iconic red-stone *Flame of liberty*! And, there is the Durgiana Mandir, as well. As in the case of the Golden Temple, the same way, in the case of Amritsar city, a rich treasure trove of literature is available recounting the past and present. The Golden Temple is much photographed; its replica is also a much gifted memento - representing Punjab, Punjabis and Punjabiat.

The city's flavour, sights, sounds, smells and history is well enshrined and well entrenched in its *Katras* inside the *walled* city, which once had 14 gates and the average height of the wall was 14 ft. This city of gates and *Katras* has much to boast about as also to rue, given the chronic insanitation, cramped living; chaotic relationships among neighbours whose dwellings and business premises are inter-locked. It is a Herculean task to navigate and crisscross *Katras'* narrow, dark, dingy lanes and alleys; some of which are impassable, difficult to maneuver and walk through. Yet, life survives and pulsates; surges forward and thrives.

Anyone interested in a quick read about Amritsar may pick up an old volume of Historian, V N Datta's book: *Amritsar-past and present*, published by the Municipal Committee, Amritsar in 1967; {now there is a Municipal Corporation.} The story of the Golden Temple is no less fascinating in any way. One of the most exhaustive studies ever on this holiest of the holy places is by Dr Madanjit Kaur: *The Golden Temple-past and present.*

*

Dr Madanjit retired as Professor, Department of Guru Nanak Studies. She had served as Professor and Chairperson of Guru Gobind Singh Chair at Guru Nanak

Dev University. Her book gives detailed information and insight into the Golden Temple. It was first published by GNDU in 1983. The latest, third edition, was published in 2013; it is revised, enlarged and comprehensive; pages: 444.

*

With the passage of time, Amritsar, a gourmet's delight, a place of pilgrimage, commerce and gateway to Pakistan, has grown and developed, albeit haphazardly; in an unplanned manner like any other city in the State. Yes, Amritsar has also been described as a *Cinderella* among historical studies in India, as Datta puts it. Thus, seen through the prism, this city offers myriad hues and rainbow glimpses of its socio-cultural, religious, commercial and historical perspectives, which have passed through many vicissitudes in its existence and life - *Sifti-da-ghar*!

With this short background, let me lead you into the *walled* city's labyrinth of winding passages to know its secrets! The gates that once controlled and regulated entry and exit are named after Sikh legendaries and other prominent personalities; these gates bear testimony to the city's eventful history. Dutta says that the 14 ft high wall {average height} was got constructed by Maharaja Ranjit Singh. This work was carried out in great vigour in 1823 at an outlay of Rs 1,400,000. The work was entrusted to the *Sardars*. From Mahan Singh Gate, on the north-east to Hakimawala Gate on the south, the remains of the wall were still visible in 1988. In fact, Mahan Singh and Ram Bagh Gates were the only ones of the 12 Gates constructed by the erstwhile Sikh government that remained. Scant attention has been paid to preserve these monuments!

The curiosity of a journalist made me explore about the Gates and Katras then. In the olden days, these gates were substantial masonry structures for defence purposes with side entrances protected by strong wooden gates elaborately reinforced with iron bolts and sheet iron. All along the wall there was a moat, five miles long, 120 yards wide and five yards deep for providing security to the city. During the British occupation, the moat was filled up with debris.

At that time, the city still retained the relics in the *Katras* or wards into which it was divided. Each of these Katras represented the State of a Sikh chief within whose limits, he was supreme. The oldest Katras were 15, all others being subsequent formations. The old trades were still concentrated in these very Katras when I left Amritsar on transfer to join duty at Chandigarh.

In fact, one of the old massive red brick Gothic Structure, which stands in the heart of the city, is the legendary Hall Gate. This 138-year-old gate, which is the main entrance to the walled city and leads to the Golden Temple, was built by and named after Col. C H Hall, the then Deputy Commissioner. After partition, it was renamed Gandhi Gate, but the people still know it by its old name. One wonders, why tinker with such names! {In New Delhi Aurangzeb Road was re- named after A P J Abdul Kalam in 2015. Earlier too, several cities'/states' names were changed to make their pronunciation as spoken in the local language.}

21

Subterranean Currents

On the face of it, life on the surface in the two border districts, Amritsar and Gurdaspur, seemed to be unaffected and flowed on smoothly, notwithstanding, on the one hand, series of curfews, restrictions, regimented orders on opening and closing of business establishments, bans on pillion riding by two males on two-wheelers etc, and, on the other hand, the subterranean currents of inter- and intra-brazen behaviour and mannerism of the civil authorities, the police and the paramilitary force, which had its own impact on the life on the surface.

The situation showed some feeble signs of calming down, in 1987-88. With that sensibilities and emotions of the common, ordinary people, began to rationalize; more so, after the Operation Black Thunder in 1988. The place and the people picked up pace, life its rhythm; amity and harmony returned. There was a shared sense of agony and ecstasy: a mixture of smiles and tears! The days of leading and living a cloistered life seemed over. With normalcy creeping back, the daily life was not strikingly any different from the life in other Punjab cities. If it was different, it was different only in the sense of restrictions still in force; it was also different and also distinctive given the religious and commercial rhythm that gripped the people. This normalcy was like a mirage; it was short-lived. Subsequent developments proved the fragility of the situation that seemed to be returning to normal!

Much before dawn, when streets were still asleep and silent, the city would stir up and come alive with hurried steps making their way to either the Golden Temple or the Durgiana Mandir. Same way, after the day's work, people would rush home with harsh commands and curses hurled by the security forces chasing them, as they pulled down shutters; this clamor and clutter would echo in the gathering dusk! It later transpired that early closure of shops and business premises was not so much from the security and safety point of view of the citizens; it was a way of making things easy for the security forces to police the empty streets and bazaars. {This was revealed to me by a close aide of the then Director-General of Police, K P S Gill.}

Despite the living having become a hazard, one did come across oases of pulsating life full of colour and vigour, like holding of a three-day Red Cross Mela in the Ram Bagh in March 1987, when one saw Governor Ray and his wife Maya mingle with the locals! It is another story that the festivity was somewhat eclipsed by an incident in which six personnel, including a CRPF inspector and a cop, had lost their lives; and 10 others were injured in an exchange of fire with terrorists. Amidst the revelry, one did hear murmurs of anguish and disapproval of such festivity, when the security forces had lost their personnel, who lay dead, not far, waiting for cremation!

As per the state craft, after the Red Cross show, wreaths were placed on the security personnel killed; and the life flowed on!

*

It would be inappropriate not to admit that in the wake of what had happened since the Army action in June 1984, the face of the city had changed: the face showed conflicting emotions - anguish, suffering, tiredness, defiance and at times strange silence! Undeniably, all this, particularly deafening silence, had been heightened by the near absence, howsoever temporary, of devotees, pilgrims and tourists/visitors, who would come in droves from home and abroad. Business in the bustling city had taken a beating; it was slump time. It, nevertheless, goes to the spirit of resilience of the people that, on the one hand, they could cope with life constraining and constricting regime; and also bounce back with energy to lead normal life anew, on the other hand!

*

The omnipresence of the security forces made one wonder if the surface amity and normalcy would remain were the forces to be withdrawn? Was what was visible only temporary and artificial or had the equations and relations between the two communities and the common people really changed for the better or what was discernible was only a pretence?

In such a scenario one heard: i*t is never late, not yet, to restore the lost bonds forged by the learned with great thought*. This was stated by none else than the University Grants Commission Chairman, Prof. Yash Pal, while delivering the convocation address at GNDU, adding that he had seen both *devotion and anguish* in the Golden Temple and in the Durgiana Mandir, earlier in the day, when he went to pay obeisance.

I remember Prof Yash later telling me: *it is time to have a proper perspective of the situation and find a solution to the present crisis for the good of Punjabis, who have lost their smiles and whose dancing feet have stopped.* Yes, those were the times where one needed nerves of steel to cope with strain and stress of living and performing duty. This applied equally to the common man, as well as to the professionals.

*

To diffuse the situation and in an attempt to restore normalcy, Amritsar had a procession of visitors, including Jain saint, Acharya Sushil Muni and actor-turned politician Sunil Dutt and his daughter Priya; the two having undertaken a long march, *Padyatra*, from Hardwar's *Har-ki-Pauri* to the Golden Temple's *Har-ki-Pauri*! All efforts came to a naught, because for the powers that be, time was not ripe, yet, to act to resolve the pending issues!

22

Demoralized, who? Police!

Let me preface the situation I am going to talk about by saying that men in *Khaki* and even civil and judicial officers, perhaps, forgot that there was a society beyond their own protective ring; whatever happened within their guarded confines, had ripple effects out there in the civil population, as well. The apprehensions and unanticipated ramifications of what tomorrow may be like created a fear psychosis in the minds of ordinary people. In the parlance of the police and security forces, the word: *demoralize* was much used and abused then, much to the consternation of higher ups in the echelons of the forces, as also civil administration. The following narration is, in a way, a sequel to - *subterranean currents*.

*

With signs of normalcy becoming somewhat more pronounced in 1987-88, the growing subterranean currents of acrimony between the police, the executive and the judiciary also surfaced, so did reports of increasing erosion of indiscipline in the police. Given the gravity of the situation, the state home department decided to step in. It came up with a periodic review plan.

Under the plan, each police range: Ferozepur, Patiala and Jalandhar was put under the supervisory control of an Inspector-General of Police, who was asked to visit each district in his range and submit fortnightly situation report to the home department for state-level discussion at the top. The idea was to monitor the functioning of the police and the paramilitary forces and remove the *irritants*. In the absence of any direct control over the forces then, the system was expected to give the government a feedback on the happenings in the field.

This situation had arisen amidst reports emanating from several quarters where the policemen, including some station house officers, had tried to *intimidate* the civilian officials in their operational areas. Despite intervention by the senior officers, reports of defiance and obtrusive behaviour of the subordinates continued to surface. The home department was worried that usually the senior officers in the field took no cognizance of *excesses* committed by their men when these were brought to their notice by the civil officers, including the deputy commissioners. In fact, several officers confided in me that many times even the senior officers in the hierarchy were also ignored, when certain decisions were taken because the senior superintendents of police had direct access to the Director-General of Police! Naturally, existence of such parallel channels affected policing. This break in the chain of command gradually eroded inbuilt controls, checks and constraints in the force; these very traits ensure discipline.

On several occasions even Deputy-Inspectors General of Police were either ignored or bypassed. So much so, in one case, a DIG's recommendation for award of a medal, the President's Medal, was completely ignored. This lowered the officer's standing in the staff and dented his image. In fact, with the passage of time, it transpired that the police had begun to misuse the term *demoralize*. That was why for fear of *demoralizing* the subordinates, officers were either hesitant or reluctant to take any action against erring officers! If, this new found term, *demoralize*, had its adverse impact on the system and made the government institutions and instrumentalities redundant, on the one hand, it also encouraged the policemen to continue with their brazen, arrogant behavior and commit excesses on anyone and everyone in the civil society and services, on the other hand.

If the police resented the usual *political interference,* there apparently, was also no *magisterial control* over the forces; the opinion of the *executive* was usually ignored with impunity. Can one imagine what all this must have led to then? Though the democratic institutions like the legislature or the council of ministers had the right to speak on behalf of the people: electorates; police brooked no interference from either. However, from reliable and responsible low profile police officers, I learned that despite all talk of *political interference*, there were scarcely any cases, where terrorists or criminals were let off at a politician's instance!

*

Looking back, I think the tragedy then seemingly was that the security forces did not realize then that there lived a society beyond terrorism and that, there were respectable, as well as common people, who were being intimidated and harassed. One additional district and session's judge had told me that his experience showed that the police was arresting, torturing and implicating *innocent youths*!

*

It was an open secret then that there was no control of the state police over the paramilitary forces, particularly CRPF. So much so that even CRPF commandants were not answerable to the district police chiefs. In fact, frankly speaking, the state, as such, did not exist then! Take the following two examples:

First, Guru Nanak Dev University Vice-Chancellor Professor S S Bal, a Historian, told me that, of late, he had received threats and had been harassed in the wake of the killing of the only son of a superintendent of police on the university campus. {Incidentally, Bal was my teacher and head of the department of languages, culture and journalism at Punjab Agricultural University, Ludhiana.} Bal's approaches to the deputy commissioner, the senior superintendent of police and the chancellor {Governor}, had made it worse for him rather than ease the situation. In fact, it is a matter of fact and record that the police *challenged* Bal to approach anyone he liked, including Rajiv Gandhi and Buta Singh! The university demi-official letter of November 1986 is a telling example of a vice-chancellor living under constant threat from the law enforcing agencies!

Second. A judicial magistrate had declared a station house officer at Tarn Taran a proclaimed offender. In return, the magistrate was threatened with *elimination*! In fact, most of the issues agitating the police, the executive and the judiciary could have been settled at the level of the officers concerned; but unfortunately were not. Such were the times then; one did not know whom to turn to for help, protection, safety and security.

23

The Mummy.....

Amidst all the upheavals, one day *The Tribune* News Editor, S P Sharma, called up. He gave me a tip-off on a story and asked me to act fast before local journalists do. The story was to be chased in Gurdaspur. Equipped with the address given to me I met Senior Superintendent of Police J P Birdi. He was in a meeting with senior officers; some local journalists were also present. Once the journalists left, I told him the purpose of my visit and sought his help. He not only willingly agreed to do but was excited to accompany me as was the Deputy-Inspector General of Police A A Saddiqui. The *Mohall*a {Prem Nagar} and the house were marked, after a word was sent to the station house officer of the area.

With cops all over in that crowded, congested locality, we entered the house and asked for Sudesh Kumari, 26. The family chickened out on hearing this! A room-to-room search followed. And, there she lay in bed with vermilion in the parting of her well-oiled hair and facial make-up. This was in May 1987. Sudesh had been dead since February 1984. However, on the asking of a *mahatma*, the family had preserved the corpse in the belief that she was only unconscious. In fact, the body was mummified! The blind faith had done its job.

The face that I saw that evening still haunts: it was a typical skeletal face, all teeth showing and eyes wide open and fixed - a horrifying, scare-inducing look! The body was evicted from the house and sent to the Medical College, Amritsar for post-mortem, despite resistance from the family, which insisted that it was no crime to keep some one dear, who was only unconscious, at home!

The forensic science head B S Ahluwalia headed a team of doctors. The post-mortem report revealed: body mummified; no blood, skin having turned dry- dark brown, more intensity of brownish colour on the backside, since the body lay on its back; brain reduced to rustic brown powder; liver, spleen, kidneys and stomach fused into mass; no blood oozed when body dissected, as it had dried up {hence no foul or putrefying odour}; hair well-oiled with pins fixed to part the hair.

The discovery of body was as shocking as was the College surprised: Ahluwalia told me that it was first such case to be dealt with in the department.

Later, the police went on to investigate the circumstances and to trace the *mahatma* and the doctor, who had found *traces of life* in Sudesh Kumari even after the Gurdaspur civil hospital had issued Sudesh Kumari's *death certificate.*

Such are the misplaced beliefs and taboos that have even in this age enslaved sections of the society in false rituals and faiths!

*

....And the dead shall live on!

Remember Suraj Bhan? He was MP: Member of Parliament from Ambala. Though not often, I did meet him on a couple of occasions at his residence. He was soft spoken, humble; a man of simple habits and life style. In November 1982 during the course of our tete-e-tete, he narrated an interesting story he had come to hear, when on a visit to the Government Museum or Madras Museum. {Suraj Bhan had visited the place in his capacity as Chairperson of the Parliamentary Committee on the welfare of the scheduled castes and scheduled tribes.} There he had met G Kesavaram, curator of zoology section, who had joined in 1961, and had concentrated on improving the collections. During his tenure, the Bird's Gallery was modernized and he also focused on preserving animals in synthetic resin. Later, he was to become director of the museum: 1989-91.

*

It is a museum of human history and culture, located in the neighborhood of Egmore in Chennai. It was established in 1851. There is a wide range of sections. It is particularly rich in archaeological and numismatic collections. It has the largest collection of Roman antiquities outside Europe. Its sections stretch from archaeology to anthropology to arms to art, botany to zoology and much more.

*

Here is the sum and substance of the narration of Bhan: He learnt that the dead could be preserved till eternity! Bodies could be embedded in transparent plastic slabs and retained in that form for an indefinite period. The technique of preserving bodies in that manner had been evolved by Kesavaram. Though, he had been approached by many persons, who wanted bodies of their dear and near ones preserved; however, because of fear of offending religious sentiments and acute shortage of funds, Kesavaram rejected all such requests. He was also under great pressure from various quarters to reveal the secret of the body-preservation techniques.

Nevertheless, Bhan felt the government should finance the research being conducted by the Madras scientist. During the visit Bhan had observed that the scientist was able to embed in plastic, a body made available to him within five hours of death to be preserved. His experiments in that regard with small specimens like scorpions, starfish, water bugs, butterflies and mushrooms had been highly appreciated. However, the technique suffered from a major flaw – the eyes of the specimens suffered up to 75 per cent damage during the embedding process.

Kesavaram had also written a pamphlet: *Method of embedding biological specimens in clear plastic in tropical regions*. Initially, Kesavaram had informed Bhan that he had used an *embedding kit* obtained from a firm in Chicago, the USA, in his experiments in preserving zoological and Botanical specimens in bio-plastic. Thereafter, he perfected the techniques he had employed through sustained research. Kesavaram was believed to have received attractive incentives from abroad for disclosing the details of the technique, but he had declined all of them, said Bhan.

*

Closer at hand, body of Ashutosh Maharaj, a spiritual guru, continues to be in deep freezer at the sect's : DJJS- Divya Jyoti Jagriti Sansthan, Jalandhar district, headquarters since January 29, 2014, when the 'Guru was declared "dead" with his followers claiming and believing that their 'Guru' was in 'Samadhi' and shall return in due course of time. Despite High Court directives the body has not been cremated, yet.

*

Print and electronic media reported on November 19, 2016, the case of a 14-year old British girl, suffering from cancer, who had expressed her desire to be 'cryogenically frozen' after her death. A British Judge Justice Peter Jackson allowed her wish. Her body was frozen in the US. Here is a report:

> *"A British teenager who died of cancer has been cryogenically frozen in the United States after winning a court case before her death.*
>
> *The girl — who can't be identified and is referred to only as "JS" — suffered from a rare form of cancer and expressed a hope to be brought back to life and cured in the future.*
>
> *She died on October 17 but details of the case at London's High Court were not allowed to be made public until now.*
>
> *In his judgment, obtained by CNN, Mr. Justice Peter Jackson said the girl had expressed her desire to be cryogenically frozen.*
>
> *She wrote: "I have been asked to explain why I want this unusual thing done. I'm only 14 years old and I don't want to die, but I know I am going to. I think being cryo-preserved gives me a chance to be cured and woken up, even in hundreds of years' time. I don't want to be buried underground.*
>
> *"I want to live and live longer and I think that in the future they might find a cure for my cancer and wake me up. I want to have this chance. This is my wish."*
>
> *According to the judgment, the girl's parents are divorced and their relationship is "very bad." Her mother was supportive of her wish, but her father — who had not seen his daughter face-to-face since 2008 — initially was not."*

Medical and legal opinion says such beliefs are doubtful and debatable.

24

High Drama

As a reporter, one is privy to many inside stories, several off the record conversations, also not to disclose the source of information; and at times is witness to the goings on at public events or at press conferences. As stated elsewhere in the preceding passages/pages, reporting was often difficult given the situation prevailing then, and the pressures that one had to bear at times.

One such incident relates to a news conference that the Punjab Director-General of Police K P S Gill had called in Chandigarh, sometime in March 1994, at the Police Officers' Mess, which also doubled up as his residence.

There was high drama, when the chief of Akal Federation, also a member of the Panthic Committee, Ramesh Kanwar Singh was presented before the media. The police had expected him to read from the prepared text. What followed caused much embarrassment to the super cop and other officers present.

This is what happened: Kanwar Singh, who was seated alongside the D-G.P, stood up and greeted the press with *'Waheguru ji da Khalsa...'* Without looking at the clutch of papers in his hand, he trained his guns at the police. It was an emotional outburst. At the very outset he said he was not present to surrender or touch Gill's feet, as he had been told to say and do but to declare that being a staunch fighter for *Khalistan*, he would prefer death to surrender.

He, nevertheless, admitted that due to their own doings the Sikhs, who always pray for the wellbeing of the humanity, had been defamed at the national and international level by indulging in killings of innocent persons. The Pakistan ISI: Inter-services intelligence agency had no sympathy for the cause of *Khalistan*. All those engaged in this movement had been misled and forced to perpetrate atrocities even on the members of their own community.

As Kanwar Singh went on, a visibly upset Gill held him by the wrist and tried to pull him down to make him sit down and, perhaps, shut up! He said the reason why Pakistan was against the Sikhs was simple: it was the Sikh Army General who had freed Bangladesh and it was before the Sikh General that the Pakistan Army surrendered. The ISI, therefore, wanted to settle scores with the Sikhs. The militants in Pakistan jails were being ill-treated and insulted time-and-again. {The Indian General in 1971- liberation of Bangladesh war was J S Aurora and the Pakistan commander, who surrendered: Gen. A A K Niazi.}

The drama did not end there. Refusing to sit down, he went to say that he had been in the Ropar police custody for the past 10 months along with his wife, Kuldip Kaur, also a member of the Panthic committee, had been picked up from Baru Sahib Akademi, where she was a hostel warden. Their six-year old son was also with them. His wife was pregnant, he added. He claimed he had been tortured and feared that he would be eliminated. He had been kept in CIA staff custody and elsewhere.

He said his arrest was in the knowledge of the Akali leaders and also the Jathedar of Akal Takht, Bhai Manjit Singh, whom he had sent a letter and that no one had helped him or raised voice for him and his family- both had been victim of police atrocities. He was taken away by security personnel but not before saying what he had to say, much to the chagrin of the police officers.

Later, individual news persons and news paper offices were approached to either kill or down play the story. It did not, however, work. That's how the police worked and the media at times played along but many times showed its independence and, if one may say, courage to defy the official diktats! Thereafter, Gill gave his usual briefing but mostly centered on Kanwar Singh alias Dhami and went on to talk of the role of ISI in Punjab since 1970s.

*

Even after two decades of normalcy having returned to the state, there is no denying the fact that the ISI has not given up its support to the anti-India elements or pro-*Khalistan* protagonists, who are still alive and in Pakistan.

Writing on the situation then, September-October 2015, former Director-general of police K P S Gill listed the surviving *Khalistan* militants in the shelter of ISI. In his article, *A vein of discontent,* published in the *Indian Express, October 27,*

2015, Gill mentioned: Wadhawa Singh, chief of the Babbar Khalsa International; Paramjit Singh Panjwar of the *Khalistan* Commando Force-Panjwar group; Lakhbir Singh Rode of the International Sikh Youth Federation-Rode; Ranjit Singh Neeta of the Khalistan Zindabad Force; Gajinder Singh 'Hijacker' of the Dal Khalsa International; and Balbir Singh Sandhu of the Council of Khalistan. Gill further wrote: *The ISI also supports and coordinates the activities of a number of Khalistani diasporas, such as Council of Khalistan, the Khalistan Affairs Centre, the Sikh Youth of America and American Gurdwara Prabandhak Committee in the US, and the World Sikh Organization, the Komagata Maru Dal of Khalistan, the Sikh youth of Belgium and number of other splinters of the Babbar Khalsa International and International Sikh Youth Federation in Germany, the UK, France, Norway, Belgium, Switzerland and Canada. These groups periodically organize demonstrations; engage in propaganda and petition governments and international organizations with grossly distorted allegations.*

There were some other occasions as well when militants were presented before the media, who would read from a prepared statement; and thereafter no question-answer session. The rest, as we say, is history.

25

Caste-War in Cabinet

Reservation in India is a process of facilitating a person in education, scholarship, jobs, and in promotion, who has category certificates. Reservation is a form of quota-based affirmative action, governed by constitutional laws, statutory laws; local rules and regulations. Scheduled Castes {SC}, Scheduled Tribes {ST} and Other Backward Classes {OBC}, and in some states Backward Classes among Muslims under a category called Backward Classes {M}, are the primary beneficiaries of the reservation policies under the Constitution – with the object of ensuring a level playing field.

Across the decades, the word reservation has had several manifestations: it has been discussed and debated. It has been used, abused and misused. There remain opinions for and against continuation with the concept of reservation. There is lack of consensus as to how long the system and practice of reservation should be continued or not continued, as also where all should or should not reservation be applicable; and if there should be a time limit or not after which reservation should be scrapped etc. etc.

Of all types of categories, the one which is, perhaps, more contentious than others is caste-based reservation policies. Casteism is neither confined to nor prerogative of the society at grassroots alone, though its roots are deep and wide. It is also not just about high and low castes' conflicts alone. It is prevalent even within the castes, say between two classes of Scheduled Castes: *Balmikis* and *Mazhabi Sikhs*, on one side, and *Ramdasias* and *Ravidasias*, on the other side. Such a sharp caste division and the growing acrimony and anger between them had cast a shadow even in the higher echelons of the government, including the council of ministers in Punjab, when Beant Singh was the chief minister. The following episode dates back to March 1994, when militancy had been fairly checkmated and controlled.

Based in Chandigarh, I was reporting on Punjab at that time. The caste-war had so much precipitated the situation within the council of ministers that even the cabinet sub-committee the chief minister had constituted proved ineffective to defuse the situation and douse the passions. This division had begun to cast a shadow over the functioning of the cabinet as well as the government. The deadlock remained indefinitely, despite several meetings but the issue could not be clinched.

The stand taken by two ministers of state, Joginder Singh Mann and D P Sabharwal, on the one hand, and of the two cabinet ministers, Jagjit Singh and Shamsher Singh Dullo, on the other hand, had created a piquant situation. The contentious issue involved more reservation for Balmikis and Mazhabi Sikhs. So much so that it became difficult to even table Bills in the Vidhan Sabha. In fact, the other ministers were, by and large, against giving any reservation to Balmikis and Mazhabi Sikhs.

The development had taken place in the backdrop of BSP: Bahujan Samaj Party gaining political ground, as also in the context of Akal Takht exonerating Buta Singh {union minister} after he had completed his *Tankha*, religious punishment. At that time, Punjab state Balmiki and Mazhabi Sikh Sangarsh Samiti was also on a sit-in demanding that a Bill on reservation be introduced in the Assembly. The draft Bill of the proposed Punjab scheduled castes and Backward Classes Act {Reservation of vacancies of posts in services} had not been approved due to deadlock in the cabinet. The BSP had decided to support the Bill in the Vidhan Sabha. This further added to the woes and worries of Beant Singh. Support for the Bill had also come from SAD.

If I recollect correctly, the moot point of discord then was an order the department of welfare of scheduled castes and backward classes passed way back on May 5, 1975. That was done when Giani Zail Singh was the chief minister. From my aging notes, I reproduce that text of that order: *I am directed to refer to the subject noted above {reservation for members of scheduled castes/tribes in services under the state government} and say that the government has decided that henceforth 50 per cent vacancies of the quota reserved for scheduled castes should be offered to Balmikis and Mazhabi Sikhs, if available, as a first preference from amongst the scheduled castes candidates.*

My enquiries then revealed that since *Ramdasias* and *Ravidasias* had more clout, both political and bureaucratic, the order was changed denying the *Balmikis* and *Mazhabi* Sikhs the right to reservation when it came to *admission to professional educational institutions, recruitment and promotions.* In fact, *Ramdasias* and *Ravidasias* had lost the long legal battles in the Punjab and Haryana High Court and in the Supreme Court. Yet, the two categories demanded that their reservation be restored by including or incorporating May 5, 1975 order in the Bill.

In the light of representations received from several quarters, Sabharwal had sent a detailed note to the chief minister in July 1992. He had also enclosed the draft of the proposed Bill. The detailed note of the minister, running into 5-pages had built a strong case of reservation for Balmikis and Mazhabi Sikhs. Obstructing such a move was a representation from the Punjab employees' welfare federation, which was strongly opposed to such a move, arguing that such a step would be in violation of the decision of the Supreme Court. This caste-war had its ripple-effect across the state with daily reports of demonstrations and strikes, particularly in Doaba area.

*

Much after the cabinet had felt the caste-war tremors, one of the ministers sent me two pages, photocopies, in May 2003, to give me an idea of number and names of scheduled castes, as well as backward classes and other backward classes in Punjab, as per a 'constitution order of 1950'. The listed scheduled castes were 38, while the combined list of backward classes/other backward classes numbered 68!

*

I have deliberately included this instance to underline that quota system or reservation has its pluses and minuses. More often than not, it is ultimately the political electoral considerations that matter, though the Apex Court has passed as many as three important judgments on the question of reservations in the past decades, the latest was on reservations in the higher educational institutions in October 2015.

*

The Supreme Court had directed the centre and state governments to scrap reservations in the institutions of higher learning. In its order, it said that national interest required doing away with all forms of reservation in institutions of higher education, and directed the central government to take effective steps "objectively".

A bench of Justices Dipak Misra and P C Pant noted that despite several reminders to the central and state governments to make merit the primary criteria for admissions into super-specialty courses, the ground reality remained that reservation often holds sway over merit.

*

The Jat reservation that flared up in Haryana in February 2016, resulting in killings and arson is yet another instance of consequences of politics of and politics over reservation and growing caste-class conflicts and chasm in the countryside in several states!

*

The caste factor is deeply ingrained in the society's psyche. The manner in which Punjabi Sufi singer Hans Raj Hans, a Balmiki, was first announced as the Congress candidate for Rajya Sabha and later his name withdrawn; and instead Shamsher Singh Dullo, a Ramdassia by caste was named as the party choice, in itself is a proof of divisions within the castes and the way Dalit vote counts in the state. Here are some statistics, if a proof is required, of the Dalit vote influence and power in Punjab. Dalit vote is concentrated in Doaba, literally meaning do aab or area between two rivers. As many as 23 Assembly seats are in this region comprising of Kapurthala, Jalandhar, Hoshiarpur and Nawanshehar. Dalits constitute 40 per cent of the electorate in this Assembly-seat belt.

*

According to census 2011, Scheduled Castes are 31.94 per cent of Punjab's population, the highest among all states. Dalits also constitute poor section of the population: over 60 per cent of their households are below poverty-line, as per Punjab's department of Scheduled Castes and Backward Classes. No wonder all political parties in the poll fray are out to woo the Dalits.

*

And, as a measure of please-all policy, in its last budget before the assembly polls, the Finance Minister Parminder Singh Dhindsa presented on March 15, 2016, he allocated Rs 1,060 crore for the Scheduled Castes and Backward Classes and minorities, including introducing new initiatives like Scheduled Caste scholarship fund with a corpus of Rs 100 crore, which will be given to the universities and institutes, besides providing uniforms, school bags and stationery to children belonging to Scheduled Castes.

*

It is not only the pleasing of Dalits alone, several other sections of the society have also been given handsome sops to garner votes even as Punjab is headed towards a "debt trap" as revealed in the latest report of the Comptroller and Auditor General for 2014-15, with total debt at Rs 1,123,66 crore. In five years, 2010-11 to 2014-15, this debt burden shot up from Rs 74,687 crore. Yet, here is a state which believes only in sops and doles! The word debt trap connotes that the state is borrowing more and more to repay its old debts and these borrowings, between 47 per cent and 70 per cent, were utilized to repay earlier borrowings.

*

In a nut shell, for garnering votes, any and every political party would go to any length and breadth to appease the voters, cutting across all sections, castes, classes, isms, beliefs etc. Wooing of Dalits is, thus, not an exception. And, as is the wont of the ruling Akalis, they exploit their constituents through every conceivable means: religious – remember the pilgrimage to religious places across the country by organizing special trains or depriving Sehjdhari Sikhs of right to vote in the SGPC elections; emotive – SYL issue; and economic - offering sops and doles worth Rs 1,200 crore in the last budget, 2016-17. And, in August 2016, SAD partner BJP at the Centre has entrusted a score of anti-Sikh riot cases to Home Minister's Special Investigation Team in addition to what it was already probing. All these measures are aimed at regaining political reckoning before the elections, 2017.

26

Change of Guard

Memories of some experiences in a journalist's life refuse to fade away, while some other get fixated in the mind. These moments obstinately stick and when one reflects on those, a faint smile or a smirk involuntarily appears on the face. And, it seems as if what one has been through decades ago had happened only yesterday. Let me share one such experience, which dates back to January 1, 1995.

It was a pleasant morning: no cold breeze, no sharp sun. There was also no let-up in the security apparatus at House no. 50, Sector-2, at Chandigarh. Armed men in uniform and mufti stood scattered around, alert and agile, as ever. Accompanied by my photographer colleague, Karam Singh, we approached the entry gate; we underwent the usual security check drill and were waived in. Present were half-a-score of other visitors, as well, talking in whispers: a kind of eerie silence seemed to hang thick and low! We were in a dilemma: as to how to wish the person whom we had come to meet. Should the wish be the usual- *Happy New Year* or should it be- *Happy retired life in the New Year*? The others too, perhaps, were in similar dilemma, as were we two!

The man of the moment on whom several of us were waiting to call on was K P S Gill. {The place was his temporary residence and commonly referred to as GOs Mess!} A routine union home ministry wireless message the previous night had ended his tenure and term, as Punjab's D-G.P, on the expiry of his extended one year term.

*

Gill had been on extension *till further orders* and there were no further orders, till those up in New Delhi reviewed his extension. The news had reached him at Patiala, soon thereafter, where he was going over the security arrangements for the 83rd Indian Science Congress, which was to be inaugurated by the Prime Minister, P

V Narsimha Rao, on January 3. It is a different matter that the PM could not make it owing to fog! Having done his day's work, Gill had returned to Chandigarh late in the evening. The new appointee was O P Sharma, who had been heading the Police's intelligence wing for a long time.

*

Unlike in the past, we waited that morning pretty long before we were escorted to the back of the building to the lawn where the tall Sikh sat in a garden cane chair; not in his civvies or uniform. Instead, there he was in a light grey track suit with a *patka*: a kind of under-turban, much shorter in length than the usual turban tied on his head! This was the first time we were seeing him casually dressed like that: ordinary next-door neighbour! Between meeting visitors, answering phone calls and aware his close relatives waiting inside, he had agreed to talk to us, briefly, though.

The question-answer session followed the speed of an AK-47. In his answers, there was no RDX, no explosion. He defused several questions, as he answered them in his characteristic style: either with a smile or feigning, as if he had not heard! He was, somewhat, reluctant to be photographed. After much patient persuasion and perseverance, also little cajoling, he agreed but with a rider: *I shall approve the photograph to be published*! Left with no choice we agreed adding, *we will inform the Editor, as well, of your wish. It is up to him.* A set of photographs was later shown to him and he approved one.

That day, he said he felt a sense of *relief*. This was on two accounts- one, not having to attend a round of farewells; two, not to shoulder anymore: a host of responsibilities that go with the profession and policing! As to *reflections*, he had *enjoyed* his entire tenure and career that was *full of excitement,* as a thoroughbred cop! He had been in Punjab, since 1988, where the situation kept changing like patterns in a kaleidoscope and terrorism in its many forms took different courses and followed different currents. And, all through the decade here, he had experimented with different methodologies for ever emerging new situations and challenges. To a question, he had replied: *yes, there were three basic factors that enabled Punjab to restore normalcy, peace and ending terrorism: activated security forces, the bravery of the common man and, united consistent stand of major political parties on fighting terrorism to the finish. This has paid off.*

*

People loved/love to hate Gill and hated/hate to love him. Yet, he is remembered as a professional cop; his loyalists remember him for his strategic thinking and tactical implementation thereof, devising overall conceptual plans, resource mobilization and motivation of personnel. His detectors, however, remember his aberrations with the media and authority, his film star nites, dribbling his way into the world of Hockey, his love for drink and so on.

On his own admission, *education* of the people of Punjab and the *economic health* of the state interested him, as much as studying the developments taking place across the world, as also national situation. Though out of sight all these decades, he is not out of mind; he is missed, yet remembered in different ways by different people for different reasons!

In fact, if earlier successes to contain terrorism were short, temporary, and in measured tones; blame the long period of the President's Rule in the state for ad hoc decision-making. Then, decision-making took place in New Delhi, everything was remote controlled and extensions in the President's Rule came in spasms. With changed circumstances, decision-making began to take place at Chandigarh with Beant Singh, as in charge; and police got better, more and quick *opportunities* and *liberties* to deal with the problems that beset Punjab.

*

Before taking leave of him, we asked: *what now and next*? He smiled and replied that he would like to catch up with his *reading - literature, English and Urdu poetry; and of course writing.*

27

Religious Means, Political Ends

It is the Sikh {read Akali} leadership that must be held responsible and apportioned the major blame for the religio-political schizophrenia that grips Punjab, on and off. Akalis are known to tie themselves up in knots, create Panthic problems, where none exist at times, and then expect the knots to get untied of their own. Across decades, well meaning individuals and institutions, both at home and abroad, have made numerous attempts to debate and discuss the two contentious issues: religion and politics; and their *mix-up*. Yet, a consensus has always eluded all such efforts.

As I sit back and regurgitate on this sensitive and emotive issue, as also the manner how Sikh leaders have failed their own institutions, my thoughts go back to Professor Devinder Singh Chahal, who taught us Microbiology at Punjab Agricultural University, Ludhiana in 1970s. Little did we know or did he ever reveal that besides his deep interest and knowledge about invisible living creatures – microbes - he also had deep-seated bent of mind about religious studies, as well. It was much later, probably in 2000 that I really discovered this hitherto unknown fact and facet of his life. It was more by accident than design.

It so happened, while working in my cubby-hole in *The Tribune* office I got a call and the operator connected me to a caller, who had simply identified himself as *Dr Chahal*. It took just a few seconds and there we were all familiar and travelling down the memory lane. We met the following afternoon and here is an account of what unfolded during our tete-a-tete:

After his PAU tenure, he had migrated to and settled in Canada on his retirement as Professor of Applied Microbiology from the University of Quebec. It was in that period of his life and times that he had set up *Institute of understanding Sikhism*, which also brought out a magazine: *Understanding Sikhism---the research journal* of which Chahal was the editor-in-chief. The editorial board had a global spread with members from Canada, Malaysia, India, the UK and the USA.

He was visiting India {May 2000} to present a paper on *Sikhism—scientific and logical religion for the third millennium and beyond* at Punjabi University, Patiala. He gave me the copies of the first three issues of the journal, which exposed me to new vistas of Sikhism. He had also told me that several journals were being published abroad in Punjabi and English. Such of the journals or magazines dealt with the traditional or conventional methods, dominated by mythology and rituals, for interpreting the Gurbani and Sikhism. That made the institute's journal different, he argued.

*

Our meeting had taken place shortly after the Sikhs had celebrated the tercentenary celebrations of the founding or establishment of the *Khalsa* in 1999, when Anandpur Sahib was the cynosure of all eyes. It was during that period that foundation stone of Virast-e-*Khalsa* was laid, which today is a major devotee/tourist-attraction. It was designed by Moshe Safde, an Israeli expert and authority on museums.

*

The sum and substance of my conversation with Chahal was that the essence of the tercentenary celebrations was in the message of the Gurus: *universal brotherhood, peace and wellbeing of all.* He emphasised that Guru's message would stand implemented, if the Sikhs achieved a consensus on issues, which have time and again: caused pain, created fear-psychosis among the principal communities, threatened peace, led to divisions within the Sikh community and ridicule of their institutions.

As I perused the copies of the journal, these gave me an insight into the labour of love that had gone into its production and the efforts that had been put in by the Sikh Diaspora in really making Sikhism intelligible to the non-Sikhs and even to the Sikhs, globally. Religion has been variously defined and interpreted since time immemorial. It is as much *man's expression of his acknowledgement of the divine*, as it is *a system of beliefs and practices relating to the sacred and uniting its adherents in a community,* as the Longman Modern English dictionary defines it.

*

There have been wars between religions - struggles seeking the right to worship. Often, these wars developed heavy political overtones. And in Sikhism, there has always existed not symbolic but symbiotic relationship between religion and politics. The question, therefore, was/is should the two be accepted as a whole and practiced as such or be compartmentalized, as, across time, one continues to hear many voices demanding such a separation? The great debate goes on.

*

In Punjab, a sound knowledge of the Sikh religion {and also History} is imperative, if one were to follow Akali politics. The roots of Sikhism are traced to Guru Nanak, who in the 15th century founded a scientific and logical religion for the benefit of the humanity. It is readily acknowledged that Sikhism has *universal* appeal and relevance. The Sikhs have failed to evolve consensus over various contentious issues, concepts, practices, rituals, scriptures and even the manner of living {*Rehat Maryada*}.

Differences of opinion persist even on the definition of a Sikh. Should only those with unshorn hair be called Sikhs or even those who have cut their hair – *Sehjdhari* Sikhs - should also be covered by the definition, as they too very much remain within the fold of Sikhism; and also arguing that symbolism, rather than substance, seems to weigh more with some scholars and theologians. Even the burning issue whether to allow or not to allow right to vote to *Sehjdhari* Sikhs - ones who are clean shaven but believe in, observe and follow Sikh *Maryada*, and bow before only the holy book: Guru Granth Sahib - is now being heard in the Supreme Court. The SGPC had moved the Supreme Court against quashing of the 2003 notification by the High court. In fact, for quite some time the Akalis have been keen to have the Sikh Gurdwara Act, 1925 amended and has been cajoling its political ally: BJP – Bhartiya Janata Party - for an amendment to the Act, barring the Sehjdhari Sikhs from casting votes in the SGPC elections. This has yielded dividend.

*

A word on the Sikh Gurdwara Election Commission, a statutory body under the Sikh Gurdwara Act, 1925, which is responsible for conducting elections to the SGPC and various management committees of the gurdwaras under it. The last elections were held in 2011, the next round was due in September 2016. There was a furor when in 2014, a non-Sikh, Justice J C Verma, {Retd.}, was appointed the Chief Commissioner. SGPC protested vociferously, as also Akali politicians, who saw a game-plan of the Congress to help Delhi Sikh Gurdwara Management Committee chief Harvinder Singh Sarna to infiltrate SGPC dominated SAD.

Earlier, Union Home Ministry issued notification on the appointment of the Chief Commissioner, Gurdwara Elections Commission, However, in October 2014, the power to appoint Chief Commissioner was vested in the Prime Minister, who heads the Appointments Committee of the Cabinet; and a three-member search-cum-selection panel, headed by the Home Minister, was constituted; the other two members of the panel being union secretaries of law and commerce. The panel was assigned to seek names of at least three retired judges from the Registrar, Punjab and Haryana High Court to be put up to ACC for final word.

As per available information, there are seven posts sanctioned by the union government, including the chief commissioner and secretary of the Gurdwara Election Commission. The Punjab government provides 12 staff members, who are attached to the commission, as secretarial support. The commission has been without the chief commissioner since September 30, 2015. No successor was appointed after Justice HS Brar (Retd.) completed his tenure.

*

There is a growing perception in several quarters that even Sikh intellectuals have failed their community by not presenting Sikhism the way it should have been by giving its meaning and substance in the manner the Sikh Gurus conceived and conveyed their message. For want of a clear, simple and reasonable explanation and interpretation of *gurbani*, many myths and misconceptions have crept into the religion, which is not being followed and practiced strictly according to the holy Guru Granth.

The sad part is that the intelligentsia has developed its own political roots and shoots. Moreover, the SGPC, which is *accepted* as the final arbiter of and on religious affairs, has also often failed and faltered. It has tripped to fully perform its assigned and mandated duties and own up onerous responsibilities entrusted to it. SGPC remains stuck in the administrative matters of Gurdwaras, with a strong political bias. It has miserably failed to end the cult of idol worship and ritualism, widely prevalent among Sikhs; thanks to the existence of Babas, Sants, Mahants, Sects and Deras; all potential vote-banks for the politicians, Akalis are no exception!

*

Consequently, across decades, many organizations have, therefore, mushroomed within and outside the country following or adhering to a variant of religious rituals and worship means and methods! Even educated Sikhs, retired or serving, representing diverse interests and coming from different professions, have also joined in; and are wont to emerge as *self-appointed* conscience-keepers of the Sikhs' religio-political affairs. On many given occasions, these people express their views and render advice to the Sikh clergy, as well as the political leadership. A few lucky ones even manage to become advisers to either a political party or outfit or the government.

Constantly changing views and loyalties to religious and political masters is now all too common. This is, perhaps, one reason why nothing tangible or worthwhile and meaningful gets done. The only saving grace is that the holy book-Guru Granth Sahib- is *codified*: it can neither be altered nor tweaked or tampered with. Some research scholars, who did come up with radical views, were summoned to Akal Takht.

*

One believes and hopes that, sooner than later, some well-meaning Sikhs and non-Sikh scholars, who have dedicated themselves to understanding and propagating Sikhism in universal perspective, would come forward and give the much needed direction to Sikhism. Unfortunately, while accepting and practicing religion and politics as one entity, the Sikh political leadership has politicized the religion rather than drawing strength and sustenance from it. For the Sikh political leadership, religion is only a means to achieve political ends. This interplay of the two and exploitation of the emotions and sentiments of the common Sikhs have been responsible for the undoing of the both. Consequently, there is much media coverage {add social media, as well} and comment on Sikh religio-political affairs, thanks to the controversies the religio-political leadership generates every now and then.

*

This, perhaps or probably, is one reason why the Sikh institutions, notably, Akal Takht, Sikh clergy {High priests} and the SGPC and its political wing, SAD, in its many manifestations, presently dominated by the Badals, have messed up issues. It is a collective failure of the Sikhs' religio-political leadership' as also quiet acquiescence of the allied Sikh scholars and intelligentsia, which has played havoc with the Sikh religion and politics.

It is observed that whenever there was a ray of hope of something worthwhile taking place, a chorus or cacophony of voices, mostly discordant, would occupy space demanding to be heard. While the issues faded away, the bitterness lingered on! The religio-political leadership has missed out many occasions when they could have sat together and sorted out contentious issues and controversies by viewing them in proper perspective. This, however, was not to be. For too long the Sikh leaders have survived and sustained themselves on Panthic sentiments and emotive issues. How long will this continue? Your guess is as good as mine. There are several examples one could quote, but just one will suffice: framing of the All-India Sikh Gurdwara Act. This has been in the making for as long as one can remember. Yet it remains a stillborn baby.

*

Besides many other institutions and organizations, despite BJP being a partner in sharing the spoils of the office with the SAD, the looming presence and somewhat growing influence of Rashtriya Sikh Sangat, an off-shoot of RSS: Rashtriya Swayamsevak Sangh in the countryside is a disturbing factor, given the fragile caste-class and ethnic line-up and fault-lines emerging in the villages. Even as controversies and contradictions remain over authenticity of the *Dasam Granth* and *Nanakshahi calendar*, several other issues also remain unresolved: crisis of Sikh identity, task of distinctly defining the role of Sikh institutions etc.

There is no common meeting ground, yet, even in respect of following and observing certain rituals and practices in the Golden Temple and at Akal Takht. At the other end of the spectrum are purely political matters: on inter-state disputes on territory; on sharing of river waters --- despite Punjab having enacted an Act scrapping and annulling all previous agreements on water sharing. Status of Punjabi language in educational institutions in adjoining states is another issue. There persist differences with New Delhi regarding Centre-state relations on devolution of funds or having a second look at the Constitution for a *federal system of government* with greater financial and administrative autonomy to the states etc. etc. {Should the term not be *Union*-state, instead of Centre-state, as this word- Centre – does not figure even in the Constitution?}

*

Thus, what Chahal and his institute had sought to do was to provide a global platform and to universalize Sikhism by bringing together scientists, philosophers, theologians and administrators to correctly interpret the *gurbani*; and represent Sikhism as envisaged by Guru Nanak. Unlike other publications that have their own place in the sun, the journals I studied were designed and produced, as any other *science journal*, where a team of experts examined each article, which was submitted for publication. The team was drawn from the streams of theology, physical sciences, medicine, natural sciences, political and social sciences, philosophy, history, languages and law.

The stress was to create interest and impart knowledge about Sikhism to the present generation, particularly, in the West, which is alien to Sikhism; and which requires to be educated on the sensitive issues with reason and logic rather than by creating fear of the unknown and the divine. The aim was to fill a vacuum, globally, by networking and keeping intact the umbilical cord the Sikhs have with the holy Guru Granth Sahib back home in *Harimandir Sahib* at Amritsar. Growing apostasy was also a major concern of the Sikh Diaspora engaged in that venture.

*

Close at home are also several Sikh institutions which imbibe similar sentiments and ideas. However, there is lack of networking and coordination among these. Consequently, the Akali leadership invariably has had a free-run and has treated such of the institutions, including Akal Takht, High priests, SGPC as their proxies or protégés or even their pocket-borough!

It is with deep sense of concern that I say that the religio-political schizophrenia, unleashed in the distant or recent past, had pointed to an Akali leadership that seemed locked in an echo chamber, relying overly only on the present SAD leadership, dominated as it is by the Badals and his close associates/colleagues, who have mastered the art to shrug off concerns expressed by institutions and experts from time-to- time, time-and-again, ascribing motives to them. The results are there for all to see.

There are diverse opinions on the role of the Sikh institutions. A section of scholars are dismissive of distracters and critics and assert that the institutions have not failed. The failure, if any, has been due to man-made distortions, corruption and erosion of ethos and ethics. Some of the institutions were corrupted as those at the helm worked for self-aggrandizement, not service and self-sacrifice. For short-sighted gains these institutions have been exploited for selfish interest by the leaders.

*

In fact, I remember the late Dr Kharak Singh of the *Institute of Sikh Studies,* identifying to me two types of institutions: one, basic and the other that evolved with time and need. The former included: the Guru, the Gurdwara, the *sangat* {congregation}, the *pangat* {queue}, the *langar* {community kitchen}, *daan* {giving of alms or sharing} etc. The latter category of institutions was: the *Gurmata* {collective decision of the congregation}, the *Panj Piare* {the five beloved ones}, the SGPC, the SAD {SGPC's political wing}, the Sikh High priests, the Chief Khalsa Dewan, the Damdami Taksal etc. {The Institute of Sikh studies is based in Gurdwara Kanthala, situated diagonal to *The Tribune* office in Chandigarh.}

The need, to quote Kharak Singh, was to make the institutions: *functional to articulate the heightened aspirations and expectations of the Sikhs; discarding or abandoning or winding up of these institutions is no solution.* The way out was reorientation, assimilation, elimination, where needed, and consolidation of the Sikh institutions. In fact, in the past as now, several of the institutions have weathered many storms and crises. Each time Panthic crises erupted, the reason was always, every time and invariably: the ego-centric internecine wars among the top Akali leaders-Jagdev Singh Talwandi, Gurcharan Singh Tohra, Surjit Singh Barnala, Parkash Singh Badal and many others with each of them backed by one or the other set of High Priests; and SGPC members, mostly of the executive committee.

The Institute also favoured an apex body, not an alternative to the SGPC or Akal Takht, but a representative group of eminent Sikhs to chalk out a scientific course for emancipation and empowerment of the Sikhs, as it believed that *Sikh and Punjab* are synonymous terms! *The Institute of Sikh Studies* was as equally concerned and worried as were some others over growing apostasy among the Sikhs with the youth getting weaned away from Sikhism.

*

Branding swords, raising slogans is one thing; working together to solve problems is quite another thing. The problems required to be solved are: territorial, inter-state disputes; unemployment, poverty, erasing socio-economic disparities in the villages, bridging caste-class chasm; providing urban facilities in rural areas, checking rural-urban migration; pulling the Sikh peasantry and farm labour out of agrarian crisis, providing affordable and quality education, health facilities; and ensuring proper sanitation, besides good infrastructure in terms of connectivity and communication; and availability of power; remunerative returns and profit from agricultural produce etc.

Finding solutions to issues that are political, social and economic is also the responsibility of the Sikh institutions, as also of the Sikh leadership. Though boldly mentioned and echoed in successive election manifestos of the political parties of all hues and ideologies, if any, these issues have been ignored with impunity, across all elections, by one and all. What remains are the idiosyncrasies of the political leaders!

28

Sulking Reserve, Sagging Pillars

CRPF: Central reserve police force was the most visible sign during Punjab's trials and tribulations with terrorism. If its omnipresence seemed irksome at times, it was perceived as partisan at other times! There was a time when nearly 40 battalions of CRPF {nearly 40 per cent to 45 per cent of the total force} were deployed across Punjab to fight terrorism and to assist the Punjab police. That there was no love lost between the two, is no secret.

Given the nature of my job, one day some officers and jawans met me to share their grievances and problems. Their only condition, if one may call it a condition, was not to disclose their identity. They swore on the authenticity of the facts of information they wanted to share. That was a moment, sometimes in 1989, when one realized that inside the *Khaki* uniforms, bullet-proof jackets, helmets, heavy boots and carrying rifles there were not just men of steel, but soft-hearted humans with families; and emotions! My interaction with them revealed many reasons why the striking reserve was sulking and why the pillars of CRPF were sagging. One is sure that more than a quarter century later things must have improved for the CRPF personnel.

In brief, this is what surfaced from my interactions with a cross-section of CRPF personnel: The deep-seated frustration and discontent was visible among the cadre officers and men of the CRPF in its golden jubilee year. Yet, the men continued to perform their duties diligently albeit with a feeling of resignation; unknown to the life swirling around them! On the one hand, the force was marked by stagnation and qualitative degeneration in the recent years; and CRPF no longer was attracting brilliant young officers. On the other hand, out of exasperation, a large number of officers, who had joined the force between 1971 and 1976, had quit, others were waiting to complete 20 years service to become eligible for pension and then exit. Such exodus was more visible at the level of commandants, assistant commandants and deputy superintendent levels.

The officers rued that all along fate and destiny of CRPF had been in the hands of the IPS officers on deputation. The cadre officers rarely reached the rank of DIG: Deputy-Inspector-General. *Clay* was the word the officers and men used to describe the way how controlling or management group of IPS officers treated the striking reserve! One learnt their frustration was genuine and well pronounced.

In CRPF, they said, besides the Director-General there were seven Inspector-Generals of Police and among them just one cadre officer, who was posted in the North-eastern sector; probably he was one M P Singh. The rest, including the I-G {headquarters} and Director Internal Security Academy were IPS officers. There were, as I discovered, many additional DIGs, from among cadre officers, who, however, had no voice. The interviewed personnel said IPS officers on deputation spent more time on getting acquainted with the force rather than pursuing policy matters in respect of cadre review or career planning. Even professional training aspect had been neglected. With one voice they said: *we have lost our {meaning CRPF} culture, continuity and luster*. They complained of working in a vacuum in the absence of time-scale promotions, resulting in erosion of morale! Moreover, no *Padma* awards were ever given to CRPF personnel, the awards, if given, went to the IPS officers on deputation {this was applicable to even BSF, which was mostly deployed on internal security duty in Gurdaspur} or to the deputy commissioners!

Then, there was no provision of payment of ex-gratia grant in case CRPF personnel got killed in action. In fact, given long distances between their posting and home place, bodies were not sent to families for performing last rites and cremation/burial; only an urn containing the ashes was sent to the bereaved family! The only consolation was Punjab government giving an ex-gratia grant of Rs one lakh to the family then, as applicable to Punjab police personnel. So much so, even rank differentiation rankled: there were instances when cadre officers were promoted but with the same rank badge. When second in commands {2 ICs} were inducted between the commandant and assistant commandant that was of little or no solace. The CRPF officers insisted on operational parity with the state police and introduction of some rationale while inducting IPS officers.

Eventually, it emerged that the CRPF jawans suffered from emotional crisis, as well, due to long absence from home and family. This had shattered them. There was hardly any family accommodation available to the force personnel, who lived out of temporary camps and tents all over the state. {Some officials said 90 per cent force had put up in these temporary shelters and led a nomad's life, given the nature of their duties and deployment.} Besides emotional vacuum, the jawans were also bitten by economic crisis, given the un-remunerative salaries, unfavorable service conditions, lack of promotional avenues, tough and long duty hours etc. Their cumulative effect was growing despondency among all ranks then. Disappointment and homesickness was all pervasive.

Some sub-inspectors and head constables had revealed that according to a conservative estimate every month at least five per cent of all ranks sought premature retirement after 20 years service. At that time the total strength of the CRPF was estimated around 1.25 lakh. Despite 1989 being the golden jubilee year, no tangible steps were on the anvil to galvanize the force. The real strength or pillars on which CRPF edifice rested were sub-inspectors and head constables. The discontent was more pronounced at their level.

Here is a telling comment of one of the head constables, who stood guard in a sandbag-walled observation post close to the Golden Temple: *I will prefer to get half the pay or pension and be with my family now, rather than wait for 20-odd years and then return to a broken home and shattered family*. With a deep sigh, he continued: *can you believe that nearly 70 per cent the children of CRPF personnel, who have roots and families in villages, are illiterate? We are losing our families as well as farms. I wish to return to look after both*. Since service rules mandated that a person could not be posted in his home state, the men in uniform found it extremely difficult to get solved even minor problems their families faced back home.

There were reports of internal disquiet impinging upon discipline within the CRPF with its personnel feeling that they be allowed to carry their weapons home when proceeding on leave. Their families were exposed to threats and terror attacks. Several cadre officers desired to go on deputation elsewhere, as that meant better status and also 10 per cent higher salary.

In a purely incidental meeting with the then CRPF Director-General P G Harlankar, I raised the issues the CRPF personnel had brought to my notice. He admitted lapses and said a high level committee had been constituted to suggest measures to end stagnation in the force, as also welfare measures required to boost their morale. That committee was headed by an Inspector-General and would take a holistic view of the issues of concern. He, however, did say that a proposal was on the anvil for setting up at least six more group centres to provide housing facilities to men in addition to 19 centres across the country, then. {Later, a centre came up at Jalandhar.} He also talked of a string of family welfare measures etc. What happened thereafter, I could not know.

That was a difficult period as much for the civilians as also for men/women in uniform out to maintain law and order to ensure peace and tranquility. Have things changed for the better?

29

The Letter

Letters, we are told, have been written and sent since antiquity. These contain messages, personal and professional. These bring us happiness and sadness. These make us laugh and cry. These lead us to hope and despair. These inform us. These educate us. These awaken us. These inspire us. These make us think. These bond us. These tell us stories. These teach us history.

Letters are literature. Letters are prose. Letters are poetry. Letters reveal secrets. Letters convey emotions. Letters are a medium of communication; teaching and learning. Letter writing is a hobby. Letter-writing is an art, a craft. Letters to the editor are a class apart: these help us to unwind. Letters help us share perceptions on men and matters. Letters are written in code language, invisible ink, as also by hand or type-written. Letters have been compiled into books, which contain instructional material.

There is an element of timeliness and universality in letter-writing. In the ancient world letters were written on different materials, including metal, lead, wax-coated wooden tablets, pottery fragments, animal skins, and papyrus. As communication technology has diversified, posted letters have become less important, as a routine form of communication. For example, the development of the telegraph had drastically shortened the time taken to send a communication, by sending it between distant points as an electrical signal. At the telegraph office closest to the destination, the signal was converted back into writing on paper and delivered to the recipient.

The next step was the telex, which avoided the need for local delivery. Then followed the fax {facsimile} machine: a letter could be transferred electrically from the sender to the receiver through the telephone network as an image. Today, the internet means of email plays a large part in written communications; however, these email communications are not generally referred to as letters but rather as e-mail messages or simply e-mails, with only the term "letter" generally being reserved for communications on paper.

Nevertheless, a letter is a product in its own right. And, as we have seen, letters have become less popular due to new and faster ways of communication. To preserve letter writing, a rich old art, motivation to share feelings and thoughts with others in an early childhood becomes essential. It is important to promote the study of letter writing showing that writing letters can be interesting and that it brings advantages.

When did you last write a letter to someone or anyone?

In fact, we all in our life, at one point of time or the other, not only have written and received letters, we have also preserved some of the letters, which we value and cherish. I remember, when I was in class sixth, I was sent to P P S: Punjab Public School, Nabha. That was in 1962. Apart from studying, it was compulsory for every student to participate in extracurricular activities and sports; so was writing a weekly letter to our parents.

On Saturday afternoons, our English teacher, Joginder Singh would distribute the light green coloured inland letter sheets; these inland letters have become extinct. {He was also Housemaster of Beas House.} Then he would proceed to write an opening paragraph on the blackboard –common to all of us - which we would copy. Each week, the opening paragraph would be differently worded. Thereafter, we would be free to write what we wanted to share or convey to our parents. He would collect the letters, check these for correct address, sender's name, House number etc; read them before these were posted. When the replies came, each letter would be opened before being handed over to us; a two-way censorship! That helped us learn how to write letters. That helped us express our thoughts and communicate the same through the power of word. That helped us innovate. That helped us take care of our handwriting. Letter-writing was a great experience. Letter-writing was great education. Is it still, the same?

Years later, after finishing schooling at P P S, I returned home to join the Government Senior Model School, Sector-16 Chandigarh. One day, sitting with my parents, my mother smilingly asked: *would you like to see something that we have preserved and cherished, while you were away? That is something which, though, never made us feel lonely; it helped us overcome emotions*! *Sure*, I responded excitedly. What she brought out from her box was a bundle of letters that I had written across the years while at PPS. Together, interspersed with sobs and smiles, we went through the pile of letters. Believe me, I blushed at seeing some of the letters; these gave me goose-flesh! In some letters there was my *art* work, as well. Memories came flooding. Such is the permanency of the impact the letters make on us, the humans. Who says, letters do not bond humans! Unfortunately, the information technology has deprived us of even sending *New Year* greeting cards, as well.

*

And, yes, History repeats itself; but at a higher plane! Decades later, in 1997, my younger son, Gauravjit was to be admitted to the same school where I had studied; though, he was not there for a very long time - as much due to *homesickness*, as also self-invited and self-inflicted *scholastic probation*. He was to return home after one year. Yet, in that period, he had written a good number of letters in which he was in a lamenting mood, all the time! Like my parents, I have also preserved his letters. Incidentally, he also handed me the ones that I either wrote to him or corrected for grammar and returned to him. I have carefully kept these - for posterity! After his marriage, I showed these to his wife, Simmi; I wonder why her eyes welled up!

*

Not only this. As I said, letters have become subjects of books, just as Jawaharlal Nehru's letters to his daughter Indira Gandhi: *Letters from a father to his daughter*. In this compilation, he educates, informs and widens Indira's horizon of knowledge by telling her about Nature, evolution of life, world history, races, early and present-day faiths and beliefs of religion, the beginning of communication using languages by making sounds that are meaningful, how writing evolved through meaningful marks, and how the different languages were related and much more.

Similarly, Amarjit Singh Hayer, my English teacher at Punjab Agricultural University, Ludhiana, has also written a book using the letters that he had exchanged with his class-fellows, fellow-travellers and others. The book: *Chithian Mittarn Dian* —Letters of friends--- {2010}, written in Punjabi, makes a fascinating reading. Some letters are personal in nature. Others are nostalgic, when friends *talked* –

through the written word - of the past and the present! The sentiments and emotions exchanged between friends just seem to meltdown on the pages. Carefully preserved across the decades, this is a precious treasure that he cherishes, which gives him strength to live on, as also inspire others!

The point I am making is simple: times may have changed. Technology may have gobbled letter-writing *per se*, especially by hand. Yet, letters have their own value and importance. Letters have their own place in an individual's life. Letters help you to reflect on the past, correct the present and prepare for the future. These are strong chains which help overcome mood swings, weaknesses; and lend strength: moral and emotive to smile and move on!

It is in this context I share the following incident; how a simple brief letter, now frayed at the edges, still makes me feel ashamed of my initial instinctive reaction: one day, *Tribune's* Associate Editor T K Ramasamy called me over to his cubby-hole. He handed me some loose papers and documents, saying: *go through these and see if you can do a piece.* He was short, straight and to the point. Yet, he was an inspiration to his colleagues. Back in my room, I studied the bunch of papers. Those pertained to a project: *The encyclopedia of Sikhism* underway at Punjabi University, Patiala. This was in 1993. My piece was published. After a few days, I received an envelope through mail. Inside was a typed four-line letter. I just casually glanced at it and tossed it aside, as it was not signed. Many weird thoughts crossed my mind about the *letter-writer* in those few seconds. I admit my carelessness in not being careful with the written word. Impulsively, I picked up the letter again.

On second look, I was totally shattered; it was the ***post-script*** that made me look sheepish: *Sorry, owing to this infirmity of mine, I cannot sign.* The letter read:

My Dear Mr Gill,

That is a very generously-worked out piece on the Encyclopedia. My sincerest thanks to you

With many thanks—and much affection,

Yours sincerely,

HARBANS SINGH

The letter on the official writing pad: The Encyclopedia of Sikhism, Guru Gobind Singh Bhavan, Punjabi University, Patiala, had university's insignia. It was dated June 23, 1993. Every time I see the framed letter, my heart fills with regret and remorse. My apologies to the learned Professor! Though, we never met, he has taught me a lesson: *be patient with the written word.*

Yes, a journalist is not only supposed to read, he is also expected to read *between the lines*; for once, I had slipped!

*

As I write this, two incidents come to mind, which fill me with self-conscious air! During one of the state assembly election, we, the Amritsar-based correspondents, were touring the border belt. At Khem Karan, we stopped at a tea-stall and engaged in conversation with some of the farmers there. My PTI colleague, Gurdip Singh, asked one farmer about the election prospects. Taking a deep sip, he said, "If you read yesterday's *Punjabi Tribune*, there is a write-up by one Gill. That will answer all your questions". We exchanged glances. I could not have got a better compliment.

The second incident took place at Panjab University's Administrative Block in Chandigarh, once I was transferred to the state capital. Accompanied by the then Public Relations Officer, Sanjiv Tewari, as we were walking out at lunch time, he introduced me to a tall, handsome Sikh gentleman. "Meet our Deputy registrar", Tewari spoke. When the DR heard my name he asked Tewari if I were the same person who was reporting from Amritsar during the terrorism days. When Tewari said, "Yes", the gentleman politely asked: *May I shake hands with you. I am lucky to have met you.* I was speechless; overwhelmed with emotion, as we shook hands!

The two incidents remind me, even today, that God has given me more than I deserved!

30

Travels and Travails

Travelling is not just going from one place to another for either personal or professional or business or other purposes. The more important part of travelling is about getting informed, educated, awakened and exposed to new interesting places, meeting people, learning about new cultures, customs, cuisines, faiths, rituals, languages, history, economy and local social life.

In this context, I remember my meeting with legendary journalist Sher Singh Gupta. He was based at Patiala. He belonged there and worked for *The Tribune.* One day, on my way to Bathinda from Chandigarh, I happened to stopover at Punjab State Electricity Board office to meet the public relations officer. Gupta was also present. It was a chance meeting, but very educative. Brief who's who formalities over, he put his frail hand on my shoulder and asked: *do you read foreign news in the paper and in other papers you subscribe to*? The question had caught me off guard. As I fumbled for the right, honest answer, he put me at ease: *you are young and have long career before you. Read foreign news and try to understand the geo-political situation in the neighboring countries, as also elsewhere. One never knows when an opportunity may knock at your door and you are sent on assignment to some foreign country. Even otherwise, our profession requires a wide exposure, involving multiple issues; including travelling within and outside the state or country is education*. His sane advice made me learn the art of reading a newspaper, the correct way; and resolve to travel.

One had, as a student, heard about books written by foreign travellers and read travelogues. People have been travelling across continents since time immemorial, exploring the world. The people undertook voyages on foot, on camels, horses and mules; used motorized means; by ship across seas and oceans and by air. Man's quest to travel and explore continues.

*

My first air travel opportunity was from Chandigarh to New Delhi for the International Trade fair at the Pragati Maidan, where Chandigarh Union Territory administration had put up a stall. The journey lasted about 45 minutes, but it was quite an experience: from check-in formalities to frisking and scanning to tying the seat-belt. Later, however, one got the opportunity to go across the country, as part of Vidhan Sabha press gallery group; and also travel abroad!

The trip with fellow journalists took place in September 2001, shortly following attack by the air-borne terrorists in Washington and New York. In the wake of that gruesome incident, a three-tier security system had been introduced at all airports in the country. I discovered that the ways of the security personnel and the manner in which the drill was carried out was both cumbersome and comic; no, I am not disputing the need for that utmost caution and safety of passengers. On that trip, I encountered security checks at Chandigarh, New Delhi, Chennai, Port Blair and Kolkata.

If the encounters with security personnel were not hassle-free, at least some were hilarious, giving a comic touch to grim situations! In fact, such security checks exposed you with privacy ripped open! Co-passengers would either look the other way or steal a look, embarrassed and nervous, hurriedly re-packing the suitcases and zipping the handbags. The airport entertainment was embarrassing and amusing at the same time with security personnel holding up lingerie's and lip-sticks or turn-over shaving kits and hair dryers, to see if there were explosives hidden inside. Those with cameras were asked to click pointing to the floor! And physical frisking, screening with hand-held metal detectors or walking through metal-detector-doors was add-ons! The lessons were well learnt and experience well gained: educative, informative and knowledgeable.

*

The first two trips abroad were a private affair, when I visited the USA and Canada in 1998; and later Europe and the UK in 2001. The first official visit came when I was assigned to travel to Pakistan for the inauguration of the *Motorway* from Islamabad to Lahore – 375 kms - in 1997, when Nawaz Sharif was the Prime Minister; the second official trip abroad was when I accompanied the then Deputy Prime Minister L K Advani to the USA and the UK in 2003.

Besides attending a press briefing at the White House, where President George Bush had met with Advani, one had the opportunity of visiting the 10 Downing Street in London; official residence of the Prime Minister. Tony Blair was the incumbent Prime Minister then.

*

While waiting for the two leaders to come out after their talks, I happened to ask a security person on duty as to where can one have some details about 10 Downing Street residence. To my utter surprise, he fished out a printed paper from his hip-pocket, showed to me and then walked across to knock at the front door, which had a gold-plated ring above the number 10! He came out after few minutes with a photocopy of the printed material that gave me enough details and background of the place.

*

And, in 2003, as I looked at the memorial under construction to perpetuate those who had lost their lives to terrorism, memories of having once stood atop one the *Twin Towers* of the World Trade Centre {in 1998} flooded my mind. I paid a silent tribute to those who had died!

*

Incidentally, during the official visit to Pakistan, I used a potable type-writer and sent the dispatch through telegraph office. Carrying that was quite helpful, as also cumbersome. By the time I accompanied Advani, I was used to working on a computer. Since then, things have changed - the media and the medium itself.

*

Believe me, official visits are taxing, as also enjoyable: a great learning experience while working to meet deadlines, keeping in mind the time difference between India and the country in which one is. Such trips are a rush job: hopping from one event to another, bleary eyed going from one city to another, rummaging through the piles of printed material, attending press briefings, finding place to sit and work to file stories; grabbing a bite here or there, lack of rest, and what have you.

There is pressure to file something exclusive, if possible, as well, and also write a travel diary: sidelights, light-hearted stuff! From experience and having been put through the paces, one can say with fair amount of conviction that the best comes out of a reporter, when hard pressed for time to meet deadlines! Of the many varied experiences and memorable moments, some vignettes of the travels abroad are still fresh in mind, as if all this had happened only yesterday. It was a different world one saw outside India: fascinating, exciting, awesome, numbing; even bewildering, at times!

Here we take-off:

The unanticipated and unexpected *detention* at Amman Queen Alia international Airport, in 2001, was quite a nerve-shattering experience with clock ticking away and the Royal Jordanian Airlines flight about to take off for Paris; and my key travel document, the passport, held by Jordan authorities in some obscure office room.

As I sat waiting and praying, an officer came over and with a smile handed over my passport. I literally ran to the aircraft. No sooner had I settled down in my seat, much to the puzzled and curious looks of fellow passengers, the plane had started taxing. A sympathetic woman, who was from New Delhi, in a consoling tone said: *relax, these things happen. Perhaps, being a Sikh put you in the awkward situation.* In return, I forced a smile, thanked her for empathy, and sighed: never to travel this route again!

*

As the plane touched down at the Orly international airport, Paris, I felt relieved. As I walked down the shimmering corridors, a burly security man smiled and motioned me into an empty room: *please open the suitcase.* As I nervously looked for the keys inside the handheld bag, he spoke again: *no hurry, take your time.* There was nothing objectionable. He spoke again: *what are you here for and where are you staying*? I replied with a forced smile: *for the world air show and sightseeing.* I showed him the visiting card of my cousin, B P S Cheema, who was posted as Deputy Air Attaché in the Indian Embassy. *Have a nice time*, he muttered, and helped me pack up the baggage. Anita Cheema greeted me. *{Thank you, Sher Singh Gupta Sahib for that valuable tip at Patiala, decades ago!}*

*

The 44th Paris air show at Le Bourget was a life-time experience. I had never thought of seeing such a wide variety of *mechanized birds* from vintage to latest airplanes - fighters to passengers to virtual flying hospitals; from squirrel helicopters to A340 Airbus; innovative aviation designs; display of killer power and what have you. That show was an affirmation that for the flying machines, aerospace was as much a playfield, as hard business and defence market for their manufacturers on the ground.

One came across companies from across the continents: 43 countries and 1800 companies! It was an international village, where one rubbed shoulders with a sea of humanity representing different continents, countries, regions, religions, cultures, relishing an assortment of cuisines and speaking different languages. It was a thrilling experience to board many of the aircrafts and helicopters on display; collect brochures and souvenirs!

Paris, as I discovered, is not just about the Eiffel Tower or the Louvre or Arc de Triomphe or Dome church, the Pantheon, Notre-Dame, Champs-Elysees, Opera houses etc. It is also not just about being a repository of art galleries, museums, architecture, statutes, sculptures, restaurants and hotels; walks and music or just about geometrically manicured trees and straight roads; or washing clean the entire city every morning; or about the vast, efficient metro net-work underground or the cars that clog the city arteries or ones that remain parked on road berms in narrower streets and roads: packed like sardines! It is much more. I learned there were about 300-odd places to see in Paris.

*

Among the suggestions given out to me by friends and experienced travellers was one to zealously safe guard my passport and wallet, besides taking along a comfortable pair of walking shoes!

It so happened, my friend, an IPS officer, and a colleague from *The Tribune* were going to the USA via Paris, where they had a pretty long halt and wanted to see the place in the given limited time. From experience, I told them to zealously guard their travel documents- passports, air tickets, and currency etc., given the smart pick-pockets who roamed the tourist destinations. They responded with smiles. Yet, I gave them my cousin's email ID, cell no. address etc; just in case! They took this albeit reluctantly.

My IPS friend lost his travel documents to the street smart pick-pockets, near the Eiffel Tower. Desperate, not knowing French, and English of little or no help and use, as a last resort, they contacted my cousin, B P S Cheema. He went over to the police station, lodged a complaint and took the officer home, while my Tribune colleague continued with her flight, on to the US. The Indian Embassy, courtesy Cheema, opened on a holiday; and issued a new Passport and other related documents to enable him with his journey. He had to spend a night in Paris and was shown around, as well. Cheema gave him money for his onwards and return trip, as well. That is Paris!

*

What, however, I wish to share in the following passages is something different, not the tourist guided spots, places and palaces. It is about my experiences and impressions about people, our own - the Indian youth - whom I met and observed during my long stay in Paris. That experience exposed me to the seamy side to Paris - *a city of dreams and reality*! That side came into focus when I visited some key tourist interest stops. This seamy side became all the more pronounced with the presence of young boys of Indian, Pakistani and Bangladeshi origin, who were spotted at the museums and churches, gardens, shopping arcades and malls; or were seen to hang around street corners in shopping plazas.

These youth would hawk souvenir, memorabilia besides mineral water bottles and Coke cans tucked in buckets filled with ice-cubes. Some others were seen either selling dancing *dolls* to the tunes of typical Punjabi pop songs or throwing sticking and prancing *human figures* on to the walls or glass-panelled show cases. The most bizarre presence, however, was of those who dressed-up as look-alikes of old characters of history and ancient civilization, adorning appropriate makeup and posing as *statute vivante or mannequins*; bending or bowing only when tourists threw coins into their plastic bowls. This was the segment of youth, who had made it to Paris after paying hefty sums of money to travel agents and middle-men, ranging from Rs 4 lakh to Rs 6 lakh, for better life outside their own country.

I spoke to several youth from Punjab. The *modus operandi* of trafficking in human cargo, including tales of horrifying deaths and long tormenting time spent in transit via circuitous, long land and sea routes had become clear not just in Paris but also back home. That was the time when people would often talk of Malta boat tragedy, whose echo persisted, as I spoke to them.

*

The Malta boat tragedy took place on December 25, 1996, in which 283 youths, mostly from Punjab, had lost their lives. The youths, who were to enter Italy illegally, were transferred from a ship to the Yiohan, a small boat that capsized in the Mediterranean near Italy. The case has been under CBI investigation. It has remained pending in a CBI court for the past 19 years, as even charge sheet has not been framed and filed against the 29 accused — all travel agents — in the case! This is not an isolated incident. Later, on April 21, 2002, 30 Punjabi youth were drowned near Turkey, when the boat ferrying them capsized. The latest such mishap took place on January 10, 2016, when a similar accident took place near Panama in which 25 youth were reported to have died in a watery grave. Behind all such human tragedies are travel agents. Across the decades, successive state governments have failed to take cognizance of such unscrupulous travel agents – though two or three travel agents have been arrested - who had enticed the youth showing them green pastures across the seas and have engaged in human trafficking, illegally; and repeatedly.

*

I gathered in Paris that there was wide-spread international awareness of such exploits, wherein, human beings were smuggled, for money. Besides the United Nations, even the Council of Europe, Parliament Assembly was in the know of this clandestine business and seized of the matter. My observation was that the blame for such trade tantamounting to violation of human rights had to be apportioned to both sides: one, dealing in human smuggling and, two, who are enticed into the snarl.

Conversations with most of the youth hailing from Hoshiarpur, Ambala, Ahmadabad and even Delhi revealed that only a small percentage of them were plus two pass. They were the drop-outs, who had coaxed, cajoled and even forced their parents, mostly living in villages and small upcoming towns, to cough up money - even if it meant raising loan from the Ahrtiya {commission agent} at very high rate of interest or mortgaging their land or property to meet the travel expenses of their obstinate children, mostly sons!

I could only pity them, as they unburdened themselves, getting nostalgic and narrated their harrowing experience and fugitive living. Their parched throats, dried lips, sheepish smiles, impoverished looks, eyes ever on the look-out for police and halting narratives unfolded their sordid stories of transit. A majority of them wanted to return home but could not, as according to them they had destroyed their passports. Others were scared of their parents and jeers that might greet them on return to the native land!

Most of the youth, certainly, were not telling the truth, as to how they eked out a living: some lied, some exaggerated. The fact was these *on-the-run* boys having shirked studying or doing work back home had landed here only with dreams and fancy ideas of making it big and rich. The agents had lured them with false hopes and tricked them that job opportunities were aplenty with good earnings in Europe, where labour was scarce, society ageing and active population diminishing, thereby, changing the demography of the region.

Some of the enterprising or lucky among them, on an average, made 200-odd French Frank every day: then, one Frank equaled Rs six. Yet, to repeated questions about the fear of the police, deportation, living like fugitives on the run, how much they were able to earn etc, the answer was always same: a wry smile! Nevertheless, they did not want either their names or photographs clicked and published. Exasperation was evident. Majority of them said their ultimate destination was the USA.

*

B P S Cheema and Indian Embassy officials concerned told me that every now and then the countries covered under the *Etats Schengen* visa opened immigration, and these youth filed documents in search of jobs. Lucky ones got one. The basic purpose, I was informed, was to obtain *Carte sejour*, equivalent of American Green Card that permitted them residence and permit to work. Their status, however, remained: *illegal*!

Though no official figures were available, it was estimated that several thousand Sikhs lived in and around Paris. Their focal point to meet, share and socialize was the Gurdwara Singh Sabha at Bobigny, a suburb North-East of Paris, where Sikhs and Hindus converged on weekends and on special occasions. To further interact with a cross-section of the youth whom I was following, I travelled to

Bobigny on metro. In French a *suburb* is referred to as *baulieus*, a sort of inner city: low income, high crime rate; and an array of social ills mark the habitats.

At the Gurdwara, I learned that the entry for the youth to France {Paris} was via Moscow, Prague, Warsaw and East European countries whose border was pretty porous, particularly, after the formation of European Union - EU.

*

The EU was not always as big as it is today. When European countries started to cooperate economically in 1951, only Belgium, Germany, France, Italy, Luxembourg and the Netherlands participated. Across time, more and more countries decided to join. The union reached its current size of 28 member-countries with the accession of Croatia on 1 July 2013. The concept of EU was conceived in 1993 to form a political and economic union under the Maastricht Treaty. EU has a combined population of just over 500 million. And, in June 2016 the UK held a referendum to stay or quit membership of EU. Following the results, the UK decided to leave EU. As a consequence Britain exited, Prime Minister David Cameron had to quit and former Home Secretary, Theresa May became the new Prime Minister. At present the effective strength of EU is now 27.

*

The youth, whom I talked to at the Gurdwara, shared their adventurous, dangerous and torturous journeys, travelling clandestinely all the time, on land, by sea and air. Normally, it took them three to four months to reach Paris and meet the earlier immigrants from their villages and towns or neighborhood. Like the migrant labour in Punjab from other states, these boys lived in cheap places and in groups.

This weighed on my mind. I persisted this with others. What emerged was this: at times, these youth were, more often than not, hauled up by the police, offered accommodation, bedding and food, warned and let off. These boys had no fear of being deported, as they possessed no legal documents to show. The law, the youth had discovered and understood with experience and brush with the authorities, was a cumbersome, tedious and long process; and that the French police would neither spend money nor waste time nor have any intentions to detain them for long.

*

At times, the French authorities would approach the Indian Embassy to ascertain antecedents of those, who had given out names of their villages and parents. The result would be the same: no village by the name given in a state and no persons claimed as parents living in that village. If the name of the place was correct that of the parents would invariably be incorrect. Verification took time. The matter would be shelved; languishing and fear-psychosis persisted day-after-day, month-after-month. These youth, who had lost opportunities to study when back home, oblivious of their future, continued to spoil their present on foreign lands. What, however, sustained them was a forlorn ray of hope that one day Paris would absorb them: turning their dreams into reality; or send them to the USA. Though, I have said, I pitied them, in truth, one really did not know whether to pity them or sympathize with them; empathy? No way!

*

Even today, when thousands of youth in Punjab are still keen to go abroad, and are making rounds of the travel agents and teaching shops offering courses in English language proficiency and meeting other basic 'academic' pre-requisites, all I can offer is a word of warning or caution, if you please: do not venture out as illegal migrants or through unscrupulous agents or traffickers in human beings! Globally, with stringent laws and restrictions, things are much tougher than say a decade or so ago.

*

At the Eiffel Tower I met with a retired joint director of Punjab's department of social welfare, H S Tuli. He too, incidentally, had just talked to some youth from Hoshiarpur. They were selling Coke cans and small key-rings depicting the Tower. He had empathy for those youth; and impromptu said: the Akali government, Parkash Singh Badal was the chief minister then, must launch a state-wide campaign to create awareness among the youth and educate them about hazards of illegal migration. In fact, the Akalis should frame a comprehensive policy on the youth that they have failed to do in the past four years, despite Punjab having come out of militancy.

*

One came across these youths doing labour in *Marche*-local fruit and vegetable markets- or trying scout for jobs with Indian families. One pitied them even more when they ran helter-skelter, hurriedly packing up and taking their bundle of software or knick-knack they sold, on seeing the police come after them. In fact, in that multi-nationality, multi-cultural capital-Paris- and on the fashionable Champs-Elysees, hearing Punjabi pop music and seeing Indian boys grinning was - amusing and sad!

Interaction with local families, like Shashi and Prem Puri, revealed that Indian youth were not alone in their misadventures. There were illegal migrants of different nationalities, as well: Tunisian, Arab, Moroccan; Algerian refugees besides those from other East European countries.

Prem Puri informed me that despite hindrance of the French language, the Indian boys had picked up words and mixed them with English to convey to the tourists, through sign language, what they were looking for. One also heard reports of human trade of girls and women from East European countries that was fast picking up. These women landed in the *pig ale* - brothels. One came across such women, some carrying small babies, sitting on road-berms or Metro entrances asking for alms.

Not all smuggled entrants did badly, though. Some were able to send home remittances, as well.

*

At that time, one learnt, human trade cargo was a world-wide phenomenon, it still remains. The then UN surveys and other reports indicated it was a global business worth US $5-7 billion! There are agencies like the Centre for International crime prevention, the UN integrated crime and justice research institute and a programme against trafficking. The slave trade picked up after 1980, world-wide. It was then estimated that some 30 million people were smuggled across the international borders and frontiers, annually, out of which 40,000 to 60,000 were in the European territories. The European countries accounted for three million illegal people. At that time Paris had nearly 6000 Indian boys.

The real focus on this aspect of violation of human rights came to light on June 20, 2000, when the custom and immigration staff at Dover, in the UK, found 58 bodies of Chinese from the trunk of a lorry bearing Dutch registration number plate, there were two survivors. The Chinese were being smuggled from Zeebruggee {Brussels}. That was to be only a tip of the iceberg.

The European Council, Parliamentary Assembly, went into a huddle and action, when presented with a detailed report of the committees concerned that summarized remedies. The action plan was adopted on June 27, 2000. The then executive director of the UN office for drug control and crime prevention, Pino Arlacchi, in his report called human trafficking as *slave trade*. The main centre for origin was the South-East Asia region heading to Western Europe and North America.

As then, even now, I for one feel that recruitment, transportation, transfer, harboring and receipt of such illegal labor or sex workers remains an international crime requiring global strategies to deal with. This menace is as threatening as export of terrorism and terrorists, as growing concerns over climate change. I was told that since 1980, some four million illegal migrants went to European countries, annually. The UK alone had checked 10,000 per year on its border posts and ports.

One may add here that apart from problem of illegal migrants, the other serious issue is of refugees, internally displaced, as well as those driven out of their country of birth; and even ones who are not recognized as any nationals, anywhere. Such large swathe of people are forced to leave their homes either due to conflicts, internecine ethnic and religious wars, famines or suffocating political conditions that impinge on their freedom of speech and expression in their native countries. UN human commissioner for refugees keeps track of such people, world-wide. The rise of Islamic state of Iraq and Syria has further complicated the problem with several countries and millions of refugees facing untold problems and crisis. These human crises pose a challenge and opportunity to the world powers to unite and act as one, rising above narrow interests: political, economic or geographical.

And following the terror created by the likes of Boko Haram or the Islamic State militants, hundreds and thousands of refugees from Syria and other countries in 2015 were headed to European countries for shelter. Germany showed the way when it opened its doors; and so did many other countries out of human considerations.

Going by the statistics revealed by UNHCR, as reported in the *Indian Express*, dated December 21, 2015, as many as 59.5 million individuals stood forcibly displaced, worldwide, due to persecution, conflict, violence, or human rights violation. The break-up was: refugees- 19.5 million; internally displaced persons – 38.2 million; and asylum seekers – 1.8 million. In other words, one in every 122 humans was either a refugee, internally displaced, or seeking asylum. Also, over half the world's refugees were children: 51 per cent below 18 years, 46 per cent between 18 years and 59 years; and 3 per cent 60 plus years!

The statistics also revealed that *top hosts* were Turkey, Pakistan, Lebanon, Iran, Ethiopia and Jordan; while, *top origins* were Syria, Afghanistan, Somalia, Sudan, South Sudan, Congo. It was estimated that 53 per cent, more than half of all refugees, were from just three countries: Syria, Afghanistan and Somalia, while 86 per cent of all displaced were housed and hosted by developing nations. The problem of refugees has further precipitated following continuing civil-war in Syria. It has been going on for the last five years, consuming 2.5 lakh lives; and another 1.9 lakh have been injured in the war-torn country. World powers are out to defuse the crisis there with UN acting as facilitator. It is difficult to say when global terrorism and hostilities will end, perpetrated as these are by the likes of Islamic State, al-Qaida etc.

In fact global migrant tide had swelled to 6.5 crore at the end of 2015. *The Tribune*, June 21, 2016, quoting latest UN report said globally one per cent of humanity had been forced to flee. In other words, counting earth's population at 7,349 billion, one out of every 113 people was internally displaced or a refugee. Such migrant crisis is the worst since World War II. Giving breakup, UN report revealed that Palestinians were the largest group of refugees at more than 50 lakh, including those who fled at the creation of Israel in 1948 and their descendents. Syria was the next on the list, with 49 lakh refugees, followed by Afghanistan, 27 lakh, and Somalia, 11 lakh.

*

And, as Tuli had suggested to me then, it was high time to make the youth aware of and educate them about the *real-life* world outside their homes. This is imperative. It was, in fact, shocking to see Punjabi or Haryanvi or Indian youth slog out in Paris with fear and anxiety-neurosis writ large on their faces. They seemed neither here nor there - back home. Obstinacy and time lag had made them insensitive, lonely and lost.

Across decades that craze of foreign lands still persists among Punjabi youth, who are jobless, shun farms and villages, are unqualified to pursue higher education and lack skills to take up required jobs. Those employed earn low salaries that result in family tensions and break-ups. The Punjabi society, particularly rural and semi-urban, is adrift.

*

As I wind up the anecdotal narrative of my travels and travails; journeys, spanning nearly three decades - within and outside India - and look into the rear view mirror, I find images of the past decades still etched there: some clear, some blurred, some evoking empathy, some sympathy, some chilling, some warming the cockles, some educative, some exciting, some informative, some life-time experiences. Travel travails notwithstanding, the explorations and adventures were worth learning. I have discovered that the best way to see a country is to travel either by road or rail. I have had experience of both in the USA, Canada, the UK and Europe.

*

Here, sample these experiences.

The bus-journey from Paris to London and passing through the tunnel under the English Channel! When the bus reached Calais in North France; and there it was put on a freight train under the English Channel tunnel. The 50.5 km journey under water was awesome! We surfaced at Folk stone, Kent in the UK; and journeyed onward to London, where water jets washed the wheels before the bus entered the bus station!

*

By the way, at Calais, Immigration authorities singled me out and minutely scanned my travel documents. After a few questions and satisfied, I was allowed to proceed to the UK. As I sweated it out and waited, I was reminded of my temporary *detention* {!} at Amman airport by the Jordanian authorities. In the meantime, I had gained confidence and was mentally prepared to return to Paris, where B P S Cheema, Anita and my nephews, Jovan and Sheenu, had seen me off at dawn!

*

And, how can one ignore to mention the unforgettable visit to the Lake District in the UK, famous for William Wordsworth's famous poem: *Daffodils*! Staying in the International Youth Hostel was educative in itself, where one rubbed shoulders and exchanged smiles and engaged in small talk with people from across different continents, of different nationalities, speaking different languages and representing different cultures. The serenity of the lake and its view from the hostel window was to put it simply – splendid!

Daffodils, incidentally, originally appeared as: *I wandered lonely as a cloud*, in 1807. The words *Daffodils* and *Wordsworth* go hand-in-hand with each other. This most famous poem in the English language was composed in 1804; two years after Wordsworth saw the flowers while walking by Ullswater on a stormy day with Dorothy, his sister.

*

Another memorable train journey was from Brampton {Canada} to Chicago {the USA}. It was for the first time that I had boarded a double-deck rail coach. As the landscape and countryside flashed past the window seat I had occupied, one got to see the interior of both the countries. In fact, it was a very lonely journey; there weren't very many passengers; and in between soaking-in the countryside, I would read or take a nap! {And as a typical Punjabi, handling foreign currency has always been an arduous task for me. Therefore, I had brought some snacks – Parantha - from Mississauga, where my uncle Darshan Basran and Aunt Mohini had bid me goodbye

*

Reaching late in the evening, the Chicago railway station simply took my breath away. It is literally a city! The loneliness and some fatigue simply dissipated when my uncle Darshan S Padda received me with a big, warm bear-hug. It was drizzling in the Windy City that night! The place, where I spent couple of weeks, was enchanting and enticing! The stay in Chicago was made all the more rewarding by my kind and tender hearted aunt Kulwant Padda, who we affectionately call: Kay! She is one person who believes in only giving, sharing and caring; expecting nothing in return but a smile and a hug! It is a beautiful city.

And, later, the drive from Chicago to Garry in Indiana State was yet another experience, as was drive to the capital Indianapolis. My hosts Ravinder and Gurnam

Sidhu showed me around. The countryside is simply beautiful. It was during that drive I saw how American farmers stored their grains and how a see-through canopy on tractors protected them from dust while plowing their fields.

*

While in Canada, the drive from Mississauga to Niagara Falls and the scenic beauty of that place is unforgettable; and so is a visit to the CN Tower, a 553.33 m-high (1,815.4 ft) concrete communication and observation tower in downtown Toronto, as one got a bird's view of the City. It was there that I for the first time saw ice-hockey as also baseball matches!

In fact, earlier, when still in the US, I had a chance meeting with my former teacher, A S Sandhu, who was visiting Washington D C. {He taught extension education at PAU.} I was staying in the Crystal City, and from the apartment one got a majestic and elegant view of the Pentagon building. Along with his family; I travelled to Mississauga and saw the US-Canada landscape, as well. It was nearly 750 kms long drive, the excitement and newness of the place, however, did not make one feel tired at the end of the journey. By the way, it was Baisakhi Day when I drove into Canada!

*

In Atlanta, my hosts Kiran and Tarsem Gupta showed me around and one of the most memorable visit remains to the 29-storey high Coca-Cola headquarters in Midtown, where after the visitors are given a visual presentation of the story - origin and history of the beverage - one is taken on a guided tour. The place has five tasting stations, geographical representation-wise of 100-odd varieties of the beverage: Africa, Asia, Europe, Latin America and North America. It was quite a scene watching school children enjoy Coca Cola samples in small disposable tumblers, which they would place on a swiveling counter and a fountain of selected beverage brand would pour into the glass!

*

From Chicago I flew to St Croix in the Caribbean Sea. It was another memorable journey. The view of the vast ocean down below was simply breath-taking! The Archipelago, off the mainland, is unique in many ways; spread as it is across 214 Sq Km area. Its terrain is hilly to rugged mountainous with very little level land. It is host to several communities: Afro-Caribbean, Puerto Rican and Caucasian. My host Harinder Paul {Ranju} Dhillon showed me around. My uncle, Darshan S Padda, who was Vice-President of the University of the Virgin Islands there, informed me that besides the Christian Carnival in December the other important fair was on Agriculture and Food in mid-February. After an exciting stay, I flew back to Chicago's O'Hare airport, one of the busiest in the world.

31

Distant Neighbours

This chapter bids fair to be a lengthy expatiation on the subject related to a *distant* neighbor, and is necessitated because the journalistic experiences that I had during the eight-day stay there have been pretty dear and close to my heart. There are several reasons, the chief being that I am going to share my memories, impressions, observations, experiences and travels in a country that is next-door, just an echo away from either the Attari-Wagha {Amritsar} or Hussainiwala {Ferozepur} borders in Punjab; yet, so far! Once a part of British India, it is now a separate, independent geographical entity called: Islamic Republic of Pakistan.

This is the place from where my grandparents-maternal and paternal- and parents migrated on Partition in 1947. I grew up listening to and enjoying their pre-Partition days' anecdotes, reminiscences and intimate talks; hearing about their life and living, schooling and play-mates, narrated at bed-time or otherwise; the tales and stories of common heritage, culture, traditions; and travails of partition!

They would talk of Sammundari or Lyallpur {now Faisalabad}, or Chak No. so and so, as districts, subdivisions, villages or habitats were then named, numbered and referred to. Or, how with no money, no change of clothes, no food, no, nothing; they had no choice and place to go to except to seek shelter with relatives and acquaintances in villages in what was to be their new home - India. They literally led the life of refugees; and that's what their shelter-giving relatives thought of them to be: a parasitic burden, howsoever, temporary!

In my heart, I would often long to visit the places where my grandparents and parents had come from, commonly referred to as *Baar*, where they had had their homes, hearths, hearts and lands; and they would get nostalgic recalling that period and time. Even today, when my 86 years old mother Gurbachan Kaur looks back to reminiscence about those days, she talks of those times either with a sigh or a smile;

or how she lost all her belongings that she had been gifted on her marriage that took place shortly before Partition!

And, as I matured and was exposed to information, knowledge and gained in experience, I began to realise that India and Pakistan had no love lost for a host of reasons; the major reason is state indoctrination being too strong in Pakistan. That there lurked mutual suspicion; and opinions were often formed by the people in the two countries on the basis of *purified* information filtered out of official and political prejudices. I also learnt, across time, that there were people, may be, perhaps, several are still around, who could then consort across the communal divides despite the subterranean magma of hatred that existed in pre-1947. There were, and there are, such people, who feel for each other, but with unspoken and suppressed feelings, as I was to discover during my stay in Pakistan.

Across the decades, despite bitter-sour-sweet relations between the two countries, somehow exchange of people has continued. Many would suggest that I visit Panja Sahib and Nankana Sahib and other shrines with SGPC-sponsored *Jathas* on key occasions. Somehow, I wanted to go in my own way in a relaxed atmosphere. Who says prayers are not answered? These are answered, if made with sincerity and submission! My wish and prayer were answered. The opportunity came when *The Tribune* assigned me to go to Pakistan for the inauguration of a Motorway from Islamabad to Lahore. That was in November 1997.

*

Incidentally, my visit took place at a time when Pakistan was in the grip of a Constitutional crisis, like of which had not been seen in the past; and, that too in the 50th year of Independence, with the two warring nations, India and Pakistan, into their Golden jubilee year! Those crises, involved the state institutions and instrumentalities---presidency, parliament and judiciary {the Supreme Court and its two benches at Quetta and Peshawar}; with the Army thrown in, not leaving the executive behind--- kept the chattering classes on the edge. It was practically a war of nerves with each side trying to find its own foothold to establish *autonomy* and find a place in the constitutional space.

And, there I was for eight days amidst rising collusion-prone political situation. Given the involvement of key institutions and powerful individuals, one saw sparks fly all over. The core institution –*democracy* - thus was swinging between feudal and dictatorial trends and spasms. Each player in the combat politics was trying to mow down the other. Was the army playing an honest broker? This question was being asked even as the then army Chief Gen. Jahangir Karamat had cut short his European tour and returned to act as *peace-maker*!

From what I saw, heard, read, observed and witnessed during the visit was, in essence, a battle for one-upmanship between the government of Nawaz Sharif, who had come to power at the crest of a popular massive mandate given by the Pakistan electorate in February 1997, on the one hand, and the institutions of presidency and the Supreme Court, both unrepresented organizations, on the other hand.

What was the crisis about? Varied answers were provided, yet much of what was being talked and written about in the media bazaar only compounded the confusion, as no one really could anticipate: what next! The political pot had been simmering for quite some time, I was told, over the issue of some constitutional amendments, including the one which had withdrawn the powers of the President, granted under section 13 of the Constitution, to dismiss the government; the appointment of five judges to the Supreme Court; the new anti-terrorism law {the Supreme Court felt this amounted to diluting its authority}; the anti-defection law {introduced by the National Assembly}; the subsequent contempt case against the Prime Minister etc. All these had precipitated the politico-constitutional crisis. Those crises saw the exit of the President, Farooq Leghari and also of the Chief Justice, Sajjad Ali Shah. The rest, as we say, is history.

Before proceeding further, I must put on record that even as part of 34-member *foreign* media group visiting Pakistan for a Motorway inauguration function, and all the attention and security provided to us, one could not overcome anxiety-neurosis or the fear of the unknown in a land, which till the other day was one entity: India included!

The twin focus, here-in-under is on: one, my visits to Gurdwaras-- Panja Sahib {situated at Hasan Abdal, 50 kms from Islamabad, the capital city on the outskirts of the Army garrison town, Rawalpindi} and Nankana Sahib {85 kms from Lahore}; two, travel to NWFP: North West Frontier Province, now called Khyber Pakhtunkhwa with Peshawar as its capital {187 km from Islamabad}. This is one of the four provinces, other three are: Baluchistan, Punjab and Sind. The country, otherwise, has four administrative divisions: Gilgit-Balistan, Federally Administrated Tribal Areas – FATA -; Azad Kashmir and Islamabad capital territory.

*

Reflections

However, before we step inside Pakistan territory, legally, let me narrate some incidents and experiences, which are still fresh in my memory, as if these took place only yesterday.

*

In August 1977, the union home minister Chaudhary Charan Singh visited Amritsar, as part of the 400th year celebrations of the founding of the holy city. One of the listed official engagements was his visit to the border posts. The names of journalists to accompany him were finalized after having been security-cleared in New Delhi. I was lucky to be part of his entourage. In fact, since the creation of the BSF, 11 years ago, it was for the first time that a home minister was visiting forward posts on India-Pakistan border. At that time, it was a *porous* border, no fencing, no cobra wire, no high-voltage lighting. Smuggling was commonplace but not rampant.

In the small convoy of BSF open jeeps, we followed the Home Minister, who was accompanied by the BSF Director-General and three chief ministers: Parkash Singh Badal {Punjab}, Devi Lal {Haryana} and Bhairon Singh Shekhawat {Rajasthan}. The two parallel tracks, dividing the two countries, ran zigzag, at times converging at some places. At one place, seeing few Pakistani farmers grazing their buffaloes, Charan Singh stopped and got into a short conversation with them and asked what if India and Pakistan was to become one again! A Pakistani farmer, leaning on his staff, raised his hand upwards and remarked in chaste Urdu: *Janab, isko to pakheru be tarste hain* – Sir, even birds years for that to happen!

Later, addressing the BSF Jawans and answering some of their questions, Charan Singh assured that depending on availability of funds, steps would be taken to provide *family accommodation* to the BSF personnel, who were posted away from their families for long periods. The more significant part of his short address to the BSF personnel was this: *the border has not been demarcated in a straight line. It runs zigzag and needs to be re-drawn for better policing and patrolling and easy identification of the boundary line and pillars.* At the end of the adventurous drive, we were all powdered with dust, making us all unrecognizable! In fact, I have had the privilege of extensively driving along the international border from Ajnala to Dera Baba Nanak and visiting many a BSF BOPs: Border Outposts/Observation

Posts, along the land as well as river bank side dividing boundary; as also having seen the misery of people who would be evacuated following spate in the Ravi and temporarily settled/sheltered on the Dhusi Bandh – a protection embankment.

*

The second memorable event that has remained stuck all these decades is the night spent at Wagha border; the land route open between the two countries. In October 1977, there was famous London-Sydney car rally. Inquiries with the Indian Oil authorities, local police and the immigration and customs staff yielded little information on the exact time as to when the first car was expected to drive through the Wagha gates.

Nevertheless, it was decided to proceed to the international check-post at mid-night to be able to cover the event's first car's entry into India. After an hour or so into the night, the staff that had set tables for quick customs and immigration clearances could be seen asleep on the tables; some had just slumped in the garden chairs, fighting sleeplessness, as also the ubiquitous mosquitoes! We passed time by having a close look at the border, which did not have that much infrastructure as it now has – for example, a large visitors' gallery to watch the retreat ceremony at sun-set. The post itself had a non-descript appearance; faced frequent power cuts, outages and failures that further added to the woes of the staff posted there.

It was a long wait. The headlights of the first approaching car from Pakistan, having traversed from Kabul {Afghanistan} touched the tree-tops and the Pakistan Rangers flung open their gates, so did BSF Jawans. The first car roared into India at 5.28 am. It was quite an experience for a 28 year reporter to meet, shake hands and talk to the rally drivers across countries and continents; see their mud-smeared vehicles fitted with powerful engines. They had trudged through quagmire of slush! The first driver said that the participants were running eight hours ahead of scheduled time!

*

Background: I gathered that the 1977 London - Sydney rally was the fourth, the longest, and the last in a series of post -war inter-continental marathon car rallies that began in 1968. The idea was simple: to drive a rally route of 30,000 kms from one Opera House to another - London's Covent Garden to the Sydney Opera House. It began with 12 days on the road through 11 countries from London to Madras before shipping the cars to Malaysia for the stretch down to Singapore; then loading the remaining cars on another ship to take them to Perth before a massive round - Australia section. As the event went along, it became even more grueling than originally advertised.

Shipping problems had delayed the Australia restart by two days. To make the original finish date, that could not be changed, the average speeds were increased and the planned rest halts were ruthlessly cut. Australia turned out to be 13,200 kms in 7 days and 16 hours; a day and night average of 72 km per hour for 184 hours. The route took in mountains, rivers wild enough for a Datsun to float off downstream, and several deserts – the Australia section was a marathon drive in its own right. When the ship arrived late into Freemantle, rather than cancel sections to get the rally back on schedule, it was decided to make up the lost time by simply running it non-stop – for seven days and nights.

*

Much before Wagha had become active and live, India traded through the Hussainiwala border in Ferozepur, where the busts of three great martyrs are displayed at a memorial, commemorating the sacrifices of: Rajguru, Bhagat Singh and Sukhdev, who were clandestinely cremated there after they were hanged in Lahore jail on March 23, 1931.

As a school boy, I would occasionally accompany my maternal grandfather, Arjan Singh Sandhu to the Hussainiwala border, which was the route through which pomegranates and grapes would arrive from Chaman/Kandahar, Afghanistan, and were transported to New Delhi. Some other goods, primarily dry fruit, were also traded. The crude *refrigeration techniques* used by Pathans kept the fruit fresh when it arrived at its destination through rail and road. Despite decades of strife and turbulence, one hears that, of late, with some signs and semblance of normalcy and peace returning to certain areas in Afghanistan, fruit exports to neighbouring regions have again picked up.

*

It is fairly well known that the coolies on either side of the border at Hussainiwala, who were engaged in off loading and loading of trucks had good relations, given the hardships they faced to eke out a living. It were the Pakistani coolies who whispered to Indian counterparts while handing over fruit baskets and packages that an attack was imminent and they better get out. Thus, it was the coolies, who first alerted Indian security forces of the impending attack by Pakistan in 1965.

*

And, then there was the farm my uncle Gurdial Singh Cheema had established in the wilderness of the Sutlej bordering Pakistan- an unmarked border. It was at a place called Dona-Telu-Mal. Even the BOP was named after this village, just a cluster of non-descript mud houses with *Sarkanda* serving as demarcation *wall* between two hamlets. Whenever the river was in spate during monsoon, it would change course, which was quite often, and meander its way at will and the direction it wished to take, washing away large chunks of fertile agricultural land that my uncle and others owned.

At that time, hunting of rabbits and partridges was quite common. We were also fed on stories that for smuggling, the *Rai Sikhs* – settled along the border - had trained horses, as had Pakistanis on the other side of the border. When loaded with contraband, horses would be given *instructions – small pep-talk while thumping and massaging them before their cross-border runs* and speed away they would and stop only at the houses of the identified and designated smugglers in villages on either side. The horses would return the same way!

These trained horses would make us wonder at the *horse- sense* man's friend displayed. On occasions, BSF and the Pakistan Sutlej Rangers would catch or intercept the horses and would return, of course, after paying gratification! Such were the times.

Time to step inside Pakistan, legally!

*

Thank you, Mr Prime Minister!

It was with mixed feelings I proceeded to board the PIA: Pakistan International Airways jet for Lahore from the Indira Gandhi International airport at New Delhi on a November late afternoon {1997}. There was slight nip in the air in the smog-soaked air in the National capital. Yet, I could feel the cold sweat on my palms, as I stood in the queue waiting to board the flight. As I moved forward, my attention was diverted to a uniformed officer near the front wheels of the jet, who had kneeled down on the tarmac to say the *Namaz*! He was the pilot! In 30 minutes the jet landed at Lahore Allama Iqbal international airport; same night, we, a small select group of journalists, were flown to Islamabad.

The next morning memories of Chandigarh came flooding – given the similarities of the two cities - as I stood in front of the white-marble buildings at the toe of Margalla hills. The stately institutions: secretariat blocks-two groups of four interconnected buildings, surrounded by Moughal- style terraced landscape; the five-storey Parliament house; *Aiwan-e-Sadar*: President's house; Prime Minister's housing complex, and his secretariat; and the building of the Supreme Court; all standing like white sentinels against the backdrop of the majestic hills show-cased the capital; the place was referred to as the *Constitutional avenue*! {Officially, Islamabad has the status of capital territory; the city was designed, after being carved out of Rawalpindi. Its master plan was designed by a Greek architect firm: Constantinos Doxiades in 1961; and first offices moved into the new city on October 26, 1966.}

The city –Islamabad - itself is well planned, well landscaped with lot of lush greenery; a reminder of Chandigarh in its early years; now the joint capital of Punjab and Haryana seems no one's baby; the foster parents, the Central government, remote controls it, as a union territory, allowing it to commit hara-kiri! As I said earlier, at the time of my visit these very state instrumentalities, which appeared calm, were in an unprecedented, unanticipated constitutional crisis

*

One of the *foreign* journalists in our group of 34, invited for the intended function was a Sikh lady from Malaysia. The following day, an official of the ministry of foreign affairs asked me to get ready to visit Panja Sahib, as another correspondent also wished to pay obeisance there. One could not have asked for more! It was there the founder of the Sikh faith, Guru Nanak, who had arrived in Hasan Abdal, contained a rock hurled by Wali Kandhari from the hill top at Him and his companion Mardana. In the Gurdwara premises is an imprint of Guru Nanak's palm, which had stopped the rolling rock; hence the name: Panja Sahib!

It was drizzling, when we reached Hasan Abdal. We were received and escorted around the shrine by Wakf official, Manzoor Bhatti. It was a dream fulfilled and prayers answered, as I stepped into the water flowing in a small stream and placed my palm in the Guru's palm print! Inside the Gurdwara, the caretakers, Inder Singh and Partap Singh, offered *Ardas* on my behalf. The quietness added to the serenity and solemnity of the place. The Gurdwara precincts were well-kept.

*

On our way back, we were taken to Taxila Museum. It is situated in Taxila, a tehsil of Rawalpindi. This is a site museum and its collection mainly focuses on Gandharan art. These sites date back to 600 or 700 BC. Construction of Taxila museum started in 1918; its foundation stone was laid by Lord Chelmsford, Viceroy of India in 1918. Construction was concluded in 1928; the museum was opened to public by Sir Habibullah, the then Minister for Education. Sir John Marshall, who was going to be retired from the post of Director- General of the Archaeological Survey of India in 1928, could not complete its original plan. The government of Pakistan constructed the northern gallery in 1998. There are some 4,000 objects displayed, including stone, stucco, terracotta, silver, gold, iron and semiprecious stones. Mainly the display consists of objects from the period 600 B.C to 500 AD. Buddhist, Hindu and Jain religions, are well represented through these objects discovered from three ancient cities and more than two dozen Buddhist stupas and monasteries and Greek temples in the region.

Taxila museum has one of the most significant and comprehensive collections of stone Buddhist sculpture from the first to the seventh centuries in Pakistan - known as Gandhara art. The core of the collection comes from excavated sites in the Taxila Valley, particularly the exactions of Sir John Marshall. Other objects come from excavated sites elsewhere in Gandharan, from donations such as the Ram Das Collection, or from material confiscated by the police and custom authorities. The whole collection contains more than 1,400 objects, and 409 have been published. The Taxila Museum is a site museum and is the repository for the majority of the numismatic material found during archaeological work in Taxila. Digging began in

1917 under John Marshall, then director of the Archaeological Survey of India, and continued until 1934. Since those excavations, work has continued to the present day. The museum contains a large collection of coins from the period of the Indo-Greeks to the late Kushans. Some of these are published in Marshall's original excavation reports, and an ongoing project exists to publish the full collection. This was a unique experience and very educative.

*

The visit to Nankana Sahib was as dramatic as it was unanticipated, since only a day was left to return home. How it materialized is fascinating; it sticks in memory as fresh as ever.

*

This is what happened: After the inauguration of the motorway, at a banquet in Islamabad, when we were introduced to the Prime Minister, Nawaz Sharif, he shook hands with me and asked me: *Nankana Sahib Ibadat kar li je?* Have you paid obeisance at Nankana Sahib? I replied, *No sir, the visa expires tomorrow and we are returning*. On hearing this he held my hand and said: *No, no, you must visit it*; he spoke more to himself than telling me. He turned to an official standing close by and gave some instructions. My air ticket and passport were taken. My travel plans were rescheduled; and my visa extended. Arrangements were made to escort me to Nankana Sahib the next day itself, a Sunday.

*

On arrival at Lahore, I was lodged in a five-star hotel, all expenses paid, and given a room in *no-smoking* area! The following morning, after breakfast, a public relations official arrived to escort me to Nankana Sahib, 85 kms away. Our vehicle followed a police pilot Gypsy. On the way, he gave a running commentary, interspersed with some polite conversation; and later he assisted me in shopping. At Nankana Sahib, Jamil, an official made passport entries in an old, tattered register, and escorted me around. The main Sewadar at the Gurdwara, Partap Singh, had been there for the past 37 years. He served us *Langar*! Another old hand there was Ishar Singh, who had been living there for the past 20 years. I learned that the tradition of *Langar* had been introduced for the past six months or so; I partook *Langar*. I was told there were about 55 Sikh families residing in Nankana; and 150 students studied in a school run at Patti Sahib.

There are seven Gurdwaras associated with the life of Guru Nanak, the first Guru. Besides Nankana, the *Janamasthan* of the Guru and the main Gurdwara, I visited two other shrines: Gurdwara Baal Leela, where Nanak played with other children, and Gurdwara Patti Sahib, where Nanak taught the *Pandha* engaged by his father, Mehta Kalu to teach him. Besides *Jatha*s from India, sponsored, supported and organized by the SGPC, the place is frequented by the Sikhs living in Peshawar and the Sindhis. A vast expanse of land is attached to the Gurdwara. The same was true of Gurdwara Dehra Sahib, where Guru Arjan was tortured to martyrdom; and, alongside is *Samadhi* of Maharaja Ranjit Singh. The ashes of this great ruler of Punjab lie in a dome adjacent to the Hazoori Bagh. {Thank you, Mr Prime Minister for the *Niwazish*!}

*

Kalashnikovs and Narcotics

The journey to NWFP is memorable for the simple reason that in this region, Michni post, 3,600 feet above the mean sea level, is closed to foreigners. It was, thus, quite a bonus to have gained entry to that area, as part of visiting foreign media team! It was a planned, guided tour.

We left Islamabad for Peshawar, 187 km away, before dawn when Sun rise was still a few hours away; the cold winter morning of November 27, 1997 was still enveloped in darkness. The early start was in view of the anticipated heavy traffic, as well due to work in progress, as a new Motorway was under construction from Islamabad to Peshawar, NWFP capital city, similar to the one that had been built from Islamabad to Lahore. The second reason, we learnt on reaching Peshawar, was to be in time for breakfast with NWFP Governor Lt. Gen. Arif Bangash {Retd.}

Meeting Gen. Bangash in the sprawling Governor's House in the cantonment area was an informative and educative experience in itself. The grandeur and splendor of the Governor House only made the event memorable. During the time spent at breakfast and conversations with other guests and some hours spent in the city late in the evening enabled me to form some impressions of what the place was like, given its geo-political location.

*

Peshawar, the capital of Khyber Pakhtunkhwa province of Pakistan, is the largest city of Khyber Pakhtunkhwa and by the 1998 census was the ninth-largest city of Pakistan. But now the estimated population of Peshawar has crossed 3.5 million making it the fifth largest city in Pakistan. It is a metropolitan city and the administrative centre and economic hub for the FATA: Federally Administered Tribal Areas of Pakistan. The city is situated in a large valley near the eastern end of the Khyber Pass, close to the Pak-Afghan border. Peshawar is irrigated by various canals of the Kabul River and by its right tributary, the Bara River. Peshawar's recorded history goes back as far as at least 539 BC, making it the oldest living city in Pakistan and one of the oldest in South Asia.

*

In NWFP, we were told, two discernible and distinct cultures were: one of Kalashnikovs {remember the AK-47 and its improved versions and variants militants used during the height of terrorism in Punjab}; and the second of narcotics, as a consequence of the war between the Taliban and nine other factions in Afghanistan. Whatever might have been the geo-political compulsions of Pakistan and other countries that meddled in Afghanistan's affairs in the past decades, the fact remained that the region was reaping what it had sown. {The situation is no better at present.} At the time of my visit, in Peshawar alone, there were estimated 1.25 million Afghan refugees, who had set up establishments and were looked upon as *parasites* on the host country's economy, which in any case was then in a shambles; {not that it is any better now}. Though the hosts gave the refugees food permits, the living conditions were appalling.

*

During a brief round of the place, one saw the small-arms bazaar with r*ehries* and shanties displaying AK series' assault rifles, hand grenades and ammunition; keeping a weapon and flaunting it was not only fashionable but also a passion {it still is} with the *Pathanas*; particularly, the tribesmen of the Province, who live in the Khyber area. As I saw the weapons and hand grenades on the pushcarts, a smiling Pathan holding an AK-47 said: *Sardar ji, tofa samajh ke le jao*: take it as a gift!

It also emerged that the area was known for poppy cultivation and after it was processed, as heroin, through India, it found its way to the West. Bangash told me that steps were being taken to check the spread of Kalashnikovs and drug culture. He was candid when talking of the two problems: AK assault rifles and drug trafficking. He said: we *are keen to develop the area as a travel or tourism hub and also to streamline the assembling of AK series rifles in the Darra area so that these could be exported after being manufactured in the Province, as part of promoting and developing cottage industry!*

In our conversation, Bangash described making of weapons by the local artisans and others as *cottage industry* in the Darra belt: home to copying and manufacturing of small arms {heavy weapons are banned and barred}, which the government was keen to promote, given the fact for the past 100 years, the belt, which leads further to Kohat, had been supplying arms to the tribesmen.

*

Darra Adam Khel, 42 km from Peshawar is a town in the FATA covering Frontier Region Peshawar and Frontier Region Kohat. It is mostly inhabited by Pashtuns of the Afridi clan, the Adam Khel. The town consists of one main street lined with shops, with some alleys and side streets containing workshops. Darra Adam Khel is devoted entirely to the production of ordnance. Located in between Kohat and Peshawar, around 40 kms south of Peshawar, a wide variety of firearms are produced in the town, from anti-aircraft guns to pen-guns. Weapons are handmade by individual craftsmen using traditional manufacturing techniques, usually handed down father-to-son. Guns are regularly tested by test-firing into the air. Darra is controlled by the local tribesmen.

Darra Adam Khel is an unkempt village of two storey wood and adobe buildings in the sand stone hills near the Kohat Frontier region. It is the *gun factory* of the Tribal Areas. Though, Darra - Adam Khel denotes a clan of the Afridi Tribe – and is inside Pakistan but has certain special laws, as compared to rest of Pakistan. The Darra arms trade first fired up in 1897. This arms trade has won fame for the Adam Khel Afridis, who are the major inhabitants of the town. Most of the people there seem to make or sell just one thing, i.e., guns, while the second largest business of the inhabitants is - transport.

In the arcades off the main road are workshops; hundreds of closet-sized rooms, where men and boys make working copies of the entire world's guns with nothing more than hand tools and a small drill press. The tools are astonishingly primitive, yet the forges turn out accurate reproduction of every conceivable sort of weapon, from pen-pistols and hand-grenades to automatic rifles and anti-aircraft guns. The copies are so painstakingly reproduced that even the serial number of the original is carried over. A Darra gunsmith, given a rifle he hasn't seen before, can duplicate it in around ten days. Once the first copy is made, each additional copy takes two or three days due to the templates created. Handguns, being more complex, take a little longer.

In Darra, almost three-fourths of the people are in the gun trade. Pen pistols and walking stick guns are popular here. Around 400-700 guns are made in Darra each day and the number is rising with the adoption of more tools. These guns are more than enough for the Pashtuns themselves. Many guns find their way to and from Afghanistan. In the 1980s, heroin was shut down in the markets after consultation with the tribal elders due to foreign pressure, but guns, known as the ornaments of a Pashtun, could not be eliminated. Manufacturing of heavy ammunition, however, has been closed down.

*

Bangash further informed me that as a result of government measures, the production of poppy had come down from 850 tonnes in 1996, to barely 20 tonnes in 1997. He went on: *There is no unit or heroin processing mechanism in NWFP now. We are trying to change the attitude of the people and offering alternative crops, which can give them, if not the same, at least the maximum returns. Compare to it the poppy production in Afghanistan, where it is 2,800 tonnes per annum from nearly 30 lakh acres. Pakistan is totally against the smuggling of narcotics and drugs and in the next five-to-six years, you will find the difference.* Bangash, who was in a reminiscent mood, said a major proposal was to set up hi-tech industry in the province.

*

In so far as poppy or opium cultivation goes, next door Afghanistan is far ahead of Pakistan's Khyber Pakhtunkhwa region. The latest survey of the United Nations Office on Drugs and Crime data on Afghanistan opium survey {2015} shows that the total value of unprocessed opium there is $572,000,000. And, a total of 183,000 hectares area is under poppy cultivation! In other words, over 67 per cent of the world's illicit opium products originate from Afghanistan, where 1.3 million Afghan adults are drug users. The other disturbing aspect of opium trade is the deep and wide spread involvement of Taliban, who now control drug cartels. The data also reveals that 97 per cent of the poppy cultivation takes place in the southern, eastern and western regions of the country with Helmand province leading the pack with 47 per cent of the total poppy area: 86,443 hectares; followed by Farah, Kandahar and Badghis. Poppy or opium is a thriving business!

*

In fact, it was a paradox to learn that Peshawar was known as the *city of flowers,* on the one hand, and a sprawling conglomerate – crowded, chaotic and polluted, on the other hand, where traffic policemen wore masks! And, its markets were stacked with perfumes, cut-glass and crystal wares. Peshawar has been a seat of learning with its famous Islamia College. Local people, I learned, were greatly influenced by Khushal Khan Khattar, a warrior-poet, and Rehman Baba, a preacher and poet of Pashto.

*

Terror-struck!

Things changed rapidly after September 11, 2001 with the terrorist attacks on the USA, which brought down the Twin Towers of the World Trade Centre in New York.

As this sensational news spread around the globe, the date, November 27, 1997, flashed in my mind: four years ago, it was a bright sunny day with cool breeze blowing across the Khyber Pass. I had stood atop the Michni post on the Pakistan-Afghanistan border surveying the hostile terrain. The place had been of strategic importance throughout the history of civilization. Name an invader, and he had marched across this Pass. From the look around the place, one could make out that NWFP was a backward area with several belts still inaccessible. Electricity, roads, education and other necessities were yet to be provided. The hills that surrounded it were brown and barren and rocky. The area, however, was rich in mines and minerals.

*

I recall that day – November 27, 1997 - because following 9/11, a war had been declared against an elusive, invisible foe ensconced somewhere in that forbidding terrain of Pakistan-Afghanistan border that I had visited. The media - electronic, print and internet - of that time was full of news of terrorism, war, warlords; and world powers had formed a coalition against the *enemy*. The live coverage of *Operation Enduring Freedom* and unending visuals had entered millions of homes: TV screens blazed with field operations and aftermath stories after the *Attack on the US*.

The war in Afghanistan had cast a dark, wide shadow over Peshawar, as more refugees poured in swelling the number of teaming millions already camping there! One wondered if by attacking Taliban the world would ever win and combat terrorism, which had manifested into various variants, across decades and time. There are a variety of Taliban dressed as they do in loose and baggy *Salwar-kameez*! They are natives of a land that bears deep scars of many a war. For centuries, violence has been as much in Taliban's veins, as in their backyards, right from the time of Genghis Khan and since the British gave Afghanistan freedom in 1919. And, lest we forget, there are no *good* or *bad* Taliban, nurtured as they have been for decades by different countries and political regimes for their own narrow selfish ends, ever arming them with arms and ammunition!

*

To understand, firsthand, the story of the Afghan warlords or Taliban, I read Ahmed Rashid's immensely readable book: *Taliban* in January 2001. It was first published in 2000, as *Taliban: Islam Oil and the New Great Game in Central Asia*. Rashid updated his book with a *new foreword* and published it in 2001. This was, perhaps, necessitated because of the tragic events of September 11 that had brought the Taliban into sharp focus, as the most radical and extreme Islamist movement in the world.

The following quote from the author's *new foreword*, post- September 2001 is worth reproducing: *Since 1989 the US and the West have ignored Afghanistan's continuing civil war. On 11 September 2001 the world changed forever, as Afghanistan visited the world in a brutal, tragic fashion. The nineteen suicide bombers, who hijacked four planes and then rammed three of them into the twin towers of the World Trade Centre in New York and the Pentagon in Washington, belonged to the Al'Qaida organization led by Osman Bin Laden, which is based in Taliban-ruled Afghanistan. Their targets were the heart of the post-Cold War world, the nerve centre of globalization and the supposed international efforts to make the world a safer, better place.*

And, eight years later, in 2009, followed two more books similar in character and description as Rashid's. One, Antonio Giustozzi's - *Empires of Mud: Wars and Warlords in Afghanistan;* and second, Gretchen Peters' *Seeds of Terror: How Drugs, Thugs, and Crime Are Reshaping the Afghan War.* The two books together provide an insight into the psyche of the Taliban and warlords –who wish to be participants in state formation - and how external interventions would never help Afghanistan, where fight or war is not so much based on either religion or ideology but on controlling sub-national territories, as it is the vast expense of poppy fields in southern Afghanistan, which yield money to the warlords to get armed. The Afghanistan poppy is transferred to processing labs; and for money laundering the trade goes to Karachi or Dubai; no wonder the convoys are guarded by stringer missiles!

*

Frankly, my understanding of the scenario, though it is inconsequential, after having read the books and talked to a cross-section of people in Pakistan and back home in India was/is that terrorism was/is here to stay, globally; things may get worse, not reverse, notwithstanding all the technology, science, arms, ammunition, weaponry available to the world governments. And, perhaps, terrorism has stayed on in more menacing and gruesome ways than one that were, largely, unanticipated.

Each time terrorism explodes anywhere, dealing death, destruction and sniffing out innocent lives, the powers that be shriek louder to show their determination to fight terrorism, terrorists, Taliban, ISIS, Boko Haram, merchants of death or mercenaries or by whatever other name or word you may chose to describe them. This inhuman cult, wherein, man slaughters man in the 21st century world, continues unabated.

Also, internecine conflicts, clashes and upheavals among different Muslim sects, communities, ethnic groups: *Shias* or *Sunnis* within and outside Afghanistan and Pakistan would only become more commonplace, frequent and pronounced; ever exporting death, mayhem and killings outside their geographical territories, as well, to strike a blow to other cultures, communities, civilizations; and the *Infidels*, as fundamentalists and radicals call others. They are also intolerant of even centuries old archaeological, architectural and heritage monuments and statues!

For centuries, the future of the *people* in Pakistan and Afghanistan, as also other nations in similarly placed situations, has remained uncertain, despite world governments' political and diplomatic endevours at forging alliances and maintaining that the war against terrorism was not against any *religion* or *innocent people.* Yet, these people have suffered and continue to suffer - internally and externally - dispossessed of their homes and hearths even as the rest of world remains vulnerable to terrorist attacks. Ripples of war against terrorism, anywhere in the world, impact one and all. And, in Pakistan, I learned that disturbed and turbulent conditions in Afghanistan were having a cascading effect even on neighbouring countries that encircle it: Tajikistan, Turkmenistan, Uzbekistan and Iran, while in Iraq and Syria things seem to have gone from bad to worse due to ISIS. Yet, Pakistan cannot be absolved of its nefarious designs and role for happenings in Afghanistan.

In fact, reports of fear of bio-terrorism, use of chemical and biological means, photographs of people in masks, mailing of anthrax, fear of mass food poisoning through salmonella or e.coli or release of nerve gases like Sarin or VX, sent a chill down the spine. However, these thoughts did not cross my mind, as I had stood at the Michni post that November morning in 1997. And, less than four years later, echo of the pounding bombs in that area had changed the geo-politics, while daily new strategies began to be drawn to meet the new enemy: *global terrorism* and *Jihad*!

*

Jihad is an Islamic term, referring to the religious duty of Muslims to maintain the religion. In Arabic, the word Jihad is a noun meaning *to strive, to apply oneself, to struggle, to persevere.* A person engaged in jihad is called a Mujahid, the plural of which is Mujahedeen. The word *Jihad* appears frequently in the Quran often in the idiomatic expression *striving in the way of God (al-jihad fi sabil Allah)*, to refer to the act of striving to serve the purposes of God on this earth. All Muslims and scholars do not agree on its definition. Many observers—Muslim and non-Muslim—as well as the *Dictionary of Islam*, talk of *Jihad* having two meanings: an inner spiritual struggle {the *greater Jihad*}, and an outer physical struggle against the enemies of Islam {the *lesser Jihad*}, which may take a violent or non-violent form. *Jihad* is often translated as *Holy War*, although this term is controversial. According to Orientalist Bernard Lewis, *The overwhelming majority of classical theologians, jurists*, and specialists in the *Hadith, understood the obligation of Jihad in a military sense.* Javed Ahmad Ghamidi states that there is consensus among Islamic scholars that the concept of *Jihad* will always include armed struggle against wrong doers.

*

There are reports that stung by terror and terrorism in its own backyard, Pakistan kicked off the *Zarb-e-azb* campaign in 2014 with military dealing blows to the *Jihadists* but the ideology continues to thrive. One is flummoxed by the dichotomy of the anti-militancy drives. While, on the one hand, known hate-mongers and preachers, who spew venom in the name of Islam, continue to roam free under state protection and patronage, rather than being arrested; the establishment chooses to switch off cell-phone net-works, on the other hand! In fact, the *war-cry* of *Jihad* has been sounded across the globe. Simultaneously, world powers have also launched a war against terrorism; not *Islam*. In this grim scenario with stark fault-lines visible everywhere, what the future holds for the world and mankind is unknown. Is geography being re-drawn? Is new history in the making?

And, yet, despite global concerns and some action, there still does not seem to be any comprehensive plan to counter terrorism for an effective peace in several distraught, destabilized and disturbed countries. Writing on this issue, Rod Nordland in one of his dispatches from Islamabad to *The New York Times* concluded that the *whole menace of terrorism cannot be dealt with purely as a security threat. The ideological* threat *still needed to be addressed.* He was quoting Muhammad Amir Rana, the director of the Pak institute for peace studies.

*

Even as Jihad alone was not enough, the world has been shocked and rocked by the rise of a new cult: emergence of the Islamic state of Iraq and Levant, alternatively translated as the Islamic state of Iraq and Syria or Islamic state of Iraq and al-Sham – ISIS; a militant group that adheres to an Islamic fundamentalist Wahhabi doctrine of Sunni-Islam. Derived from its Arabic name *ad-Dawlah al-*

Islāmiyah, the group is also known by the acronym *Daesh*. It proclaimed a worldwide caliphate in June 2014, with Abu Bakr al-Baghdadi being named its Caliph. As a caliphate, it claims religious, political and military authority over all Muslims, worldwide. The UN and several countries reject such a claim. Such resurgence of religion in the 21st century reminds one of the passive intensity the militia of Islamic State follows, adheres to and wants to propagate, globally. Islamic State's diktats on how to or how not to treat women slaves - taken hostages- as objects of sex, has shocked the civilized world community.

*

Romance of Khyber

It was a panoramic view from atop the Michni post of the Suleiman hills, which form the western border of Pakistan with Afghanistan. The post, manned by Khyber Rifles of Pakistan-KR, as I said earlier, is not open to foreigners! During the day-long stay in that region I found that prime attraction of Peshawar remained the Khyber Pass, which at places was as broad as 1.5 km, and at another point, as narrow as 16 meters. There was a time when only two camels, one loaded, the other unloaded, could barely pass through the narrow part.

KR Captain Mudassar Raza Siami, assigned to brief us was articulate, knowledgeable and affable. Yet, he kept the briefing short, concise and to the point. He pointed to a village, not very far, and said *Torkham is the last border village.* The word Khyber is from Hebrew language, meaning - small fort or fortress.

*

Since the invasion of the Aryans around 1600 BC, all the invaders, except the Europeans and the Arabs had used the Khyber Pass, as a western entry point to the Indo-Pak subcontinent. This Pass is witness to history and many a conquest of man in his hunger to expand territory and rule. This Pass had seen hordes of Aryans, Greeks, Seljukes, Tartars, Huns, Mongols, Mughals and Persians entering the plains of India. Some of the great captains of war, who had passed this way, include: Alexander the Great, Sultan Mehmood of Ghazni, Sultan Mohammad of Ghaur, Changez Khan, Taimur the Lame, Zaheer-uddin Babbar, Nadir Shah and Ahmed Shah Abdali. History tells us that while Alexander himself used the Hawa Pass to cross over, his troops marched through Khyber. Remnants of Timaur's *torture chamber* could still be seen from the post down below. Capt Siami gave details how it operated. It was bloodcurdling narrative!

*

Before we left Peshawar for onward journey to Michni, after breakfast with the Governor, a pilot vehicle with armed personnel of the KR preceded our bus. Travelling and crossing low stony hills, marked by historic places, and capped by KR jawans was quite a sight! The people who worked on the roads or in the fields in low hills looked rugged, tough and strong. The villages or habitats spattering the hills were mud-plastered; box-like structures presenting a forlorn look. One barely saw any women, save at places taking buckets of water, as they trudged through nearly dried up streams and rivulets. Children could be seen playing cricket with crude out of shape tree branches cut to serve as wickets; simple sticks! Frankly, the place, the landscape, the environment were awesome.

*

En route one also saw the Jamraud fort, right at the entrance of Khyber Pass. It is located besides Bab-e-Khyber at the entrance to the Khyber Pass in the FATA. In October 1836, Jamraud was conquered from the Khyberis by the Sikhs. Hari Singh, 1791-1837, a well-known Sikh general, proposed to build a big fort at Jamraud. The proposal was opposed; nevertheless the foundation of the fort that has survived was laid by him on 18 December, 1836; and the construction was completed in 54 days. The fort is noted for its 10 feet {3 m} thick walls. In the fort area is the grave of Hari Singh Nalwa, who died after being killed by Yousafzai of Peshawar in 1837 in a battle of Sikhs, Punjabis and Pashtuns. The gravestone at Hari Singh's tomb reads that Nalwa was cremated on April 30, 1837 and the place was built in his memory by a commoner: Babu Gujjumal Kapur of Peshawar in 1892. The writing on the tomb is in Urdu, English and Punjabi. Ahead of Jamraud is the Shagat fort, built in 1929 by the British to guard various approaches to the Pass. One had a distant look at even the Ali Masjid fort at the narrowest portion of the Pass: just three meters wide once; now 33 meters.

*

As we climbed up the almost barren, brown rugged hills ringed by high rise Hindukush mountain ranges, a railway track running alongside all the way from

Peshawar to Landi Kotal also came into view. It was visible from Michni post, as well. This track, Siami told us, is a wonderful miracle of engineering and passes over 92 bridges and through 34 tunnels. It took 19 years to build. It was commissioned in 1921 by a British engineer, Victor Bally. It had cost Rs 210 million {$5.5 million}. If one combined together bridges and tunnels these would add up to a length of five kms. What was more interesting to know was that the first train that chugged into Landi Kotal from Peshawar was driven by a woman: Lady Victor Bally!

*

Landi Kotal is a small town of the FATA. It is at the western edge of the Khyber Pass that traditionally marks the entrance to Afghanistan. It is the highest point along the pass at 1,072 meters above sea level; it is the headquarters of the FATA. It is on the route across the mountains to the city of Peshawar. Landi Kotal is a tourist destination. It is accessible by road from elsewhere in Pakistan or from the Afghanistan border just five kilometers to the west. It is also the terminus railway station of Khyber Pass Railway. A tourist train, the Khyber train safari was run on this railway. It was closed in 2006 due to washing away of railway track and bridges by flood. The place is the main shopping centre for both the Shinwaris and Afridi tribes.

*

On way to the KR's Mess, we were informed that the Khyber Pass road, right up to Afghan border was two-way international highway that further leads tourists and visitors to Central Asian states of Uzbekistan, Tajikistan and Turkmenistan. The road was constructed by Emperor Jalal-ud-Din Akbar in 1581; the British carpeted it in 1921.

The KR Mess turned out to be more of a museum, where right from its origin up to the last visitor, including the late Lady Diana, find a mention. Depicted through pictures, maps and souvenirs, the Mess mirrors the past and recalls the role and the part played by the Rifles, since 1878.

*

Talks with locals in Peshawar later that day, revealed that Khyber Pass is inhabited by several tribes: groups of people with common race, belief, customs, languages, culture and traditions. The most common were: Afridis, Mullagories, Shilwasnis and Shinwaris. In fact, 70 per cent of the Shinwaris live in Afghanistan and the remaining 30 per cent in Pakistan. These tribesmen are best of friends and worst of enemies!

*

Last word

The eight days spent in Pakistan, away from home, yet so close, remain memorable, as much because of the pilgrimage I was able to undertake, as travels right up to Afghanistan border. And, of course, the experience gained, as a journalist. The background material that we were given at the Foreign office, the longest briefing that I have ever attended anywhere and later interaction with the common people revealed that problems the two countries faced were not very dissimilar. From bureaucrats to diplomats to ordinary shop-owners, whom I met in Islamabad, Lahore and Peshawar, every one kept mentioning, time-and-again, just one word - *Kashmir*. Some even talked about *Khalistan*! Even during polite conversations invariably Pakistanis would drop in the line: *Let us have a no war pact.*

*

In fact, during the Lahore-Islamabad motorway inauguration ceremony, while we stopped en route at a point for refreshments and where several other people had also stopped to stretch their legs and greet the Prime Minister, Nawaz Sharif, an unexpected incident took place. One of the non-resident Pakistan media-person walked up to me and said, with a twinkle in his eyes and a faint starchiness in his voice: *we have built this road for your use; ultimately it will benefit your troops more. Let us be friends.* He had said the obvious unsaid. I understood. I just smiled and kept quiet.

*

And, there were several scores of other people, who spoke about of the sameness in the two countries: galloping population, growing pollution, corruption, joblessness, economic crisis and even the need to downsize the respective governments, spreading network of education and health facilities coupled with civic amenities, besides, of course, rural development and paying greater attention to agricultural productivity and production.

*

Reverting to the foreign office briefing, I must say here that major time and attention there was, naturally, focused on *Kashmir*, putting across Pakistan's view point and asserting that it remained a *disputed* issue. India was lambasted for not conceding the same. The briefing, if I correctly recall, was by the Additional Foreign Secretary {Asia-Pacific}, Tariq Altaf, who was otherwise also the official spokesperson of foreign affairs; and Aftab Hussain Sayed, another Additional Foreign Secretary looking after the economic coordination and economic countries' organization. {Like many a commoner, who spoke of need to downsize the bureaucracy, the two foreign officials had also repeatedly talked of the government policy of offering 'golden handshake' to bring about austerity, financial prudence and cut down on unproductive expenditure, bring about fiscal discipline and curb financial profligacy.}

*

In the kit given to us at the foreign office briefing, there was a 24-page tract: *India's True Face- Myth and Reality.* Its author was a columnist and news analyst Ahmed Hasan Sheikh. Then, there was another small booklet, six pages in all, titled: *Kashmir Issue-in a nutshell.* The never-ending and nerve-wrecking *briefing* was the longest one had attended in years, as a journalist, anywhere. We had no choice but to listen!

*

On occasions, when we were faced with unexpected encounters with motor mouths, in or outside the system {government}, and which were unavoidable and required speaking up and speaking out, we became diplomatic using tact and politeness. This, however, proved only one point: an average Pakistani was obsessed with *Kashmir* and nurtured a psychological fear of a war with India. Thus, invariably, he asked for a *no war pact* between the two neighbors. As a matter of policy, indoctrination against India at all levels seemed wide, deep and an on-going process - this much one could sense from the polite conversations and judging from the media reports. Yet, the impression given was that Pakistan diplomats felt the *dire need for operationalization of the mechanism to resume talks in the light of the Male spirit.*

*

Interestingly, the exit of Prime Minister I K Gujral was taken cognizance of by the Pakistan media and the people. Rather than worrying about the on-going Constitutional crisis and conflict of interests in their country, the establishment and the people talked more about the untimely exit of Gujral that really seemed to have shaken them!

Enquiries of this state of mind revealed that between the two Punjabi Prime ministers, Gujral and Nawaz Sharif; and the two-establishments, the people had found new hopes of co-existence in the future. Such hopes had rekindled following efforts by the two leaders across several months to find a solution for mutual development and economic prosperity under the umbrella provided for by the SAARC agreement and the SAPTA- South Asian Preferential Trading Agreement- and SAFTA- South Asian Free Trade Area provisions. That was the time when the *Gujral doctrine* was framed.

*

The Gujral Doctrine is a set of five principles to guide the conduct of foreign relations with India's immediate neighbors, notably Pakistan. The United Front Government's neighborhood policy stood on five basic principles: First, with the neighbours like Nepal, Bangladesh, Bhutan, Maldives and Sri Lanka, India does not ask for reciprocity but gives all that it can in good faith and trust. Secondly, no South Asian country will allow its territory to be used against the interest of another country of the region. Thirdly, none will interfere in the internal affairs of another. Fourthly, all South Asian countries must respect each other's territorial integrity and sovereignty. And finally, they will settle all their disputes through peaceful bilateral negotiations. These five principles, scrupulously observed, will, Gujral had enunciated, would recast South Asia's regional relationship, including the tormented relationship between India and Pakistan, in a friendly, cooperative mould. Inder Kumar Gujral, born December 4, 1919, passed away on November 30, 2012. He served as the Prime Minister from April 1997 to March 1998. He was the third PM to be from the Rajya Sabha, the first being Indira Gandhi and the second H D Deve Gowda.

*

Across decades, India and Pakistan have had an estranged relationship rather than an engaged partnership that would have been in the larger interest of their people and for the economic emancipation of the two countries. Peace alone can ensure development and good neighborly relations, including people to people exchange programmes, trade, commerce and resource sharing etc.

As of now, the two nuclear states, India and Pakistan, remain distant neighbours! The situation in Pakistan is more complex than it appears, since Army there plays an important role. Experienced political and defence analysts make us believe that despite all provocations and export of terrorists and terrorism, the two countries have no option but to ensure talks continue; and talking the two sides have been; outcome, however, remains as distant, as the two distant neighbours remain!

32

Twin-cities

Posting to Ambala was the last thing to ever cross my mind. I was sent to Amritsar when the city celebrated its 400th foundation anniversary in 1977; the city was founded by Guru Ram Das, who established Chak Ramdaspur in 1577. Though a short stint, it was educative in more ways than one, giving an insight into the life of the *Amritsari or is it Ambarsaria!*

I was back to Bathinda. And then it happened: in one of the not so cordial meetings with Prem Bhatia, he had bluntly told me that he would send me: *to a place in interior Haryana, where you would not get even a glass of water to drink!* With the passage of time, things got sorted out and I stayed put in Bathinda for some more years. Then, one day, the orders came for Ambala. Never ever having had a god-father, I packed up; reached Ambala, a city divided in two distinct parts: the old and the cantonment area – the twin cities about three km apart - in January 1982. All offices of consequence were in old city *–Ambala Shehar*; courts were divided between the two cities with some courts of judicial magistrates housed, as these were, in old, dilapidated buildings in the Cantonment area.

To know Ambala, the district and the twin cities, I ventured into the central state library, where the technical section had kept all the 11 volumes of 102-year old Imperial Gazetteer of India. I found that the Gazetteer was priced at 3 Pound 3 Shillings. Morrison and Gibb, Edinburgh had published it in 1881. Its pages had turned pale yellow. Every time I opened a volume and held a page from the corner, a small chip of the crisp paper tore off. Despite utmost care, the corners of pages kept snapping every now and then; so brittle were the volumes! I asked the person in charge about digitizing such a rich treasure trove so as to preserve it for posterity. He shrugged!

Going through the volumes at random, I came across small pieces of printed papers of varying shapes and sizes tucked between the folds of the Gazetteers. Several pages had already been damaged and torn, as if someone had cut them with a pair of scissors. I smelt that something valuable was missing from the precious treasure stacked before me.

The volumes, based on various statistical surveys gave interesting facts of each of the administrative and political divisions of the country. It had been compiled *within moderate limits of time*, as the secretary of state to the government of India wrote in a dispatch dated February 22, 1877. Volume IX contained what I was looking for: it was on Ambala city and the district, as a whole.

I learnt that the cantonment the British had set up in 1813 was on 7,220 acres. The well laid out town had *peepal* trees planted on important roads. The most beautiful landmark was the Church – an architectural marvel. St Paul's Church in Ambala Cantonment, I learnt, was one of the oldest churches in the region. The work on the St Paul Cathedral began in 1855. The building work was carried out by the British Army, who first built a wooden model of the church. During the first war of Independence in 1857, the British had taken refuge in the church. It was consecrated on January 4, 1857.

It was bombed during the September 1965 Indo-Pak war. The bombing by a Pakistani aircraft considerably destroyed the beautiful church building and all that I saw each time I passed that way were remains of the church towers. The church had sustained extensive damage due to the bombing. Previously, the church compound was spread over 21 acres of land and later a large area was acquired by the Air Force authorities for a school and other purposes. It was widely believed that the aircraft which bombed the church had actually missed nearby IAF airfield and had hit the church, as it was situated close to the air force station.

Ambala, the Gazetteer recorded, derived its name from an Amba Rajput. It was founded in the 14th century. As to the city, the streets were narrow, dark and torturous; an elephant could not pass through them. The water supply was insufficient. The place was, however, suitable for commercial purposes. Being close to the hills, Ambala was known for trade in ginger and turmeric. Its exports included: cotton goods, grains and carpets. The imports consisted of cloth, iron, salt, silk and wool.

Race-wise, Jats dominated; both the Hindus and the Sikhs were known for their industry and frugal habits; pottery was their hereditary handicraft. Bordering the hills were Gujjars, both Hindus and Muslims with cattle rearing and breeding as their main vocation. A considerable chunk of the population belonged to the lower castes. Fever was the most common disease and bowl complaints were common complaints. The gazetteer further stated that smallpox was endemic and blindness prevailed to a large extent: the ratio of the blind to the healthy for the district was 1:126; against 1:1037 in England of those days! Ghaggar is the natural dividing line between Punjab and Haryana, now.

I discovered from the volume that goiter and cretinism were common on the banks of the Ghaggar, where diseases of the spleen were also prevalent. Consequently, villagers along the Ghaggar were unhealthy. Death rate, as a result of health problems was 23 per 1,000 of the population; this was in 1872. When cis-Sutlej came under British protection in 1809, Ambala was held by Daya Kaur, widow of Gurbakash Singh, a Sikh possessor. Though she was elected by Maharaja Ranjit Singh in 1803, she was reinstated by General Ocherlony. She died in 1823. Then, residence of the political agent was set up here. Now, 34 years later, I wonder what has become of that rich treasure and how *well preserved may be* those 11 volumes, which provided me a volume of information and knowledge!

*

Ambala posting showed me a new dimension of reporting. There not being much of *spot reporting*, as we say in our profession, this left me with plenty of time to travel and discover new territory; which I did. And, thanks to my senior colleague O N Garg, who represented the *Indian Express* at Ambala, we became permanent companions on the move, as also family friends; and never had any quarrels over professional issues. We worked independently and in an autonomous manner, yet with proper understanding of neither stepping on the other's toes, nor betraying!

The new dimension of reporting resulted in doing over a hundred-odd photo-features for *The Tribune* based on sojourns into the interior of Haryana, on to its forest areas, remote villages and small towns and choked, unlivable *Bastis* or shanties and development projects under way stretching from Kalka to Hathni Kund Barrage to Nanak Dairy in Gurgaon; getting to know one of the oldest IAF station and much more. The visits to Pinjore, Morni hills, Kalka, Naraingarh and Yamuna

Nagar, Kalesar forests, Chacharauli villages etc. and drive up to Ponta Sahib were added attractions!

Ambala was then also known for its electronic goods, mixes, scientific instruments, models and equipment. Much has changed across the decades. One does not have to fear crossing the Grand Trunk road from Railway station to the Bus station opposite it. The passage to the National capital no longer gets clogged and chocked with frequent traffic jams. There are flyovers for smooth flow of traffic on this *Shahi* road! With this preamble, I share some experiences of stay in the Haryana city.

*

The last mango!

That day, as we came out of district public relations office in Ambala city, I asked O N Garg why he was unusually quiet and not his usual self. He sighed and kept silent. Then, as an afterthought, he said he wanted to share something that had disturbed him the previous night.

His story:

The superintendent of the jail happened to know him pretty well and had asked him to come over to see what he always wanted to: the psyche of a person condemned to the gallows shortly before the actual day!

There was a man waiting to be hanged. As per jail procedure and protocol, his family had been called over for a meeting - the last one! The convict, his mother, his wife and son were huddled together, engaged in small talk interrupted by sobs, silences and sighs. On Garg's asking the jail superintendent had called away the jail guard and agreed to let the family be together for as long as they desired. What really moved Garg was this: *the mother of the convict had brought some mangoes for him. On the one hand, mother was giving her son one or two mangoes for the one last time and insisting that he eat them; on the other hand, her son was keen to pass on those mangoes to his son; as a parting gift; it was triangular show of love and affection. In this mother-son, father-son kashmkash –struggle- the man's wife was a mute witness; sitting quiet all the while watching the melodrama.*

Unable to bear the burden of emotions on display, with moist eyes Garg had turned away; so had the superintendent – helpless!

We both fell silent trying to interpret life, fate and destiny in our own ways!

*

Stifled poetry

One had often heard of a tradition unique to Ambala. It was the Indo-Pakistan *mushiara*. The event attracted poets from both sides of the border and the audience would get soaked in their poetry, rich as it was in adjectives expressing love, friendship, sentiments and emotions – full of immense substance and deep thought giving rise to smiles and sighs! I had the opportunity to not only attend the *mushiara* in 1983 but also to meet with famous writers like Ahmed Faraz and Ms Shamim Ikram-ul-Huq.

That was as much a prized opportunity for me, as it was a total surprise for Hussain Askari, Cultural Attaché at the Pakistan Embassy, New Delhi, when he saw debonair, tall and handsome Faraz. Askari had inaugurated the mushiara. Faraz had arrived from London to participate; in fact, it was his first visit to India. At one time, he was Director-General of Pakistan Academy of Letters, as also Director of the Pakistan National Centre, a representative body looking after cultural and literary activities in his home country; both organizations were government controlled. Prior to leaving for London, Faraz was working on an assignment pertaining to the Copyright Act.

Our conversation was intense and informative. Faraz, for one, strongly espoused that a writer must stand for truth; as truth alone matters. True, people were used to Martial law administration in Pakistan. Previously it meant a clean environment, reasonable prices and better civic amenities. Now {Pakistan was under Martial law then} it was different: besides censorship of newspapers and bulletins, the government had started keeping even literary magazines under the thumb; *after things had gone very far, I went abroad*, he sighed!

*

He went in self exile during the military rule of Zia-ul-Haq and spent time in the UK Europe and Canada. He later returned and was appointed Chairperson of Islamabad-based National Book Foundation. He was nationally and internationally recognized, as modern Urdu poet. He returned the Hilal-e-Imtiaz award in 2006; it was given to him in 2004. Posthumously, he was honored with Hilal-e-Pakistan. He died on August 25, 2008.

*

In fact, we had met when the voice of the poets had been *stifled* in their own country. It came as a shock, when Faraz said that even passages from the holy *Quran*, which were unpalatable to the administration, were left out by the publishers! In a reflective mood he had recalled how the literary scene had changed vastly within a year. The worst kind of laws were then sought to be imposed. That environment suffocated him; it pained him. {Faraz being from Peshawar, he was born at Kohat, he conversed in Pashtu with a local colleague, D S Sarhadi, who also hailed from there. Sarhadi was a correspondent based in Ambala.}

*

The other writer who I met was Shamim, besides being a poet she was also special correspondent of *Aqbar-e-Qawateen*; a magazine with a circulation of 60,000, published from Karachi; she was its representative in Rawalpindi. Her professional experience spanned 12 years. The magazine, she explained was more or less on the lines of India's *Eve's Weekly*. During our interaction Shamim had said society women were not fond of playing cards or attending kitty parties. They preferred social welfare service and activities rather than the club culture. Women there vied for equality with men in all walks of life. I took her views at their face-value!

*

For Ms Parveen Sayed, coming to Ambala was like *homecoming*, as it was here in mid-forties that she had attended school. Her father was a jail official. Yet, children would not be allowed to enter jail, she laughed! This was her first visit to Ambala after 1947; she also had an emotional attachment with the place, as her brother was born at Ambala; he was born after four sisters!

Dark-haired, almond-eyed, the ever smiling Parveen had another fond memory: her in-laws belonged to this area, her husband hailed from Kharar {in Punjab and falls in Mohali district now, earlier it was part of Ambala division}. She was also from the tribe of new-wave poets and had appeared on the literary scene in 1974. She wanted to raise her voice against tyranny and oppression; and believed in *insaniat* - humanitarianism!

Seeing Faraz and Sarhadi talking in Pashtu, Parveen chipped in: *see, love and understanding have no boundaries; one falls in love for one's language; and loves to share the past!*

33

The beginning

Wild West!

Having come thus far, beginning with my last field {*district*} posting at Amritsar, it is time now to share some of the reminiscences of my first district posting, as an independent staffer of *The Tribune* at Bathinda in 1975; it was my first *exposure* as much to the world of functional media, as rubbing shoulders with high and mighty, ordinary and less privileged; and the commoners! And, with the passage of time and across the decades, one learns much from one and all!

In fact, the spice of life is in visiting places, meeting people, building bridges that connect us and inculcate in us the habit of sharing and caring. The profession that I had pursued for over 30 years gave me ample opportunities for all this. People also teach a lesson or two - how to live life; may they be known, unknown, absolute strangers, yet, with a humane heart, compassion, sympathy and empathy; as also those indifferent and intolerant or with attitude, arrogance and ego.

It took time to develop confidence, time to frame questions, time to write clean copy and time to understand the complexities and intricacies of the profession, as also to decipher the psyche of the people, who one met as part of professional responsibilities and duties. It also took time to understand the motives and mannerism of fellow journalists besides to learn to cross-check the information obtained or given.

Since learning is a continuous process; so it continues even now, as also the process of unlearning to learn more to accommodate, absorb and practice new learning. That enriches one's ability to garner information, acquire knowledge and develop skills to form an independent perspective and perception of men and matters. This eventually helps to analyze and understand men and matters, as well as grasp the genesis of a given situation, happening or development.

*

Let me share vignettes of posting at Bathinda, where, in addition, I was assigned to *cover* adjoining Faridkot and Ferozepur districts, as well: in fact the entire Ferozepur division. That was my *beat* way back in 1975, when that heartland of Malwa still led a cloistered life, anyone getting posted or transferred there was construed and considered to be a punishment, akin to having been sent to – Kala Pani: Andaman Nicobar Islands!

*

Incidentally, a visit to Andaman and Nicobar, as member of Punjab Vidhan Sabha Press Gallery, is memorable, particularly, a round of the Cellular jail, which is a grim reminder of those who sacrificed their lives so that we may live! It is an enchanting place and fills one with awe, emotion and admiration for our martyrs. No wonder, it was called – *Kala Pani*!

*

Yet, the romance of the Ferozepur division had its own charm and plus points. From news and media coverage point of view, Ferozepur was a virgin territory, as I soon discovered during the bus journeys that I undertook exploring new niches. That experience had its own educational value. Looking at that period, one can say that more out of political exigencies rather than administrative reasons, Ferozepur division was split. Not only new districts were carved out: Mansa and Muktsar; even a new Division was created with Faridkot as headquarter, simply to assuage and placate the people, mostly the members of the Bar and politicians. Punjab today has 22 districts and five Divisions: Ferozepur, Faridkot, Patiala, Ropar and Jalandhar.

*

In mid-1970s, hiring of a taxi was almost a no, no! Even during elections, both Parliament and Assembly, one travelled in rickety PRTC: Pepsu Roadways Transport Corporation buses. The Public Relations Department used to issue *free* bus passes to journalists to travel in the state-owned buses. And to transmit press messages and news dispatches, the Telegraph office issued special cards, countersigned by the News Editor of the newspaper or news agency concerned; it was an authority card to send news without paying any charges.

On occasions, however, when chief minister would be visiting the division, even during elections for campaign, we *enjoyed* the rides in respective district public relations officers' green-coloured dilapidated vehicles; we had nicknamed them as: *Rampiaris*! The present crop of journalists would never be able to comprehend what it meant to be travelling with fellow journalists in those vans. One could not forget that duty was first, excuse: never! It so happened, once driver of DPRO Faridkot was on leave. And responding to the call of duty, DPRO Capt. Gurjeevan Singh Sidhu himself drove all the way from Faridkot to Bathinda! And, as an unwritten rule or understanding, we, the media persons, would carry our own lunch-boxes – working picnic.

*

In geographical and physical terms, Ferozepur division put up with several problems: underground or sub-soil water was brackish, which caused health problems besides yellowing of teeth; irrigation was canal-dependent in the absence of tube wells, as the water level was very low, and un-potable; irrigation water would get lost due to seepage and a massive programme, financed by the World Bank, had been launched to brick-line canals and water courses; connectivity would get hindered due to frequent faults in manually operated telephone exchanges. That was also the time when rural electrification programme was underway on a war-footing, as was the programme of setting up focal points in villages for *in situ* development; and also establishing of village model or *Adarsh* schools!

Water-logging was another grave problem that caused immense damage to buildings, and drains were seldom cleared of wild growth – hyacinth - and encroachments; vast swathes of saline and alkaline affected soils impacted farm productivity and production; educational and health delivery systems were in a shambles; post-delivery system {Dak} was insufficient; if drinking water facilities were woefully inadequate, sewerage system was almost absent or only partially available even in major towns and cotton-rich mandi towns - stretching all the way from Fazilka-Abohar to Muktsar; road net-work was insufficient, what existed required to be mended, strengthened and widened.

*

More so, blinding dust or sand storms would occasionally break electricity supply lines and disrupt normal life! One other feature that stood out in the villages, particularly of Bathinda district, was the *Purda*-system: drawing of veil, as women seldom ventured out without covering their faces. One taboo that was widely observed was not selling milk! People were against this, as they put milk and sons at the same pedestal arguing: no one would part with the two: *dudh te putt; the two were not for sale!*

Bathinda, besides being cotton trading centre with chamber for forward trading, was also famous for gold and wholesale medicines trade; private clinics and nursing homes mushroomed, catering to the needs of not just locals but people from adjoining areas and states: Haryana and Rajasthan!

*

And, how can one forget to mention snuff {Naswar} industry in Gidderbaha. That industry has just vanished with the passage of time. The owners or makers of snuff would not reveal the secret of the ingredients used. It is another matter that the industry provided employment to women, enabling them to supplement their family incomes; and in a way become partners in decision-making at home! Did they? Were they allowed, as equal partners, to participate in decision-making at home?

The belt was/is known for cotton - *white gold*. It took quite a while before proper cotton varieties were introduced that were less susceptible to inspect-pest attacks. Much later was introduced BT cotton; and in 2015, the *white gold* was gobbled by *white fly*! In previous years too crop failures, as well as volatile prices, would ruin farm economies; and the Cotton Corporation of India was dubbed as the *Corruption Corporation of India!*

Industry was in its infancy; all one came across were cotton-ginning mills! In the entire Ferozepur division, Bathinda was like an oasis of commercial development, a seven-line railway junction and Thermal plant and a fertilizer factory. The establishment of Asia's biggest Army cantonment and Bhisiana Air Force Station added to the further development of Bathinda.

*

And when Harsimrat Kaur decided to contest from Bathinda for the Lok Sabha, after the constituency was de-reserved, the place has under gone complete metamorphosis and transformed into a new-look place. It is now host to an oil refinery, a Central University; and an AIIMS: All -India institute of medical sciences is proposed; and much more. After all, she is Badal's *Bahu* –daughter-in-law!

*

This vast canvas of what was dubbed as the *backwaters* of Punjab offered infinite opportunities to report, and report development-oriented, positive news stories and features to give the people and the place an exposure to the world outside through the medium of *The Tribune*, which then had monopoly in the state; a wholesome newspaper. {With the launching of city-centric pull outs and separate editions for adjoining states, it has confined and constricted, across the decades, much to the chagrin of its die-hard readers; generations have grown reading this newspaper!}

The kind of journalism that I was taught at PAU came in handy to pursue the profession the way one wanted to and attempted to do so – focusing on positive and developmental aspects; reporting on people-based stories and what was in their interest!

*

Men, machines and animals

In the initial days in Bathinda, some visible features attracted my attention. This was because lot of construction activity was in progress: underway were private works and big projects. These included the expansion of Guru Nanak Thermal Plant, setting up of National Fertilizer Limited plant, acquisition of and work on land for the Army cantonment, Bhisiana IAF station, and the like. {Several years later, Guru Hargobind Thermal Plant was established at Lehra Mohabat on Bathinda-Barnala state highway.}

A huge work force from several states had converged at Bathinda, including skilled engineers, technicians and the like. As hub of intensive construction and building programmes, for most part of the year, a dust cloud hung low over the city; add to this the fly ash emitted by Thermal plant's chimneys, which spewed the grey-black dust causing respiratory problems besides settling down on the habitats and inhabitants. At work in the hot, humid, dry weather were men, machines, women, camels and donkeys. Contractors preferred Eisher tractors and camel carts for carting away soil and raw material; and donkeys which could climb down into the lakes being dug up for the thermal and fertilizer plants.

*

More than anything else it was the ubiquitous donkey that caught my attention: wherever one went from bazaars to administrative-cum-judicial complex to housing colonies, one would see the donkeys busy grazing in the lawns or asserting their right to passage on the roads! Working together men, machines and animals were to change the face of Bathinda city and its surroundings. One could see growth not development: planned or symmetrical.

*

{I reached Bathinda on June 1, 1975. My first single column news appeared in the newspaper dated June 5: *over 95 per cent harijans get* plots. The district public relations officer Jagmohan Singh Brar had taken news persons to a function at village Budhladewal, 16 km away on Bathinda-Muktsar road, where the then minister for housing development Gurbrinder Kaur Brar was the chief guest. I had begun my innings! }

*

Daily mail!

It may sound incredible. Well, that's how it was then – 40 years ago – in Ferozepur division, comprising of Ferozepur, Faridkot and Bathinda districts. During my years of posting in that region – w*ild- west*, as it was notoriously referred to – one came across many colorful personalities in the course of professional duties: from politicians to bureaucrats, both civil and police officials to commoners!

One of them, who gave me many nuggets of news and inside stories on administration and politics, sprinkled with personal anecdotes, was the then Divisional Commissioner Joginder Singh, a stocky, jovial personality ever agile and with wide mood swings! Invariably, he would tell me: *you know PPS, these people*, referring to officials assigned to look after him whenever he moved out of Ferozepur on tour to the districts and during his stay in government PWD: Public works department guest houses, *offer me copious quantities of Kaju – cashew nuts- and serve chicken, so as to choke my heart's arteries! I am, as you know, a person with simple eating habits, Daal-roti type; and lead a simple life. But then, out of courtesy, I cannot say no; and oblige by accepting what they serve*; he would chuckle with a wink!

And, then there was the Faridkot Deputy Commissioner, Gurnam Singh, who went overboard to get written Prime Minister's 20-point programme atop even water reservoirs - that was the *Emergency* period!

*

Some months after I had been at Bathinda, I came across a report based on a survey PAU had conducted. It concluded that Bathinda was the *wettest* in Asia; real bottle- guzzler *Malwais*! Besides liquor, opium {afeem} and its derivatives were copiously consumed. In fact, there used to be separate auction of opium vends on the pattern of liquor shop auctioning. Bathinda city has a street called *Afeem-wali Gali!*

To wean people away from intoxicants, drugs and particularly opium, periodically, special drives would be launched to educate the habitual, backed by medical assistance. Special field camps would be organized, as part of that drive; and addicts would be addressed by the officers and medical staff.

I accompanied the Divisional Commissioner Joginder Singh to one of the camps at Mansa. The proceedings proceeded well, there was enthusiastic response, people, seemingly, had listened to the advice carefully and appeared in a mood to give up opium. As the function concluded, one person in the audience stood up and sought to speak, rather make a request. When he spoke, all he demanded with folded hands was to increase the quota of opium of those allowed consumption on medical grounds; it was distributed by the civil surgeon. The logical reason given, he went on to say, was that in the open/black market opium was available at a high price! So much for those efforts and where Punjab and its youth have landed today is anyone's guess!

*

The uncommunicative: Besides the state-level, divisional and district officials and politicians of all hues that I came across in my journalistic career, the experience of meeting with CPI: Communist Party of India, leaders was unique in many ways. The opportunity came when the CPI held its 11th Congress at Bathinda in March 1978. Even before the leaders had descended, I had always found their twisted language and vocabulary incomprehensible! {By the way, Bathinda was known to be a stronghold of the Communists. A joke one often heard was: when it rains in Moscow, Communists open their umbrellas in Bathinda!}

For exhaustive and intelligible coverage of CPI Congress, attended by nearly 1,500 delegates, my senior colleague Sukhdev Singh had been sent over; he was considered to be good at interpreting communist ideology and policy-statements besides having known some of the key leaders closely. It was at that Congress I had the opportunity to listen to, much less to speak to, CPI stalwarts: Sohan Singh Josh, Bhupesh Gupta, N K Krishnan, Ramesh Chandra, A S Malhotra and many others. After exhaustive efforts and with Sukhdev's helping hand, I managed to talk to the stalwarts, who I still call: *the uncommunicative ones*!

*

It was also during that period I got an opportunity to meet Sheikh Abdullah. He had been invited to Faridkot by the Chief Minister Giani Zail Singh. At an informal interaction with the press at one point, someone reminded us of the Emergency and hinted we avoid asking certain questions. At that Abdullah spoke up: *These poor journalists cannot write freely, I know. At least let them ask openly and unburden themselves.* There was laughter all around!}

*

Reverting to Joginder Singh, who was affectionately addressed *Sir, Joginder Singh*! Let me share his efforts to get the *Dak* – post - delivered daily in division's villages, which otherwise was distributed bi- or tri-weekly. He had assiduously followed up the matter with the Post-Master General, Ambala Circle. It was he who made me aware of the difficulties and hazards of non-delivery of post to village people every day. This is what the situation was like then, in 1976:

A survey by the three deputy commissioners, on the asking of the Divisional Commissioner, revealed that out of a total of 2291 villages in the division, 1579 villages did not have a post office! The delivery was bi-weekly {*in 381 villages*} and tri-weekly {*in 659 villages*}. The survey had taken two points into consideration: one, no village was located at a distance of more than two miles from the existing post-office; and two, no village with a population of more than 2000 should be without a post-office.

On this score, Faridkot submitted a *nil* report; Ferozepur report stated there were 75 villages in as many as nine blocks, which came under either of the two stipulated clauses {considerations} or both; and Bathinda reported there were 38 villages, which were either more than two miles away from the post-office or in which the population was more than 2000, but there was no post-office. In all 113 villages in the two districts –Ferozepur and Bathinda - the population was, on an average, more than 25,000; and there was a primary or a middle school- the distance from the nearest post-office averaged three-and-a-half miles; and school teachers were willing to work as Branch Post-masters, if a post-office was opened!

Besides post delivery problems, the other communication drawback was telephone services. The division was served by manually operated exchanges! Talking of need to improve these services, Joginder Singh wanted at least two important sub-divisions, Fazilka and Abohar to have STD: subscriber trunk dialing services, not only with the district headquarters but also Chandigarh and New Delhi. The deputy minister for irrigation and power, Balram Jakhar, who belonged to Abohar {Khuian sarwar was his native village} was making efforts at his own level with every home in villages willing to own a telephone and panchayats were willing to foot the bill. The clamor for direct dialing linkages was heard everywhere in the division.

*

There were exceptions and some of the mandi towns in the three districts had direct telephone links with Chandigarh but these were marked by plenty of irritating call drops, break-downs and delays in making connections. Requests poured in daily for teleprinters services as well for quick transmission of messages, including press dispatches, from cotton and industrial hubs of the division. A hope to either set up new automatic exchanges or expand the capacities of the existing exchanges by upgrading them was raised when the union minister for communication Shankar Dayal Sharma had visited Bathinda in October 1975 to inaugurate the new telephone exchange. However, the things seemed to move at a snail's pace, despite availability of land to set up exchanges. There was also demand for more public call offices for better communication. This could happen only when capacity enhancement took place. Such was the communication scenario in the division, where I had worked and sent dispatches to Chandigarh! {Philately, I learnt was another weak point in the division. Whenever new stamps were released, these would take pretty long time to reach the division's post-offices and stamp collectors and stamp-lovers were deprived of new introductions.}

*

Another noticeable feature of the division was the role of small and marginal farmers' and agricultural laborers' agencies. This nomenclature was later changed and it was known as Small and Marginal Farmers' Agency. The wide range of activities the agency propounded propagated and indulged in were well received and appreciated in villages, as these were aimed at ameliorating their socio-economic status. From goat-sheep and camel rearing, the agency promoted dairying farming, weaving of *Khes, Phulkari and Bagh* etc.

*

I remember visiting Balram Jakhar's village to join a visiting Press party from Chandigarh. The purpose was to see the works undertaken to supply irrigation water to the tail-end villages and brick-lining of water courses. He was a good host, open and friendly. What surprised us most was that in scores of villages that we traveled to with him, he knew the Sarpanches by their first name and greeted them as such. As host, he insisted in travelling with us in our bus rather than in his official car! He was, indeed, a leader of the masses and enjoyed good rapport and reputation. It was again at his asking that I revisited his home, when the then union minister for power, K C Pant had visited in connection with 100 per cent electrification programme of villages in his area of political operation. I remember, when he contested Lok Sabha election from Ferozepur in 1980, I called him up for an interview. He insisted on meeting me where I was staying: *65-Jhoke Road*, Ferozepur, my maternal grandfather's bungalow. He became Speaker after that election. He died on February 3, 2016; he was 92.

*

With the passage of time and political patronage, things have changed; once dubbed *backwaters* of Punjab, the division is in the process of shedding that tag! Much has improved, more is required to be done; it is being done!

*

Call from Gulmarg

It was a hot, humid morning with no wind at all. It was July 16, 1980. I was going over the day's work schedule when the phone rang. It was a friendly source from the police control room who informed that some trouble was brewing in Dabwali, and asked me if I was interested in going there. Instinctively, I said: *o k thank* you; and hung up!

I boarded the first available bus and off I set on the approximately 50 minute's journey for a 42 km distance. A short distance from the bus stop, one could see a surging crowd and hear sloganeering!

Popularly known as Mandi Dabwali, it is an interesting town on the border of Punjab and Haryana. If the front door of a house opens into Punjab, its back-door or service lane is in Haryana. It is a typical cheek-and-jowl setting.

Opposite the bus stop was the police station, target of the crowd, as I discovered within minutes of alighting. Even before I could get to talk to people at the bus stop, the crowd had come closer and suddenly everyone seemed to be running helter-skelter for shelter. Then I heard *tuck-tuck-tuck* sound! A Haryanvi driver pulled me down and made me sit behind the rear wheels of his bus, hissing out: *police have opened fire, lie low*! All hell broke out! People ran for safety leaving behind whatever small missiles {wood staffs etc.} they were carrying; the place was soon littered with shoes and slippers; and abandoned cycles and unattended rickshaws.

What had triggered the public anger was *rape and killing* of one Sheela Devi, wife of a Haryana judicial courts peon, Naffe Singh; and police taking no action against the accused! In that police firing one, Kartar Singh was killed and 22 others injured. The firing, it later transpired, had been ordered by the station house officer without seeking permission from any civil authority/official.

As I looked around for transport to go to the hospital, where the injured had been rushed, a young Sikh offered to take me on his bi-cycle. I hopped on to the carrier and he pedaled fast. {That young Sikh boy was Ram Singh Brar, a correspondent, who later became Media Advisor to chief ministers O P Chautala; thank you Brar.} Thereafter, I met the sub-divisional magistrate, P K Chaudhary, who was very forthcoming with all the information I sought. {Later, he became chief secretary of Haryana.}

I filed a detailed first-hand report; it was banner headline the next day. I followed up the story for few days; and even appeared before the inquiry commission. The newspaper of that day was flaunted in the Parliament. Next morning I got a call from the Editor-in-Chief Prem Bhatia, who was holidaying in Gulmarg. He congratulated me for the news coverage. One could not have asked for more! It was a rare gesture on his part, who kept tab on the newspaper and its correspondents even when on leave!

That call and crisp conversation, even after 36 years, still resonates in my ears, coming as it did from the cool climes to the parched, sandy tracts of Bathinda!

*

A word about Gulmarg: *Meadow of Flowers* is what the place name means! It is a town, a hill station, a popular skiing destination and a notified area committee, in Baramula district in Jammu Kashmir. The town is situated in the *Pir Pinjal* range in the western Himalayas and is within miles of the LOC: Line of Control between India and Pakistan. Originally Gulmarg was named Gaurimarg: The fair one by shepherds in honor of the Hindu goddess Parvati, the resort was renamed Gulmarg by Sultan Yusuf Shah of the Chak Dynasty, who frequented the place with his mistress Habba Khatoon in the 16th century.

Wild flowers of 21 different varieties were collected by the Mughal emperor Jahangir for his gardens in Gulmarg. In the 19th century, British civil servants started using Gulmarg as a retreat to escape summers in North Indian plains. Hunting and golfing were their favorite pastime and three golf courses were established, including one exclusively for women. One of the three golf courses established survives to the present day; and at an altitude of 2,650 meters (8,690 ft) is the world's highest golf course! In 1927, British established a ski club in Gulmarg and two annual ski events were hosted, one each during Christmas and Easter. Central Asian explorer Aurel Stein also visited Gulmarg during this period.

34

Sikh institutions at a crossroads

Besides sharing my experiences, memoirs and crucial moments in my 30-year long journey as a journalist, in this and the following chapter- Punjab: theatre of atrocities, permit me to share my honest opinions and thoughts on two aspects that deserve attention of one and all: the Sikh institutions and the state of affairs in Punjab. The impressions and interpretations that follow are the outcome of my personal beliefs, not that these are of any consequence. Yet, I, in my humble way, feel that one need to have courage of conviction to express one's views keeping in view the larger interests of the state and its people; hoping, expecting and praying that someday, somewhere, someone, would take up the cudgels and raise a voice for a better tomorrow, a better future so that generations next do not accuse us of not having cautioned them! In short, idea is to leave behind, in print, thoughts for posterity enabling our future generations to pause, ponder, analyze and act.

*

The din to restore dignity, independence and autonomy of the Sikh institutions that have been denigrated with the passage of time, especially after the Army action at the Golden Temple in 1984, refuses to fade away. What is the way out or what are the possible or probable alternatives to the existing institutions or how can these be strengthened and galvanized to respond to the ever rising aspirations and expectations of their constituents? Does the Sikh community need to fix and manicure the existing ones or need to look out for new institutions or opt for new-look institutions to ride out the occasional storms that arise, much to the disillusionment of the *quom*?

Of primary concern are such of the institutions as SGPC, Akal Takht and High Priests; besides the Shiromani Akali Dal. And the way, across decades, these have been either used or abused for personal and political purposes by powers- that- be within or outside the religio-political fold, aimed at subverting them at will and at any given point of time. It calls for serious introspection. Then there is also the Sikh Gurdwara Judicial Commission at Amritsar, which too, at times, was/is used for parking favorites of the Akali leaders

Have there ever been any attempts to put the institutional houses in order? The answer is yes, and no! Yes, because some steps were initiated, like the World Sikh Sammelan in Amritsar in September 1995. Or voices that arose time-to-time from the Sikhs settled abroad for a broad-based SGPC by enlarging its ambit, making it more representative in character. No, because several attempts made at different times were effectively scuttled by those who held sway over them for fear of losing their hegemony and control, since they drew their power from these institutions.

Consequently, all such attempts have remained stillborn, and many issues remain pending. For example, the Sikh leadership – religious and political - has failed to either get an All-India Gurdwara Act enacted, in the past six decades; or rein-in growing cult of *Sants, Mahants, Babas and Gurus; Sects, Cults and Deras;* what to say of other key, emotive and sensitive issues like voting rights to *Sehjdhari* Sikhs.

Among the many attempts and suggestions to realign the Sikh institutions was one made by a retired Army officer, the late Gurdip Singh Grewal, between 1994 and 1996. One day, I walked into the cubby-hole office of T K Ramasamy, Associate Editor of *The Tribune.* {He also looked after the book review section of the newspaper, besides writing on financial and economic issues. A voracious reader and a commentator, he commanded huge respect, both for his style of writing, as also his humane approach and unassuming nature; absolutely unpretentious!} He motioned me to sit and passed on to me a small and slim lemon coloured booklet with the words: *Global Sikh Senate* printed on the cover. He asked me to read it carefully and craft a story out of it, *as it is something new, we can, perhaps, initiate a debate on what is conceptualized in the given hypothesis.*

*

Since enough had/has been said and written on the grievances or otherwise of the Sikhs, so I wondered what new Col Gurdip Singh had to offer. One had read a lot about the myopic vision of the Sikh leadership - lacking in perspective and overly obfuscated by religious overtones - eruption of militancy and its consequent carnage in Punjab for over a decade. Also, the issue of attempts to establish a political system based on religious revivalism orthodoxy. And the role of the various Sikh organizations has also been a subject of intense debate and discussion, obviously with no consensus or conclusion within the community. In fact, the Sikhs have been conscious of their *identity* but not so much of their *minority status* in the mainstream of national politics, thus, suffering debilitating misjudgments regarding their assertions to uphold their status. However, as I read the small booklet, I realized that it was a new, different approach, not the usual run of the mill stuff that Col. Gurdip Singh had followed in writing the treatise; thereby, floating the idea of a *Global Sikh Senate*; quite a break from the beaten path many other scholars had followed on the issues mentioned above.

*

As a social activist, his ideas, as I discerned, were to enable the Sikh community in India and abroad to meet the prevailing challenges and adapt itself for optimum viable prosperity moving into the 21st century. He believed that such a senate was important and imperative for globally integrating secular Sikh social order. The proposed senate with elected representatives from within Punjab, the country and even abroad has to be in a position to comprehensively and competently manage all affairs of the community. His belief was: *Sikhs being a consensual society, the senate should be able to create a virtuous circle of consensus for prosperity of the entire community.*

Col Gurdip, who had given a deep thought to the Sikh problems, firmly held the opinion that the existing imperfections in the extant Sikh polity were on account of two factors: one, the casting of Sikh politics into an archetypical mould of thoughtless and perennial attitude of confrontation, more so for mostly archaic issues - there had been no pretentions to farsightedness and such posturing had been singular by any tangible achievement -; two, the core factor being that the guardians of gurdwaras-based politics, generally ultra-orthodox in their approach, maintained that stranglehold on the Sikh affairs, in the process obstructing enlightened minds from participating. Thus, world renowned and highly competent persons shied away from contributing creatively.

In his hypothesis, in the absence of synergy and synchronization of concurring functions, the intended senate should fill that need. The senate in his thinking was not the least tended to be something monolithic in status or stature, created out of the present set-up, but to evolve their overall amalgamation into an intelligible mainstream and ensure commonality of purpose from their fractional contribution, thus, eliminating all chasms and asymmetries. The senate of his dreams was to be *coalesce* of community organizations, a virtually omnium unit with the senate as its fountainhead and adhere to the constitutional bonds of law of the land.

The global Sikh idea was revolutionary, aimed solely at prosperity and wellbeing of the Sikhs around the world. The senate was to have its headquarters at Damdama Sahib, initially, to provide the nerve centre of multimedia communications. The issues/questions he raised then are relevant even today. What was essential at that critical juncture is even more desirable now in the Sikh history and politics: clear mind and conscience; and taking conscious decisions as to why and where we want to go. How to get there can be worked out with consensus. However, such a consensus has remained elusive since time immemorial!

In one of our meetings, Gurdip Singh told me that the senate would, rather should, therefore, take care of higher education leading to provision of job opportunities. His dream was that the senate should emerge by 1999. And, that should be a fitting tribute to the great occasion: 300 years of the founding of Sikhism or the *Khalsa*! Alas, that was not to be. And, today we have a cacophony of voices demanding institutional reforms. All that one sees is lot of heat, no light; not yet!

*

At the 1995 *World Sikh Sammelan*, besides several other resolutions, say on religio-political, administrative, socio-economic, agricultural and educational aspects, it was also resolved that a *World Sikh Council* {WSC} be set up under the Jathedar of Akal Takht, Professor Manjit Singh. Some progress was made and even Zonal World Sikh Councils were set up. All this was later to end in whimper with differences cropping up among the power-holders, power-seekers and power-brokers. Consequently, when Giani Puran Singh was the Jathedar of Akal Takht, he disbanded all WSC zonal units in March 2000. Later, Prof. Manjit Singh also got embroiled in partisan groupings, courting controversies and had to quit, rather was made to quit.

In fact, in less than three years, the envisaged World Sikh Council, wedged as it was into the existing Sikh religio-political institutions then, had shown signs of fatigue with little or no forward movement from the moment the resolution was passed. The council had failed to find its feet. Rather, the very first few steps it took led it to the doors of the court, engaging it in a controversy, not of its own making. Within no time there had arisen two councils: one *original*, the other a *clone*! As the written constitution stated, the council was to be a *global organization aimed at promoting international brotherhood among the Sikhs and to work vigorously towards the abiding glory of the Khalsa and to the wellbeing of the mankind*. Yes, the council did work towards that goal, but for *self-destruction* and *self-demotion*; throwing all talk of brotherhood out of the window!

That the council had remained a non-starter did not come as a surprise to either the Sikh intellectuals of that time or the Akali leadership. Though the listed aims and objectives were pretty ideal, their accomplishment was seen as rather difficult. Such apprehensions proved to be correct.

And as to the aims and objectives, these were and still remain the same- unmet: preservation of and respect for Sikh identity, safeguarding Sikh cultural heritage, protecting their socio-economic, agricultural and industrial interests, ensuring acceptance of SGPC outlined *Rehat Maryada*, promoting literacy, providing quality education in general and technical/professional in particular, elimination of caste and sectarian appellations, integrating, totally, backward sections of the Sikh social order into the mainstream, propagating and strengthening faith in fundamental human rights and dignity of humans, equality for all and working for the wellbeing of the humanity. All these aims and objectives are still *work in progress!*

Resultantly, the WSC, thus, also failed and remained a mute witness till the entire edifice was destroyed- at the instance of the Akal Takht Jathedars. That was *The End* to the five-day long Sammelan's efforts to give a new direction to the Sikhs. This event had been organized with much fanfare and financial spending. Fate of the idea of *Global Sikh Senate* was no different, though it died a natural death, as there was no positive response from any quarters! For both ideas, however, it was nothing short of foeticide! So much for *reforms* of the Sikh institutions, which continue to court ever raging controversies?

Why WSC idea got killed? One may turn around and ask this question from the pseudo-crusaders of Sikhs' politico-religious matters. As also, where are the promised universities, educational institutions, chairs in the universities, daily newspaper, magazine, journal etc. that were to signal or initiate the process to achieve the self-assigned aims and objectives? No attempt was made to acquire financial, movable and immovable assets for the council from any lawful sources.

The lineup of the council had disintegrated of its own even before any work could start. This further widened the existing vacuum, which had remained unfulfilled despite presence of several Sikh institutions, then. No one worked then, no one is working now, to find ways and means for preparing the Sikhs to meet new challenges in the next century. With Akali leadership having parceled various religio-political institutions between themselves for decades and believing fervently that their hold would last forever, showed little or no interest in the council or *Global Sikh Senate*! Consequently, while council got afflicted with such infirmity, resulting in fractured decision-making; *Senate* idea dissipated without a trace!

Besides, no visible attempt was seen to have been made to groom second-line of Sikh leadership either in religious or political matters. Attempts made, if any, were either scuttled or remained stillborn, thanks to the vested interests of the opinion-makers. One wondered then, as also now, if a new class of educated Sikhs would ever emerge to change the ground situation. That question, as then, still remains unanswered as to how will this happen, who will make it happen, where and when would it happen and a beginning thus would be made.

*

As one looks back at those attempts, made by a miniscule minority of well-meaning Sikhs, so as to galvanize the Sikh institutions that were clearly at a crossroads, one can say that those attempts have remained unsuccessful till now, despite best of intentions and diligent hard work done to espouse the Sikh cause and cleanse the religio-political system for the sake of the Sikh *Panth*.

Why? Simple: The so-called enlightened individuals, who had either constituted or dominated several of the Sikh institutions then, as now, had adhered to different ideologies, if any; and owed allegiance to different individual Akali leader{s}, who protected their factional interests and protégés; the leadership continues to do so even at present. Consequently, all these decades, there has been no occasion or an effort to attempt provide a *common* meeting ground, as also an *acceptable* agenda for diverse Sikh institutions to get together and work together on any agreed common minimum objective.

*

Sad, as it may sound, the fact is that across decades and despite severe setbacks to the Sikh *Panth* in the past, the Sikh institutions and individuals enjoying different political patronage have worked in isolation and continue to work that way. Thus, these have remained insulated or quarantined from hard realities. Ego hassles have been a major stumbling block in ensuring cooperation and coordination all these decades, while conflict, contradiction and avoidable confrontation have dominated and continue to dominate the Sikh institutions and Sikh psyche! As a result, either out of respect or indifference, ordinary Sikhs remain aloof. And the ones who were/are wont to or were/are keen on something being done to vest in the Sikh institutions dignity, independence, autonomy etc. have failed to change the mindset of the Sikh leadership, so far!

*

Another organization that comes to mind is the Institute of Sikh Studies in Chandigarh {established in 1989}. It too has across the years pitched in making wide-ranging suggestions on galvanizing the Sikh quom, as also Sikh politics and religion. Among its founding members was Dr Kharak Singh. All of them had made tremendous efforts to propagate Sikhism and erase misgivings that had crept in. The founders felt concerned over the large scale misrepresentation of Sikh doctrines, misrepresentation of gurbani and the lack of understanding of the message of the Gurus, its import on history and its contribution towards the development of mankind. It is non-political and voluntary international organization dedicated to the correct interpretation of gurbani and Sikh philosophy as also of propagation of Sikh religion and culture. It has a long list of specific aims and objects. Yet, it could not achieve what it had set to in the absence of the desired response from the powers that be – the Akalis, the SGPC. Nevertheless, its literature and journal – Abstract of Sikh Studies - do bear a stamp of sincerity and authenticity.

*

And what happened at village Chabba on Amritsar-Tarn Taran road, on November 10, 2015, is too recent to recapitulate in detail here. That gathering of self-styled radical Sikhs and groups had called itself Sarbat Khalsa and passed 13 resolutions. The main highlight was the sacking of Jathedars of Takhts, including Akal Takht, and appointing a new set of Jathedars. The replaced were Giani Gurbachan Singh {Jathedar, Akal Takht}, Giani Mal Singh {Jathedar Takht Keshgarh Sahib}, and Giani Gurmukh Singh {acting-Jathedar Takht Damdama Sahib}. These were replaced, respectively, by Jagtar Singh Hawara, Amrik Singh

Ajnala and Baljit Singh Daduwal, a preacher. Since Hawara was undergoing life imprisonment in Tihar Jail in New Delhi for his involvement in the murder of Beant Singh, so Dhian Singh Mand was named as acting Jathedar of Akal Takht. It was Hawara, who had escaped from Burail Jail in Chandigarh through a tunnel he and his co-accused, Jagtar Singh Tara had dug up. Tara is in Burail Jail. The Chabba congregation had also removed Giani Iqbal Singh {Jathedar, Takht Patna Sahib} without naming his successor.

As expected, the ruling SAD leadership, as well as the SGPC, rejected out of hand the resolutions passed on that occasion. The event itself had created religio-political ripples and a fierce debate, discussion and divisions. A controversy erupted, as a consequence of the not totally unanticipated outcome of the event. The November 10 occasion was a crude reminder of mid-1980, when similar gatherings would queer the pitch for the Sikhs and create confusion and add insult to injured susceptibilities, sensibilities and sentiments of the Sikhs, whenever such *Sarbat Khalsa* were held at Akal Takht by rabble-rousers of that time. The most striking being the one held in 1986, when Khalistan was announced and established Sikh institutions denigrated. In fact, time-and-again, those who had enjoyed power and pelf - acquired, bestowed or snatched - have often run roughshod over laws, institutions and individuals, which were found inconvenient. Chabba convention was no exception. On such occasions in the past, several elements had fiddled with established practices for vested interests and selfish motives. The Sikh leadership, divided as it has always been, refuses to learn any lessons from the past. It has always been the implosions that scalded the Sikh image.

In an attempt to overshadow Chabba event and decimate those who had sponsored that event, the ruling SAD, led by father-son duo: Parkash Singh Badal and Sukhbir Singh, decided upon holding series of *parallel* gatherings, calling these *Sadhbhawna* rallies with emphasis on: *communal harmony, peace, tranquility.* The move, as many analysts had stated then, was aimed at further queering the Panthic pitch and prepare the ground for 2017 Assembly elections; divisive politics and religion at their best!

A perusal of the course of speeches delivered at the ruling party-sponsored *Sadhbhawna* rallies showed new lows in political vocabulary and personal attacks on the opposition parties and leaders! In the course of the run-up to the 2017 Assembly elections, such speeches are likely to further surcharge and vitiate the political atmosphere. As earlier, when such developments take place, there are likely to be no winners; all are expected losers; all the way. Well, what has happened in the past decades, as we say, is history! And a new dusty history is, perhaps, in the making.

And, it sounds audacious and even looks outrageous, when one looks at the manner in which the SGPC-appointed five beloved –*Panj Pyaras* – had directed the removal of the Jathedar of Akal Takht and the two other Jathedars –of Keshgarh Sahib and Anandpur Sahib - and served an ultimatum on SGPC setting January 2, 2016, as the deadline to act; the way SGPC executive committee dismissed them all, except one, who had retired; and the latter the five reacting by giving a call to the Sikhs to *socially boycott* the Jathedars further compounded the situation and made the Sikh *quom* and institutions look askance! The Panj Pyaras were: Satnam Singh Khanda, Satnam Singh, Mangal Singh, Major Singh and Tarlok Singh. Major Singh had since retired from SGPC service.

Such unsavoury developments in themselves show how the Sikhs harm and hurt their own credibility and cause irreparable damage to Sikh community. Such of the moves may appear to be like a mirage on the politico-religious landscape, yet these do have a ripple effect. For instance, it was/is widely believed that to divert and deflect attention from unstoppable farmer anguish over ruin of their cotton crop by *white fly*; and other problems that beset farming sector, religion was evoked; a case in point is introduction of special *Mukh Mantri Tirath Darshan Yatra* –Chief minister's pilgrimage! This rail service was to enable the Sikhs undertake pilgrimage to their holy places; and in this political venture, aimed at garnering votes in 2017, the Hindus, Christians and Muslims were not been ignored; on the time-table were places of their interest, as well. This sort of situation would be avoidable were there to be discussion and debate to re-orient the Sikh institutions.

*

One comes across many Sikhs who are anguished and feel helpless at the turn of events, and how politics has cast a dark shadow over religion and religious institutions. It is time someone took up the cudgels to give a semblance of respectability and recognition to the Sikh institutions in the larger interest of the future of the Sikhs, Sikhism and broadcast the true message, which has universal appeal and relevance, of what the holy book Guru Granth Sahib conveys to the humanity at large, as ordained by the Gurus. SGPC is projected as the sole repository of the Sikh ethos and aspirations; also, custodian of Sikh *Rehat Maryada* and rituals etc; yet, it seems to be failing in its assigned responsibilities, given the stranglehold of a strong section of the Akali leadership on it.

It is high time to reform Sikh institutions.

35

Punjab: theatre of atrocities!

For Punjab, neither did the religio-political-militancy syndrome of 1980s auger well, nor did the political set up in 1999, when Parkash Singh Badal became the Chief Minister. As in 1999, so now, towards the last year of his two consecutive terms, the government has been shy of taking hard and bold decisions concerning administration; economic policies and other matters, religious or otherwise. People, as then, so now, find lack of confidence and competence in the ministry, which has failed to deliver. All one finds all over are only strands of despondency and despair!

Atrocities are not committed only with guns and boots! Deprivation also constitutes atrocities, deprivation in terms of lack of balanced development, economic distress and near absence of equitable distribution of welfare benefits. In fact, as a consequence of such deprivation, people feel rejected and unwanted; there is class and caste conflict; there is a tug-of-war between haves and have-nots; there is unequal application of law and inordinate delay in delivery of justice; there is intolerance to dissent or contrary opinion; there is unequal opportunity to education and health care; there is cry for basic civic amenities; there is frustrating wait for remunerative prices for farm produce and products or for pay and pensions or committed grants; there is delayed payment for agricultural produce procured by the government/ahrtiya; there is clamor for clean, potable drinking water; and what have you!

Political parties that have ruled Punjab by turn across decades have failed to either assuage the hurt sensibilities of Punjabis or attend to and address these atrocities or deprivations, effectively and permanently. This has made Punjabis, across all walks of life; feel like abandoned children of the State!

And, what a coincidence that after a gap of almost 17 years, the old political war horse, Parkash Singh Badal, again found himself caught in a piquant situation of running the government, as well as controlling religious organizations: SGPC and Akal Takht, on the one hand, the re-charged radical Sikhs, and agitated and anguished farmers, on the other hand. One need not to repeat the utter failure, flip-flops and missteps of the state on its inability in anticipating subterranean currents that have their epicenter in people's aspirations, frustrations, hopes and despairs. For once Akali leadership has failed in judging men and matters.

*

Here, one's thoughts go to what George Bernard Shaw had once said: *Reminiscences make one feel so deliciously aged and sad*. Yet, the fact is that as I plunge into the past, I am inclined to compare and contrast what Punjab was then, what it is now. Even after 17 years, one observes that while the people may have turned wiser; what about the Akalis, have they?

Though only a small proportion of villages were seriously affected, when terrorism was at its peak in Punjab in the mid-1980s, the cascading effect it has had on various aspects of state's life continued to be felt even in mid-1990s. The echo of terrorism may have partly faded into silence; it has not been completely silenced! Among its manifestations is deprivation - the atrocities people are subjected to!

In fact, in the present times, the state is battling another type of terrorism -- youth falling prey to drug or substance abuse - which is consuming more families than bullets did!

*

An AIIMS - All-India Institute of Medical Sciences - recent study, 2015-16, on drug or substance use in Punjab has revealed that four in every 100 persons in the age bracket, 18 years to 35 years were opioid-dependent, while 15 in 100 could be opioid users. Opioid is a wider term used to cover all types of *drugs*. The most commonly used drug was heroin -53 per cent; and 35 injected drugs! In fact, study claims that drug business was worth Rs 20 crore, daily; incredible, indeed! This comes to a drug-related lucrative business worth Rs 7,575 crore, annually. And among the 80 per cent who tried to kick the drug-use habit, medical facilities were available to just 35 per cent, notwithstanding government claims of running, de-addiction/rehabilitation centres, across the state. The study had put a question mark on government's seriousness in combating drug trade and consumption, whereas, the study says that only a miniscule percentage of persons were jailed; against 57,150, who were reportedly arrested! In fact, Punjab is home to 2.3 lakh drug users: 99 per cent males and 54 per cent married! Vast majority of these addicts or users were unemployed, while a small percentage possessed some formal degree.

That Punjab is embroiled in a multi-million drug scandal involving politicians is another story! Remember, alleged drug smuggler Jagdish Bhola putting drug illicit trade at Rs 6,000 crore, annually, in Punjab? The AIIMS study figures jack-up this figure to Rs 7,575 crore, per year!

*

Across the decades, Punjab has grown, not developed. Urban-rural divide has widened: former a picture of chaos, congestion, pollution and insanitation; latter a picture of abject poverty and wanton neglect with education and health delivery systems having virtually disappeared and infrastructure in a shambles. One, however, does not deny presence of oasis of development and faint rays of hope. This is truer in the case of individual Punjabi entrepreneurs, may they be working in the farms or factories.

The factors that allured youth then to pick up the gun have only accentuated across time. Social and political scientists had concluded that out of a total of 14,000-odd villages in the 1980s, the ones deeply embroiled in terrorism were around 270, a mere two per cent; majority of those in Amritsar and Gurdaspur. Professor Harish K Puri, formerly of Guru Nanak Dev University Amritsar, spent years studying the turmoil that engulfed Punjab and tried to understand why. I had the privilege of interacting with him on several occasions to learn what went wrong where and the operating reality at the grassroots.

A sample survey of 28 villages in four police districts: Amritsar, Tarn Taran, Majitha and Batala, for example, presented a broad spectrum of the scenario prevailing then. The people had identified, in all 232 terrorists in these 28 villages. It came as a shock to Professor Puri that though the youth were motivated by the idea of *Khalistan*, seven per cent were influenced by Operation Bluestar, anti-Sikh riots or were under the spell of Sant Jarnail Singh Bhinderanwale, while, as many as 38 per cent youth joined the *movement* only out of fun: *Shaukia*! The sense of adventure or love of weapons made them terrorists with little or no hope of returning home. At least 12 per cent of the youth were sucked into the vortex of terrorism only to make money!

*

As to the background of these youth, who had then struck terror, 65 per cent were from landless, marginal and small farmers' families. The average age was 22 at the time of joining the movement. About 25 per cent of them were illiterate, 26 per cent had studied up to the middle class and 41 per cent were matriculates. Just three out of 232 boys were graduates or had studied beyond. Before joining the AK-47 gangs, these youth were doing nothing: *Vehle awaragardi karde san*—vagabond time-pass! None was from well-to-do-families.

Puri would sigh: *most of them are school dropouts, unemployed and have low self-esteem and estimation. None belongs to a political or a notable family nor has anyone any religious orientation, exceptions, if any, are few. A majority of youth, 86 per cent, are Jat Sikhs, 66 of them are relatives and 45 real brothers. And among those killed in 28 villages, 77 per cent belonged to their own community, mainly Jats.*

*

When one studies the ground reality today, it is no different; it is almost the same - signs of disquiet are all pervasive in Punjab villages. In fact, rural landscape is laden with pollen of new problems: religious, class and caste overtones; cult of drug abuse; and mushroom growth of *Babas* and *Dera*s, whose business goes uninterrupted, having become immune to political upheavals, and who enjoy political patronage with mix of religion. All these pose new challenges to politicians and administrators of the future.

My own apprehensions are that there will be infringement of peace, communal harmony and tranquility, as a consequence of the developing competitive and combative political postures; societal disquiet and multiple caste, class and ethnic conflicts and socio-economic divisions and tensions; growing frustration; non-articulation of people's aspirations; atmosphere of intolerance; corruption, unemployment and stalking unemployable youth, including school dropouts; drug addiction etc.

Not much has changed since 1994. In fact, Professor Puri had lamented even then that the SAD-BJP government, despite having been in power for the past two years, had done precious little for the youth. Same is true even now in 2016.

Let me substantiate my point by quoting from the Akalis' election manifesto of February 1997, as to what was promised to be done for the youth: *we will pay special attention to the problems faced by the youth of Punjab, especially the educated unemployed. Towards this end, every effort will be made to generate more jobs and provide incentives for self-employment. Large villages will be provided with sports stadia to encourage sports. Outstanding sports persons will be given suitable grants……The sale of intoxicants and drugs will be banned. Existing laxities in the sphere will be eliminated to save youth from leading the path of self-destruction….*

All this has remained an election *jumla*; political cliché! There is no drop in school dropouts, no self-employment opportunities; neither have any of the promises been kept nor drugs and intoxicants banned, as mentioned in the election manifesto! The youth stands betrayed. The youth is still groping in the dark alleys of drugs and joblessness.

*

Quality education system has collapsed at all levels: school- to-college-to-university. Villages are the worst affected. There are schools sans teachers and teachers sans students. There are teachers, who do not teach. There are students, who do not study. There are teachers without salaries, who teach. There are teachers with salaries, who do not teach. There is, in fact, nothing to attract students to schools and teachers to classrooms, given the ground realities: lack of infrastructure in educational institutions; what is available is in a shambles! No wonder, students in schools get promoted without being able to read books of the previous classes or do simple sums!

What has become of Punjab is anyone's guess. And where it stands in the comity of the states is too well known to be repeated here. Suffice to say that it is a state gone astray, thanks to misdemeanors and pusillanimity of successive governments, since 1966, including long spells of the President's Rule. One can say with fairness that the Akali Dal's Pyrrhic-victory in 2012 has further failed the state, when upright leadership was dire need of the hour.

*

The Akali Dal created a sort of history by winning two consecutive elections to retain power in Punjab: in 2007 and 2012. This made Parkash Singh Badal Chief Minister for the fifth time. Earlier, he has been Chief Minister from March 27, 1970 to June 14, 1971; June 20, 1977 to February 17, 1980; February 12, 1997 to February 26, 2002; March 1, 2007 - at present; this includes his second term after 2012 elections. The only other Akali chief ministers were: Gurnam Singh, Lachchman Singh Gill and Surjit Singh Barnala. Incidentally, Ms Rajinder Kaur Bhattal was the first and the only woman Chief Minister of Punjab!

*

As in the previous Akali governments, so now, economic hardships coupled with unemployment, pose a big challenge to politicians and bureaucrats. It is pertinent to note that besides the sameness in factors, cause and effect, which ushered in terrorism, almost the same political line-up, same systems, red-tape and smug bureaucracy are still around. One wonders if anything would change in favour of channelizing the state economy and its farmers- small and marginal, and youth.

*

When I said *people have turned wiser; what about the Akalis, have they*, there was a purpose in so saying. Punjab has refused to learn any lessons from the past. Whereas, political analysts, social scientists and economists have remained busy studying the past for better present and future. Their reports and recommendations on reinventing education, health delivery systems, economic revival, resuscitating financial and farm sectors, rejuvenating rural development, innovative, out of the box ways to create employment, particularly off-farm, and ending financial profligacy at the hands of the politicians and bureaucrats have remained unheeded and unheard, across the decades!

*

While looking at the past to study the present, one observes there is very little evidence to show the kind of seriousness that should have been the hallmark of all the successive powers that be to help Punjab arise from the ashes! The state has fallen from grace and dignity because of what man has made of this state. Loss of economic power means, loss of political voice. Economic power loss has been due to stagnant agriculture, stalled industry, missing infrastructure; and wanton corruption in the political administration.

Interestingly, during my stay and sojourns through Amritsar and Gurdaspur in 1994, one heard the same refrain as one hears these days: people were/are fed up with divisive politics of all parties, as well as of internecine wars within them. Consequently, there is growing feeling of estrangement between the people and the politicians in the state.

Hope of *ache din* has yielded space to cynicism. People worry, as they did 17 years ago, that the government has neither time nor inclination for them. If, then, the action and over-reaction in the camps of Parkash Singh Badal and Gurcharan Singh Tohra had held people in awe and fear; lack of governance now, has created apprehensions in the minds of the people, as to what tomorrow might bring with moderates and radicals having often come face-to-face, itching for other's scalp!

People remain skeptical of the moderate Akali leadership, knowing they would strike a strident posture only once out of power! Has the Akali leadership become a laughing stock that cannot rule? Historically, Akalis have never needed any outside help to get destabilized or split into factions and fractions. There is always an implosion! Unfortunately, the Sikh *quom* remains as divided today, as it was in yesteryears, over any given issue that takes centre-stage.

My reading of the Akali politics is that the leadership's dilemma has always been twofold: one, to project itself as political party wielding power, it has to put up a secular front {SAD ever yoked to BJP}; and two, to draw sustenance, it requires to revert to its roots in the *Panth*; the *Panthic* outlook that wears a religious cloak. Thus, party leaders lacking dynamism can neither break the shackles of the traditional past nor establish linkages with a progressive future. In the process, Akali leadership has always rued and ruined the present! In fact, any *one family* rule anywhere in any political party is dangerous for healthy democracy, as it results in poor housekeeping. Such a situation that is omnipresent, omnipotent and omniscient does more harm than good. Because those who cling on to power for too long, cherish only -- *frog chorus*!

One wonders and is puzzled, why Akalis have failed miserably in their second term, 2012-2017, not that they had achieved anything spectacular in the first term: 2007-2012. This is one rare occasion where there is neither a hostile opposition

{Congress is divided, AAP: Aam Aadmi Party, new infant struggling on the political threshold is still to find its feet; and BJP is having a nice piggy-ride, as usual} in the state nor at the Centre, where Harsimrat, Badal's *Bahu*: daughter-in-law, is a cabinet minister.

As such, there is no serious challenge to the Badals from within or without. Inconvenient fellow travellers and relations have either parted company or the party has shed the excess baggage! The reason for the failure of the government is not invisible or inconceivable. The perceptible and visible reason for the failure is that SAD-BJP has failed to have a constructive look back, which could have been instructive for necessary course correction.

Consequently, Akalis' thumb rule for *governance* has been to keep up *rhetoric without action* and treat the opposition parties and every other politician, including those within their own party, as – *political midgets*. Governance has been a major casualty in Punjab. Such rancorous attitude would harm any political outfit. Yes, unquestioningly, Punjab has been harmed in every way and, thus, reduced to a theatre of atrocities!

There is, however, one big difference in the situation now and in 1994. One, farmers in the past decades were seldom in such aggressive mood and agitation-mode, as they have been in recent times, despite failure of their crops; second, the *engineered* sacrilege storm that swept the state administration off its feet, leaving Akalis shattered, may not calm down too soon! Going by the vicissitudes through which Punjab has or is passing through, one can only keep one's fingers crossed, as to who will give a healing touch to Punjab's self-inflicted injuries and bruised sensitivities, post-2017.

*

All said and done, has Punjab got stuck in quicksand of its own making? Or has it also adapted to dysfunctional systems – government institutions and instrumentalities – that seem to work only for *self, pelf and power*. Hopes that Punjab and Punjabis would leave behind the churn of the past unfortunate decades of their history are dissipating; while ad hoc palliatives may not be enough to confront the enormity of the new challenges that stare the state in the face.

*

In place of hope of reconciliation, regeneration and rejuvenation of a resurgent Punjab, one sees new political storms gathering from many directions that threaten to further cloud Punjab's prospects to spring back to its prime positioning in the comity of states; this is so, practically, in all spheres: political, administrative, law and order, agricultural, industrial, social, economic, religious; providing basic civic amenities -health and education delivery systems; unemployment, drug and substance abuse, besides growing disenchantment among the people with the ways of governance, which is marked by trust deficit, despair and disappointment. All one sees are shades of grey!

It is time all Punjabis braced up to save Punjab from falling into the vortex of uncertain future, caught as it is in the toxic nexus of religion and politics, and afflicted as it is by economic strife and social tensions, agro-industrial paralysis, caste-class and ethnic conflicts, vanishing sub-soil water, polluted soil, water and air; and quicksilver climate changes that impact farm sector and rural economy.

Does such an observation and warning ring an alarm bell? It does: it is loud and clear! Is someone out there in Punjab listening? Punjab is precariously teetering at the edge of a precipice. One prays, because of political floundering, Punjab does not march into Kakistocracy!

36

Epilogue

Punjab is still to arise from the ashes, so it seems, as one travels down the memory corridors of past decades. Even after 69 years, may it be the painful partition in 1947 or the scalding decade of terrorism, mid-1980s to mid-1990s, or yellowing of the green revolution, deceleration of agricultural growth, stalled rural development and prosperity, or despair in industry, all one sees and comes across are only shades of grey; more agony, less ecstasy; more sighs, less smiles; more dissatisfaction, less satisfaction; more government, less governance. The entire system looks discredited; peoples' aspirations remain unarticulated and politicians' promises un-kept. Consequently, still raw and fresh in the memory is the turmoil, the trials, the tribulations and the turbulent trauma we all have been through, collectively and individually.

Growing political deinstitutionalization has been stark and striking, across the decades.

Yet, somewhere, Punjab still seems to be trying to gasp for fresh air, catch its breath to regain its lost rhythm of life and gaiety; the indomitable spirit that helped Punjabis to soar to new heights, economically and socially, has apparently evaporated but not their resilience and perseverance. Like many of you, I too have been through the same tormenting, torturous and scary times, watching and wondering about why and how of eruption of insurgency, emergence of religio-political Sunami and why these issues, by and large, keep occurring time and again and have remained unresolved, so far.

Comparisons are odious. However, one cannot help compare Punjab then and now: difference, if any, is not much. Yes, the major difference is that it is the new weapon – drugs - that attract the youth, not the AK rifles; the former is more deadly and ruinous than the latter. In fact, the same or similar strains of persistent disaffection are still at work, gnawing at the Punjabi ethos: religio-political and socio-economic. Prevalent corruption, joblessness, criminalized countryside, societal divisions and disparities are yet to be effectively tackled.

The same political dispensations, barring change of several characters and actors are still at play. The situation then and now can be described in the words of Stewart Morris, who, in his essay, 'How did India's Punjab crisis arise and how has it been resolved', says:.... *It seems more reasonable to suggest that the main cause of the crisis was the failure of either congress or moderate Akali leadership to adopt a solution which did not present them with political advantage or which threatened political damage, and that its eventual solution lies in genuine 'statesmanship' when the good of the region and the nation is placed above the interests of the party and the politician....* {This was published in the Sociology and Politics of South Asia}.

Punjabis have had a chequered, bloody history, dusty geography and unaffordable lifestyles. Their efforts to fight and resist terrorism have been bitter and fierce. They have faced terrorism in its many facets. The present face of terrorism, though different and mostly invisible, is serious and has discredited even the ruling political classes, given the omnipresent dissatisfaction, disillusionment and disquiet in the society.

What brought turnaround in the Punjab situation then was a consequent of clear political direction. When it comes to taking decisions in the larger interest of the state and its people, what lacks in today's religio-political and societal leadership is maturity, grace, sagacity, as also capacity and capability to think clearly and cogently. And, what one hears and sees now in politics is the syndrome of I, me *and my self*!

Despite normalcy having been restored in mid-1990s, basic problems of the people still persist even after two decades. Though finding a solution to these is imperative, it is not happening. With both ruling and opposition parties engaged in internecine wars, their growing estrangement, polarization and marginalization does not portend well for a state like Punjab. Besides much else, need is to reconstruct the civil society, which remains dormant. The very absence of a strong civil society movement in Punjab is also a negative factor.

Unless all political parties join hands and engage sans their ideologies, if any, and idiosyncrasies and work in lock-step for the empowerment and emancipation of the people, things are only going to spin out of control resulting in further tensions in the society and, thereby, give a severe set-back to economic development; after all, peace and development go hand-in-hand, as these make a remarkable combination. If proof is required, turn to the absence of a bond between the two in the decades lost to terrorism, when Punjab suffered an economic output loss of more than Rs 13,000 crore, as the World Bank had estimated {2004}!

As then, so now, conflict between police and civil administration and mafia-like operations and functioning of the politicians of all hues, has also to be viewed with concern. It remains a serious matter. In fact, even when it comes to financial help to the state, the Centre continues to remain circumspect and acts smug, as it acted and did in the past decades - *not responding positively to state's clamor for economic and financial packages or bailouts*. Perhaps, the reason why the Centre has remained in a denial mode is as much due to loss of credibility of the successive state governments, as the endemic countrywide financial crises. In the past, New Delhi often made promises and all the right noises of helping Punjab. Yet, those promises remained unmet or were only partially met; but were largely un-kept. The promised economic and financial packages, if any, were seemingly lost in transit!

The Centre also continues to dither over Punjab's other demands {or state's rights?} for which the Akali leadership had struggled all along since partition; and eventually the struggle morphed into terrorism; injected as much by religious fundamentalism and fanaticism, as economic considerations. Punjab has to develop and explore avenues and possibilities of *consensus politics* so that economic progress and development are better taken care of. It is time to visualize Punjab's problems and prospects in proper perspective.

As a consequence of multiple factors and multiple dimensions of the Punjab *problem* as then, so now, state's economy and finances are in a shambles, agricultural growth is stagnant, unemployment coupled with drug abuse is heading north, rural and urban divide is widening and powers- that- be appear to be abdicating their responsibilities, engaged as these are in blame-game and finger-pointing. Politicians continue to indulge only in vacuous word-war, insinuations and barbed diatribes; and feather their own nests: all at the cost of common man, the tax-payer.

Epilogue

Despite loss of 25,000 innocent lives in 13 years of terrorism, Punjab and New Delhi-based politicians do not seem to have any qualms to learn from the past and mend their ways. Punjab is precariously balanced on the rim of a precipice and may go down the abyss, if things continue to remain adrift.

Punjab, as we all know, has emerged from phase of darkness. Sadly, even two decades later, it is still struggling to fully open its eyes in the new found light, when more effort is needed to keep the fire in the hearths burning, the wheels of industry running, the tractors chugging in the fields; and the power generation continuing in Hydel and Thermal plants to rotate the wheels of life, livelihood and economy. As then, so now, Punjabis remain enterprising, ready to adopt new technologies, new advances and undertake new ventures and adventures. However, the impediment is the prevailing political atmosphere, which is anything but conducive. It is stifling.

No doubt, Punjab does not easily forget or forgive those who play with its modesty; unfortunately, its modesty has been violated - repeatedly. The ones responsible are, by and large, its own sons-of-the-soil! Yes, Punjabis are made of a different stuff; it is that stuff which must be taken care of by the government{s} by involving people in decision-making, implementing promised and urgently needed development schemes and projects. The clock has to be put back, again; and Punjab has to march ahead – with head held high and magnanimity in the heart!

As I wrap-up, I do so with a feeling of conviction, positivity and optimism that during one's life span Punjab would come out of the woods; regain its lost prestige, status, dignity and self-respect in the comity of union- states; Punjab's once killing fields, which had turned red then would again turn green; Punjab's peasantry and farm workers would attain financial and economic empowerment, social dignity; and villages would avail of and enjoy the same facilities as are available in urban settlements in terms of: health, education, sanitation, connectivity, communication, information technology, skills and so on. One also hopes Punjab's youth would be weaned away from the drugs, off-farm job avenues would be explored; farmers would get rid of debt, awakened and educated not to splurge money on non-productive events and social occasions and stop committing suicides.

As an incorrigible optimist, one prays the dark clouds that hover over Punjab would dissipate and a resurgent Punjab would re-emerge: as a sunshine state!

Believe me, for someone who has been in the thick of *that* phase of history in Punjab, those hair-raising reminiscences even today send a shiver down the spine. As I rummage through the print media clippings of that time, including my own writings, the cold, small dark print against the off-white or yellowing pages, it is like walking through a mine-field; like revisiting the theatre of militancy and religio-political turmoil. While the all-consuming effect of militancy was felt by both Punjab and Punjabis, affecting their physical being, psyche, emotions and economy; the religio-political vibrations continue to reverberate even at present, given the political leaders' machinations and Sikh clergy's vulnerabilities.

One may choose to turn a blind eye to the past, the fact remains that scars left behind by *that* phase are still raw, visible and bleed. Much has been written about cross-border terrorism perpetrated, aided and abetted by Pakistan's ISI: Inter-services intelligence agency. The state-wide, decade-long violence that shook the very roots of Punjabiat and the horrors of that period are still embedded in the sub-conscious of the Punjabis. And, these bruises and wounds have only coagulated and not healed, when scratched these still bleed, as and when anniversaries of those who have departed are observed!

The questions that have haunted me and many like-minded persons all these decades are: why did Punjab undergo such tragedy and trauma and who should the blame be apportioned to? There are no easy answers to such unending questions, ifs, buts and whys. As I have said before, the blame for Punjab tragedy must be apportioned as much to the Sikhs, their leadership, which has had myopic vision, as also to the Centre/Congress and its agencies and agents outside the Sikh orbit, whether at home or abroad.

In short, there were only two actors or characters or you may even call them villains: the militants and the religious and political leaders! Thus, in the entire sordid drama, wherein, script and dialogue was written with bullets and in blood, innocent lives snuffed out, there were no winners. There are plenty of losers.

All these decades, scholars, scribes, authors and others have struggled to define what happened in Punjab and why. Each writer has come up with as many theories and hypothesis as there have been blood drops on the literature describing that period. Was it a problem of political violence or was it violence, as political discourse? Or was it Sikh militants' movement? Or was it dialectic of militant violence?

The debate is open on every burning issue that kissed Punjab: historical, administrative, legal, economic, political, social, religious, regional, cultural etc. One common denominator, however, which repeatedly finds reference in what writers and analysts say in regard to Punjab, is - *discrimination*. This is said on the analogy that Punjab and Sikh are *synonyms*. Any discrimination by the Indian state against one is construed as discrimination against the other, as well!

*

Have there been different phases of violence? Birinderpal Singh in his 2002 book: *Violence as political discourse: Sikh militancy confronts the Indian state* talks of four distinct phases: 1978-80-when the Nirankari episode took place; 1981-84; 1984-85 and 1986-1992. We are familiar with these aspects. So are we with four *major events* that the author refers to in the context of the four phases of violence that had identified.

These four *major events* are: Partition of India in 1947 and establishment of Pakistan; reorganization of Punjab in 1966 and formation of Haryana and Himachal Pradesh; the Sikh Nirankari-clash in Amritsar in 1978; Operation Bluestar at the Golden Temple in June 1984; and the massacre of the Sikhs that followed in the wake of killing of the Prime Minister Indira Gandhi in October 1984. Again a familiar ground for argument sake.

Interestingly, Birinderpal describes the first two major events as *division of body*, while he calls the latter two stages as *division of soul*! Taken together, these four *major events* in his view had: *hermeneutic significance in influencing the psyche of the Sikhs in general and militants in particular*. The author has tried to prove his hypothesis hoping policy-makers would take appropriate decisions, so that violence as political discourse does not re-visit Punjab. And, like many other writers, Birinderpal Singh has also welded economy and emotions, regional and religious identities and sentiments into the pluralistic Punjabi society.

*

The journey, as a reporter, was across a wide and lengthy arch - stretching from: administration to agriculture, politics to religion and socio-economic up and down swings, deteriorating universal and qualitative education and health delivery systems to stunted industrial development to corroding infrastructure to eruption of clutter, chaos and clamor in urban settlements to perennial disquiet and drug abuse and suicides in rural areas to psychological pressures on the Punjabi society to cult of growing short-fuse nature and intolerance, coupled with people's inability to cope with and come to grips with problems that beset them.

Punjab also faces problems of ecology, falling sub-soil water table, toxicity of soil, water and air, diminishing returns from farming, widening chasm between urban and rural settlers, resulting in internal migration; and changing demographic profile of the state.

*

The world we live in is like an oyster and, we the people, its pearls, each with a distinct trait, quality and personality; each with an independent and different thought process, a different perspective, a different interpretation and a different take on men and matters; and the ways life swirls around us. Our opinions are not only varied but are also at variance. Yet like the rainbow, we continue to live and co-exist; such is the interdependence of humans on one another, around the globe. Each one of us looks at the life and the world around through a prism. That is why there are myriad hues of views on the day-to-day developments, situations, events, happenings; and even inter and intra human or people-to-people or nation-to nation relations. In that sense humans tend to either agree or agree to disagree; it is high time to respect each ones views and thoughts and opinions.

As such, what has been presented in these pages and passages is how, as a journalist, one looked/looks at the world, the society and situations one have been through or exposed to or have experienced. In such a narrative and recall, there are bound to be different takes, depending upon from which angle of the prism one sees and perceives. These are personal impressions and interpretations. One has the right to differ and have a different take; it is everyone's right. We all must respect that right, so should you mine! If I may add, I can say with a fair degree of truthfulness, that my journey as a journalist has been quite educative, enriching, informative, knowledgeable, rewarding and remunerative.

*

Let me conclude my impressions, born as much out of conviction and affection, as concerns for Punjab, with the following passage; a reproduction from the *Indian Express* column that Tunku Varadarajan wrote in the wake of the terrorist attack on IAF base, Pathankot. It was published in the *Sunday Express* on January 10, 2016, as - *Five Lessons from Pathankot.*

The passage in question: *Pagdi sambal, Jatta.* 'Punjab is a cesspit of corruption and smuggling, ruled by a venal family and party that have brought India's most dynamic province to its knees. India cannot afford such mismanagement of a strategic border state. Corruption not only distorts the local economy and politics, it destroys morale, creating the perfect conditions for terrorist infiltration and attack. Now that it is apparent that terrorists, and the ISI, have widened their incursive focus beyond Kashmir, India cannot let any of its western border states to be so rotten.' {The writer is Virginia Hobbs Carpenter Fellow at Stanford University's Hoover Institute.}

*

Post –Script: Why do people write books? This question had haunted me for a pretty long time, as friends and family implored me to write one, given the exposures and experiences I had had as a journalist. I would ponder: Where do I start? Which topic should I choose? How do I go about it? Moreover, I am unknown. What is the fate and future of a new writer's book? How do I get the book published? Such questions would cloud and crowd my mind, and I would banish the thought.

One day, out of curiosity and for the fun of it, I *Googled*: why do people write books? I was foxed: in 0.49 seconds, my computer screen showed 15, 00, 00, 000 results! I found many answers. By and large, people wrote because they wanted to share experiences, to educate, to influence and inform, to help or to convey a message. Some took up the pen to become famous, others to earn money. One result mentioned that *everyone has a book in them*. One writer said that there's really only one good reason to write a book: *because you can't stand to not write it*. You have a story or an idea that you truly must share with the world, or you will just die.

*

And, when I did decide to write my first book, I found it was hard, getting it published was even harder, more challenging.

Well, that be so, one is still looking for a credible answer to the basic question: w*hy do people write books*? And *why did I write*?

Let me conclude with a stanza from Robert Frost's poem: *Stopping by Woods on a Snowy Evening:*

The woods are lovely, dark and deep,
But I have promises to keep,
And miles to go before I sleep,
And miles to go before I sleep

Is it The End? No, for me, a new journey has already begun….!